Pagoda, Osaka

JAPAN

AND HER PEOPLE

BY

ANNA C. HARTSHORNE

ILLUSTRATED

IN TWO VOLUMES

VOL. II

THE INTERNATIONAL PRESS

THE JOHN C. WINSTON CO.

PHILADELPHIA

CONTENTS

VOLUME II

iii

LIST OF ILLUSTRATIONS

VOLUME II

———

Photogravures made by GILBO & Co.

———

JAPAN AND HER PEOPLE.

CHAPTER I.

THE AINU ABORIGINES.

PROFESSOR CHAMBERLAIN, writing of Ainu folk lore, gave three good reasons for which this strange people is worthy of being studied—"because its domain once extended over the entire Japanese archipelago, because absolutely nothing is known of its origin and affinities, and because it is, so to speak, almost at its last gasp."

This last proposition, at least, is evident to any one who goes to the Hokkaido. Years ago, when Miss Bird followed her "Unbeaten Tracks" into the north, there were still plenty of Ainu not far from Hakodate, at Mori, on the south shore of Volcano bay, and elsewhere in southern Yezo; but as the Japanese have come, the Ainu have gone, always northward—where else, indeed, could they go?—clustering, some of them, in squalid villages on the upper shore of Volcano bay, but mostly along the remote coasts and up the rivers, in out-of-the-way places, where they can still hunt and fish. Some there are even in the dreary Kurile islands, though, according to Romyn Hitchcock, these are another people, akin to the Mongolian pit-dwellers of Saghalien.

Mr. Batchelor, first and special missionary to the Ainu, has collected many curious animal tales and bits of folk lore, some of them as unlike Japanese folk stories as possible, while others are attributed to Chinese and Japanese influences. The ethnologists, too, have been busy among them—the German Scheube in 1882; Hitchcock, of the Smithsonian Institute, ten years later; Professor Milne, Professor Chamberlain, and lately Mrs. Todd, who took a collection of clothing and utensils to Professor Morse, at the Peabody Museum, in Salem; while Captain James, of the "Coronet," arranged for a collection for the national museum in New York. Probably the Sapporo Historical Society does as much or more in collecting material than the rest of the agencies put together; but as few of the members publish out of their own tongue, it will be long before their researches get before the world at large.

Certainly the hairy Ainu should be the joy of all who delight in ethnological puzzles, for, as Professor Chamberlain says, nobody knows anything of their origin, and so far nobody can find out. Physically and in every way they are totally distinct from the Japanese; they are nearly the same height, but more chunky and thick-set, with straight eyes and

level eyebrows—not arched and far above the eyes,
like the brows of a Japanese—and above all, heavily
bearded, while the other race is notably smooth-faced.
The Ainu are as dirty as their conquerors are clean,
as slow-witted as these are quick; the two races seem
to be alike only in having high cheek-bones, dark
eyes and inky-black hair. Beards indeed are so
necessary to the happiness of an Ainu that, since
nature has neglected the women in this respect, they
are allowed to tattoo themselves fine blue-black mous-
taches. The process is begun in childhood and carried
on year by year, so that by the time a girl is " out,"
so to speak, she has a magnificent curve across each
cheek almost to her ear, and a pair of marks also on
her forehead. Modern Japanese law forbids the practice,
but it is still done in all the more out-of-the-way places.

The long beards and general cast of features of the
Ainu are so strikingly like Russian peasants that the
comparison has been made very often, but so far no
racial affinity has been proved; certainly not the least
trace of Aryan descent can be claimed for them, however much one of these dignified old chiefs may look
like a kilted Scotch Highlander. The venerable
beards give their mild countenances an air of great
dignity and even refinement, as is especially noticeable
in their photographs—this, perhaps, because one can
study them more judicially when undistracted by the
appeal to the olfactory nerves, which is generally
made by the living subject.

Not all of them are actually hairy all over, though, indeed, Henry Savage Landor insists that around the north coast and in other wild places they are universally so, and argues that those who are not hairy have an intermixture of Japanese blood. There used to be a theory that the children of Japanese and Ainu were not healthy, and that the mixed race soon died off; but of this there seems to be no definite proof and little probability. A curious physical trait is that the Ainu skeleton has the bones of the forearm and leg noticeably flattened.

Language is not much help as to their origin, even if the modern ethnologists would allow that it ever proved anything in any case. In general structure Ainu is rather like Japanese, but Professor Chamberlain says the resemblances are less than the differences. Naturally very many words have been adopted from the Japanese, with or without modification; for instance, *Kamui* (a divine being), Japanese *Kami*; *mai-dare* (an apron — literally, a "hang-before"), which is Japanese, pure and simple; *pi-shaku* (a bark dipper), in which last case both word and thing are copied from a bamboo *hi-shaku*, or Japanese dipper. The change from *p* to *h* and back again is not uncommon in the different parts of Japan proper; the northern Japanese dialect uses *pi* instead of *hi* for fire, and in the southwest—Nagasaki, for instance—they say *fi*. In Tokyo, again, people commonly make yet another change in this slippery syllable, and say *shi*

Ainu Aborigines

instead of *hi*. The northern dialect is quite rough, the peasants speaking as if they had their mouths shut, and slurring or suppressing vowels. Merely in listening to it, Ainu sounds much more harsh and consonantal than Japanese, and certainly looks so when it is written down in English letters, as Mr. Batchelor has done for them with great thoroughness and patience.

One theory of Ainu origin brings them from the north, chiefly because their inferno is cold, and their best wish for a friend, "May you be kept warm!" As we only know their beliefs and traditions as they exist now, after centuries of banishment from warmer regions, where we know they lived till historical times, this evidence cannot be considered very conclusive. On the other side, there is an Ainu tradition that in the beginning all the world was very hot—which of course may very likely be a memory of some volcanic region. At this time, says the legend, the Ainu would have fared badly but for Okikurumi, a being who appears in many stories as a culture hero, teaching and providing for the Ainu forefathers. Okikurumi caught fish and sent it to the Ainu by his wife, Turesh or Tureshi, who put it in at the window. The Ainu were forbidden to look at Turesh or ask any questions, and for a long time they obeyed; but at last one man became very curious, and one day, when Turesh came to the window, he caught her by the hand and pulled her inside. Okikurumi was very

angry at this, and sent no more fish, and since then
the Ainu have had to take care of themselves as best
they can.

I was told much the same story by the Japanese
in Sapporo, but according to them it was the Koropuk-guru (the dwarfs) who used to bring the Ainu
food and other good things, and were frightened off
by some one's rudeness. The Ainu have many
legends about these Koropuk-guru, who, they say,
were plenty in the land in the good old times. They
had blue eyes, and were so small that they could live
under a big dock leaf, whence the name. (It should
be remarked here that Hokkaido dock leaves are two
feet or more long.) They were the "Good People,"
as the Scotch say, and did many kind deeds, but did
not like to be spied upon or thanked, and conducted
themselves altogether like the Brownies of our own
folk tales. Among the Ainu somebody always has a
grandmother who has seen one, but in these degener-
ate days they are all quite gone, leaving only another
puzzle for the archæologists.

On the whole, the weight of evidence seems to be
that there really was another race, probably older than
the Ainu even, perhaps the same as the "Earth
Spiders" of Japanese tradition, who lived in caves
and fought with Jimmu Tenno and the first ancestors.
At any rate, there are mounds all over Japan, whether
of the Ainu or another people, in which stone implements and pottery are found, which bear no resem-

blance to anything the Japanese have ever made ; more-over, the Japanese certainly had iron weapons when they first reached Japan, and must have passed through the stone and bronze ages elsewhere. And, finally, all over the Hokkaido there are remains of pit-dwellings, which the Ainu declare they never have used, nor have the Japanese any tradition connecting them with the Ainu. Of course, it is not impossible that at some time the Ainu might have lived part of the year in such places ; just as the Australian blacks used to have straw huts for summer and holes for winter, and the Chinook Indians of British Columbia dig what they call " kergwilly holes " and roof them over for the cold part of the year, but return to their skin tents in summer. But so far as has been found there is not a legend among the Ainu to point this way.

A few years ago Professor Tsuboi, of the University of Tokyo, opened one of these mounds, which was on the side of Akusa hill at Oji ; he found first of all a bed of clam shells, mixed with bones of animals and charred fragments, and then four polished stone axes, some chipped ones, stones round and square, having holes through the middle, much broken pottery, and two earthen vessels quite uninjured. The articles resembled those found at Omori, near Tokyo, and elsewhere throughout the country. The pottery is very light in weight, unglazed, and made with the hand, not the wheel. Professor Tsuboi believes these remains to belong to a race identical with the legendary

Koropuk-guru, probably related to the Esquimaux, who are small, full-faced, use stone implements, and tattoo the face and hands, much as the small images are marked which are frequently found in these mounds. But Professor Milne thinks the designs in the pottery resemble Ainu patterns, and points out that the shell heaps are found in places known to have been inhabited by Ainu.

Of course the evidence that the Ainu did not once make pottery is only negative; they certainly never did in historical times, but that does not of itself prove anything; they may have had the art and lost it after contact with the more advanced race, as witness several tribes of our own Indians. Their own legend on the subject is this: Once, a very long time ago, an old Ainu woman was struck with the idea of making vessels out of clay, and she actually did make one. She was so delighted with it that she started out for the village to show it to her neighbors; but on the way it dropped and broke all to pieces, and she was so disgusted that she never made another.

This story has an air of having been invented to account for something the Ainu were rather ashamed of, like the one which relates how a stranger came from no one knew where, and stayed with Okikurumi, and taught him several things, such as rowing with two oars instead of paddling, but who finally ran away with Okikurumi's wife and his two treasures, which were a book and a counting board. "And this is the reason why, ever since, we Ainu have not been able to read."

In the version given by Mr. Batchelor, it was Yoshitsune, Japanese hero and Ainu deity, who lost the book, and with it the art of reading and writing.

It is certainly very clear that the Ainu character must have greatly changed in historical times, and it is difficult to realize that these harmless, good-natured, stupid creatures are the same race as the Ebisu, or Emishi, whom Yamato-take and Yoshiiye and the rest had so much trouble to subdue. Still, many of our American Indians present much the same picture of degeneration, mental and physical. There are very definite accounts of battles with them, and evidence, too, in the quantity of stone arrowheads found in some places, notably near Mororan, where it would seem there must have been a tremendous fight at some time, though it may possibly have been between Ainu and Ainu, or Ainu and pit dwellers, and not with the Japanese at all. They were assuredly once scattered all over the land, from the north down to Kiushiu; for if they are ruled out of the pottery question, there remains abundant testimony of their presence in the geographical names found everywhere in old Japan and not of Japanese origin. The names are disguised, sometimes past recognition, in much the same way as the Danish Mere of Buther got changed into Buttermere, and Dun-y-coed became Dunagoat; but Professor Chamberlain has traced out enough of them to more than prove their presence on half the mountains and rivers in Japan.[1]

One way in which the names were disguised was this : In old times people called the places by the names their ancestors had given them, without feeling any need of writing them down ; or when they did write them, say for purposes of taxation, it was done either phonetically or with the Chinese character denoting the thing the place was named for ; thus Takayama, the high mountain, would be written with the two characters for mountain and high. Later, for convenience of registration, an order of the government went forth that every place-name must be written in characters, not phonetically. Now the difficulty was that the places which had Ainu names often did not mean anything in Japanese, and consequently had no character with which they could be written ; and the only thing to do was to use the characters which made the right sound, whether there was any sense to it or not. So Yamashiro might be in Japanese "mountain white," or in Ainu " place of chestnut trees ; " but Tonami in Japanese will make nothing better than " hares in a row," while in Ainu it would be " stream from the lake," and entirely appropriate. Besides dozens of well proved cases there are probably hundreds more which are so covered up that it is impossible now to

---

[1] "The Language, Mythology and Geographical Nomenclature of Japan, viewed in the light of Ainu Studies." By Basil Hall Chamberlain, University of Tokyo.

say whether they were originally Japanese or belonged to the first owners of the land. Even Fuji, the peerless mountain, was almost certainly the Ainu Fuchi or Huchi, the goddess of fire.

Like the Japanese, the Ainu begin to build a house roof first, making the horizontal frame and placing the supports and ridgepole, and laying shorter pieces for rafters; all these are tied together with rope made of bark fibre, or with vines. Then they drive poles into the ground a few feet apart, and tie short horizontal pieces from one to the other; the poles are about five or six feet high, and have each a fork at the top. When this is ready, they lift the roof-frame bodily and set it on the forked poles and tie it fast, and the framework is ready to be thatched.

So far it is not unlike a Japanese house, except that the gable ends slope back much less, and the roof slants a great deal more. But instead of filling the walls with woven reeds and daubing it with mud or plaster, like the Japanese peasant, the Ainu thatches his house from top to bottom, tying the straw in bundles and fastening it to the frame with bark ropes. On the roof the bundles of straw overlap one another, making four or five horizontal ridges in place of the smooth Japanese thatch; the ends project, forming deep eaves, and the sides of the house often slope out a little toward the bottom, like a haystack. There is a small porch at the west end, which is used as a kind of outhouse for storing wood and doing rough work;

the outdoor opening of the porch is on the south side.
There is a window in the south side of the house
proper, high up under the eaves, and another in the
east end; this last is the sacred end, and outside of it
they set the "sacred hedge"—a row of sticks set up
roughly, on which they place the skulls of bears and
other animals. Mats hung before the windows and
door, and a smoke vent in the west end of the roof,
complete the house-building arrangements.

Each family has usually a detached store-house—a
small thatched affair set up on piles—to keep out dogs
and foxes; they also put a flat piece of board at the
top of each pole to keep the rats from climbing up
and eating the stores of millet and beans and dried
salmon put away for the winter. Rats are quite as
bothersome in the north as in the rest of Japan, but
the Ainu seem to have a good word for them nevertheless, to judge by one of Mr. Batchelor's tales. It
seems the missionary made some impatient remarks
about these animals, and an old Ainu reproved him,
saying, "After the creator had finished making the
world, he came down to see how everything looked.
As he was reviewing his works, the evil one appeared,
and derided him, saying, 'Doubtless you think you
have done a very good deed, and made all things for
the best. But look at this bramble bush and thistle;
what can be the use of such things as these?' The
god was angry at these remarks; so he put his hand
behind his back and created a rat. As soon as the rat

was made it rushed into the evil one's mouth and bit out his tongue. Hence the evil one has no tongue to this day, for it never grew again." The story goes on to say that the evil one was very angry, and made the rats increase greatly, so that they were a great nuisance on the earth; wherefore the Ainu petitioned the creator to take them away, but instead he let the rats live and to keep things even created cats. " Let us, therefore," said the old man, " bear with the rats a little, for they did a good thing in biting out the tongue of the evil one. Moreover, do not speak against anything that God has made, for see how he punished the evil one for doing so."

A very large proportion of the Ainu stories are tales of animals who take human form or speak with human voices. To the Ainu these are not mere fairy tales, but sober historical facts, or explanations of natural phenomena, such as "Why the Cock cannot Fly" and "The Origin of the Hare." One of the neatest is the story of the "Stolen Charm," which also gives a good character to the rat.

A certain man had a charm which he valued more than anything he had. One day it disappeared, and the man was so troubled that he refused all food, and lay down to die.

Now the man had a fox cub and a puppy, to which he was very kind. When these creatures saw their master was sick, the fox said to the puppy, "If our master dies, we shall starve. We had better look for that charm." So they looked and looked, but it was nowhere to be found.

Then the fox cub bethought him of the wicked ogre on the mountain, and he said, " Beyond a doubt the ogre has stolen our master's charm." So they determined to go and steal it back, but fearing they could not manage the matter alone, they asked a wise old rat to help them. So the three set out.

When they came to the ogre's house, the rat and the fox dug a passage under the house, and they all crept through. In the house was a large chest ; so while the rat gnawed a hole, the fox cub and the puppy turned into a pretty little boy and girl and began to dance and amuse the ogre, who had been watching for the man to die, but now turned to look at the two supposed children. He thought there was something queer about it, because the door was shut, and he did not see how they got in ; but he thought he would amuse himself for a little while and then eat them up. Meanwhile the rat made a hole and got into the box, and found the charm; so he took it in his mouth and ran away, and the fox and the puppy slipped out after him. The ogre started to chase them, but when he saw one was a fox, he thought it would be safer to let him go, and he went back into his house. So the fox cub and the puppy brought the charm to their master's house, and put it under the bed, and then they played about him and pulled his sleeve till he looked down and saw it ; and he was so pleased that he became well at once.

The way people knew all this was that the puppy and the fox cub appeared to their master in a dream, and told him all about it; and he worshiped the rat, because it had helped out of pure kindness, not being one of the family, as the fox and the puppy were. Therefore you see the rat is not such a bad animal, after all.

But to come back to the houses. The floor of an Ainu hut is bare beaten earth, in the midst of which a long, narrow space serves for fireplace, being marked off by pieces of wood laid along the sides and ends. The east end of the house is the guest's place; the master sits on the right and the mistress by him. The northeast corner is the place where the family possessions are stored, treasures of lacquered saké cups and sword-handles and such things, and the spears and arrows and fishing things. The bed-places are platforms, slightly raised from the floor and hung with mats, and mats are also used to sit and sleep on—not thick ones like the Japanese tatami, but ordinary thin ones woven of rushes and elm bark, part of which is stained black, and the dark and light used cleverly to make exceedingly pretty basket-work patterns.

Their household utensils are of the simplest. An iron pot hangs over the fire on an iron chain, both obtained from the Japanese; or sometimes they cook in bark kettles covered with clay, and the pot hook is quite as often wood as iron. The mistress of the house sits by the pot, and ladles out the food to each person

in his or her own dish—a kind of large wooden cup
or deep trencher. These dishes acquire a fine black
color, as dark as any bog oak, by the simple process
of never washing them! A wipe with the finger is
considered all that good manners require.

They still live almost entirely by fishing and hunting, the fish being still plenty, the game yearly more
scarce. For deer hunting they used dogs, which were
trained to keep the herd back until the hunters could
come up and shoot them with poisoned arrows. They
also use a kind of primitive bagpipe, made of fish-skins
tied over a piece of wood, to imitate the cry of the
deer and decoy them within reach. Nets and fish-
traps they once used, but these are now forbidden, and
they stand on the shore or in their long, narrow dug-
outs, and cast a spear or harpoon with great skill.
Japanese law now forbids the use of poisoned arrows,
which is a sad handicap to Ainu hunters; their former
plan was to set a spring with one of these arrows, and
then drive the game to it. The head of the arrow was
lightly fastened on, and broke, leaving the poison
inside, even if a bear or fox managed to pull out the
shaft. They would go out in winter, when the big
grizzlies were lying up in their holes, and by shouts
and smoke drive them out into the open; or even venture into the den if Bruin refused to be disturbed.

The bear is their special admiration, the greatest of
their animal gods, and a bear feast is the highest delight an Ainu can conceive. Formerly these feasts

used to be held every year in each village, but they are
growing rare, both for want of bears and of saké—the
last being almost as essential as the bear. Their plan
is to catch a young bear and keep him in a cage for a
year or two, feeding and watching over him most carefully. Mr. Batchelor could not get his Ainu to ac-
knowledge that the women ever suckled them, but
Mrs. Todd saw one do it at Esashi. When the proper
day comes and saké is plenty, the whole village assem-
bles; the cub is let out of the cage, chased to the sacred
hedge, and killed with arrows so that he falls in front
of it. Once dead, politeness begins again; saluta-
tions, praises, greetings as lord, crownings with white
willow shavings and bamboo; finally a feast of his flesh
and a colossal drinking. The chiefs wear crowns of
willow shavings, the cups are wreathed with them, and
so, too, was the bow that shot and the knife that finally
dispatched my lord bear.

Just what these willow shavings mean is not at all
clear. The Ainu use them almost precisely as the
Japanese use cut paper gohei, as a symbol of divinity
in the most general sense; but except similarity of
purpose, there is no traceable connection between the
two—and for that matter, the meaning of the gohei
themselves is exceedingly vague and indefinite.

The Ainu have no idols, and the "sacred hedge" is
their nearest approach to a temple; but when they
are about to worship, they set up what they call an
inao—a willow stick, about three or three and a half

feet long, carefully pealed, and shaved up toward the thicker end, so that the shavings curl up and hang like a tassel all about it. The lower end is sharpened so that it will stick in the ground easily. For certain occasions the shaving is done in three bunches, instead of only at the top. These inao are in no sense gods, or even symbols of individual gods, but the placing of them is in itself an act of worship, as appears by the following tale:

A little boy frequently had another little boy and girl come to play with him, but no one else could see them, because they were spirits. By and by the child fell sick; and when he seemed to be about to die, the little boy and the little girl came to him, and said, "The reason you are sick is this: Your grandfather had a beautiful axe, and with it he made a tray and a pestle, such as Ainu women use to pound millet. But your father threw away the axe, which was our chief, and it is rusting under the floor; and because the axe was angry, it has made you ill. So if you do not want to die, you must tell your father to find the axe, and polish it, and make it a new handle, and set up inao in its honor."

So the boy told his father, and he searched under the floor and found the axe, and he polished it and made a new handle, and set up inao to it. And his son was healed, and became a great soothsayer, for the pestle and the tray and the axe came to him in human form, and told him things hidden from other mortals.

The story shows another point—namely, that the Ainu believe all sorts of things have spirits, and may appear in human form, and help or hinder people as they are disposed. Accordingly, they worship gods innumerable, both small and great, spirits of places and of fire and water and springs, of animals and plants, and inanimate objects. Hitchcock calls their religion "a very primitive nature-worship," and their gods "invisible, formless conceptions." The fire god is the greatest, then the god of the house; after them the earth god and the sea god, and the gods of rivers and mountains, and as lesser deities the gods of the sun and moon. As they have no temples, they simply place the inao in the ground wherever they wish and worship before it, as at the hearth for the fire god, in the sacred corner—the east—for the house god, and for the rest of the deities before the sacred hedge, outside the house at the east end. This orientation, by the way, is by no means always an exact one. Probably they do have the intention of placing the door to the south, and the window to the rising sun, and the other parts have always the same general relation; but Mrs. Todd tested many houses at Esashi, and found few of them stood really east and west, and Hitchcock also doubts it.

The bear feast is their one great festival and religious exercise combined, though they pray and make libations invariably before drinking saké. The drinking at a bear feast is the crowning ceremony of all, and the most absolutely unique. When the time comes, the chiefs sit solemnly in a row, the lesser men likewise; before each man is a large lacquered cup, holding nearly a tumblerful of saké, and across each cup is laid a flat stick, which looks like a paper knife, and is carved all over with triangles and lozenges and other characteristic devices, or whittled with clean new shavings, like the inao and the shaving crowns of the chiefs. After proper bowings and strokings of the beard — the Ainu mode of salutation — each man dips his stick into the saké, throws a drop from its tip as an offering to the earth god, dips again and throws another to the fire god, and so to any other whom he desires to worship especially at this time; then, holding the stick across his mouth, he solemnly lifts his long moustache with it, and solemnly drinks. These libations accomplished, ceremony is satisfied, and the drinking goes on freely till every one is drunk, or there is nothing left.

The women have no part in these drinking feasts; they are not allowed to drink saké at all, nor to have any religion—or at least to offer any worship, which is not quite the same thing. They must greet a man by rubbing one finger over the lip, and they may not speak till he gives permission. Yet, with all this submission, they say an Ainu fears nothing so much as an old woman's tongue.

The ghosts of old women seem to be considered particularly malignant; indeed, the Ainu are exceed-

Ainu Poling Boat

ingly afraid of ghosts of any kind, and put the graves of their dead far away in the forest, taking great pains to avoid going near the place. If for any reason one has to come in contact with the dead, or visit its grave, he is careful to wash his hands and rinse his mouth before entering any house, and to brush himself with an inao, so that, if the spirit has cast any disease or defilement on him, the water and the inao may take it away.

When an Ainu dies, the first thing that is done is to build up a great fire in the house. Mr. Batchelor says that they think the heat may possibly bring back life, but though this may be their idea now, it seems more likely that some other ceremonial reason has been forgotten. He also mentions the secondary object of cooking the funeral feast. The body is then neatly dressed in good clothes and laid on a mat by the fireplace, and a dish or two and a drinking-cup laid beside it; also appropriate implements—if it is a man, his flint and steel, bow and arrows and knife, and a few moustache lifters, of which every man has good store. Beside a woman they place a cooking-pot, and her beads and other ornaments; for both men and women there must be a pipe and a well-filled tobacco-box—I had almost said pouch, but what the Ainu uses is a carved box, which hangs by a string to the pipe-case, which he thrusts into his girdle. A cake of millet (or a cup of rice, if they have any) and a cup of saké are also placed by the body. Their belief seems to be that of the ancient Egyptians, that the spirit of the food—its *Ka*, as the Egyptians called it—will nourish the *Ka* of the person to whom it is offered. At the feast which follows, all the family and guests throw a few drops of saké as a libation to the departed spirit, and break off a little piece of millet cake and bury it in the ashes of the hearth. After the burial, these pieces are gathered up and put outside the house before the east window.

The body is carried to the grave wrapped in a mat and slung on a pole, the mourners following in single file, each carrying something to be placed in the grave. These objects are broken before being laid with the body, so that they may go to the other world, where the dead are believed to live very much as they did in this life.

The grave is sometimes lined with stakes, and a mat is laid on the bottom and others at the sides ; after the body has been lowered, another mat is spread over it, and a roof of sticks laid across, on which the earth is piled   Finally a great deal of brush and larger pieces of wood are heaped on top, to keep away the bears, wolves and foxes, and a pole set up in the midst. When everything is finished, all who have taken part wash their hands in water brought for the purpose; the water that is left is thrown on the grave, and the tub in which it was carried is broken and thrown at the foot of the grave post.

The object of this post seems to be less to serve as a memorial of the dead, whom the Ainu consider it safest to think about as little as possible, than as a warning to hunters and other people to avoid the spot, lest the spirit should defile them and work them a mischief. The man's post resembles a spear, though the Ainu themselves told Mr. Batchelor it was meant for a paddle; a woman's is rounded off at the top, where it has a hole made through, sometimes used to hang up some article of her dress. The specimen in the museum at Sapporo is carved all over with the characteristic Ainu patterns, which seem to be entirely conventional and general, not individual totem marks.

A widow shaves her head and puts on a kind of bonnet; this she must wear always, unless she remarries, which is permitted after a suitable interval. A man cuts his beard and hair, and sometimes even plucks some of it out in token of his grief; he is supposed to stay at home till it has grown again.

Several of the Ainu stories deal with visits of living people to the world of the dead. It is reached by entering a cave and going a long, long way under ground. The living can see and recognize the dead, but to these the living are as spirits—they can only smell what seems to them a horrible odor; but the dogs see and begin howling, just as dogs do in the upper world when there are spirits about, invisible to men. Then the ghosts of the dead are horribly afraid, and they throw offerings to the living—hor-

rible offerings of carrion—for everything in that world
is dead and corrupted. In one of these stories, as
recorded by Professor Chamberlain, a young man who
goes down there tries in vain to make his father recognize him; when he speaks, the father throws himself
on the ground, crying out in terror. In Mr. Batchelor's version, the young man went to ask his father
to compel the older brother to share the inheritance
with him, and not being able to make his father
understand, he bethought him to enter into one of
the people in the village of the dead, just as ghosts
enter into the bodies of living men and speak through
them; which he did with entire success, so that when
he returned to the living world, his brother was
afraid, and repented, and gave back his share of the
goods.

Another of the stories is the world-old myth of the
food of Hades. A young hunter shot a bear, but it
ran away and entered a cave. The hunter went in
after it, and followed a long way under ground, until
he came to a light, and passed out of the cave into a
very beautiful region, where there were trees and
houses and people. But there was no sign of his bear.
He followed it for some time longer, and as he went,
being hungry, he plucked the grapes and mulberries
by the path and ate them without thought of danger.
But suddenly he looked down at himself and saw that
he had turned into a horrible serpent. In terror and
despair he crept back to the cave, and made his way

through it, and, lying down beside a great pine tree, fell asleep.

In his dreams a woman appeared to him and said, " I am the spirit of this pine tree, and I am sorry for you. This has happened because you ate the fruit of Hades; and the only thing you can do is to climb to the top of my tree and throw yourself down; then perhaps you will become a man again."

The hunter woke, and finding himself still a snake, decided that anything was better than to live in such a state, so he glided up the tree, and threw himself from the topmost branch. When he came to himself he was standing at the foot of the tree, and by it was the body of a great snake, with its side ripped open. The hunter gratefully set up an inao, and thanked and worshiped the pine tree, and then went home.

But that night the pine tree came again to him and said, " I have come to tell you that you cannot stay long in the world of men after once eating the grapes and mulberries of Hades. There is a goddess in Hades who wishes to marry you. She it was who, assuming the form of a bear, lured you into the cavern, and thence to the under-world. You must make up your mind to come away."

" And so it fell out," continued Professor Chamberlain's narrator. " The young man awoke, but a grave sickness overpowered him. A few days later he went a second time to Hades, and returned no more to the land of the living."

The pine and the oak are held in special reverence by the Ainu. They say the reason is that in the early time, when the world was hot, these two trees were the only ones which could grow, and they are therefore the oldest trees. It is the elm, however, which would seem most worthy of honor, since it is from two species of elm that they get the bark fibre of which they make their clothing. This fibre is carefully picked from the under side of the bark, and soaked in water until it is pliable, when the women spin and weave it on small wooden hand-looms as if it were flax. The cloth looks rather like a hempen stuff, quite stiff and very closely woven; it is nearly the color of what we call cocoa matting, but a little less dark.

The dress is nearly the same as a Japanese garment or kimono, but shorter, reaching little below the knees on men and rather lower on women; they cross and belt it with a narrow girdle or belt, the men's often made of leather and ornamented with pieces of metal; the sleeves are much smaller than those the Japanese wear, and instead of being the same width all the way down, as the latter's are, they become quite narrow at the hand. Women often wear besides the dress a narrow straight apron, precisely like those Japanese women wear to work in; at least this is so with the Ainu I have seen, but in the more remote places I suspect this evidently Japanese addition is not known. A woman's favorite ornament is a string of heavy beads for the neck, with a large metal disc for a pendent in the middle; if she can get one three or four inches across, she is happy indeed. The beads are a curious mixture of bits of metal, glass and stone, and colored beads from Japan or Europe. She also wears metal ear-rings, not heavy, but very large.

The men's dress is much more ornate than the women's. The adornment is made of strips of dark blue Japanese cotton cloth, set on in appliqué, and further decorated with patterns in outline done with white thread; the effect is certainly primitive, but exceedingly good. They say that different villages have their own particular designs, so that an Ainu can tell where another man comes from by the patterns on his coat. In all these patterns that I have seen, the triangle and double spiral—Goodyear's famous "lotus motive"—appears persistently in all work done in carving or embroidery—their only arts, except mat weaving. In both, the most characteristic feature of the pattern is the sharpness of the angles made when two lines meet; a quality very natural in appliqué, and not out of the way in low relief wood carving.

Besides the dresses made of woven fibre, the men have rain-coats of salmon skin, very thick and strong; and these, too, are lavishly ornamented with outline embroidery in Japanese cotton thread, dark blue and white, with occasionally a little red worked in. These coats are quite warm, and must turn the rain perfectly. For winter they use leggings of Japanese cloth or their own fibre, and high boots made of straw; Japanese coolies often wear these in the north to keep out the deep snow.

In the north, too, the Japanese sometimes adopt the Ainu way of carrying burdens. Like the Mexican women, the Ainu puts his bundle into a loose rope net, the ends of which pass into a broad band; this band is adjusted across the forehead, so that the load rests partially on the shoulders and is partly supported by the head. I believe the Chinook Indians of British Columbia carry burdens in the same way.

More precious to a chief than even his fine embroidered coats are certain treasures handed down as heirlooms from generation to generation; they are finely wrought sword handles—for centuries now the Japanese have forbidden the Ainu to possess swords—Japanese lacquer drinking cups and stands, bowls almost in size, and of a shape seldom seen in Japan now; and most valuable of all large lacquered saké tubs with lids, Japanese of course, which are used to keep all the smaller articles in. Some years ago they could hardly be persuaded to part with these precious articles, but now they are more and more ready to sell everything they possess for a drink of saké.

A pathetic chapter in Ainu history concerns the transfer of a number of villages of them from Saghalien to Yezo. When the lower half of this island was ceded to Russia a few years ago, the Ainu population, being regarded as Japanese subjects—wards of

the government, as we say of the Indians—were taken
over to Japanese soil. But in many cases people from
neighboring villages were separated by a considerable
distance, and some were settled inland on the rivers,
instead of by the sea that they knew ; and in their dull
way the poor things were homesick and unhappy. It
might have been worse though to leave them to Russia's tender mercies, for the Japanese are at least
kindly, and mean to treat them fairly ; they have no
such abuses to repent of as have marked our " century
of dishonor " in the United States. There are good
laws, and some schools, and in Sapporo an Ainu
Preservation Society ; and a few of the people have
begun to farm a little under a kind of " land in
severalty " act. The missionaries, too, are hard at
work, doing their best for both soul and body. But
little can be done, except for a few individuals ; it is
a doomed race, lessening year by year, passing to those
shallow graves hidden far away in the swamps and
forests, where the living never go. Yet let not the
too zealous collector try to seek out these lonely burying places. Some years ago, soon after the opening
of the country, some English and Continental scien-
tists went out from Hakodate and rifled some graves
near Mori, taking away skulls and bones which were
sent safely off to London and St. Petersburg. But
the Ainu were very angry, and complained to the
Japanese government, which required the consuls to
punish the offenders pretty severely. Modern Japanese

law is even more strict; however hardly modern progress may press upon the living Ainu, his dust is safe;
no man may move a post or trouble so much as a bone
of him.

CHAPTER II.

MIYANOSHITA.

THEY say in Tokyo that if you can see Fuji San at sunrise, floating alone above the clouds which hide all the lesser mountains, it is sure to be fine weather. Later in the day the mists rise in horizontal bands, disclosing the blue saw-tooth of the Hakone range across Fuji's base, and the white cone grows fainter and fainter, paling into the pale sky, to reappear at sunset, dark against the gold. They are fifty miles away, those mountains; part of the great barrier stretching right across the island and cutting it nearly in half. The western part of the range is wild and rugged, little inhabited, and even now very difficult traveling; but the region around lake Hakone is perfectly accessible, and is one of the loveliest parts of Japan—not grand, but of the sort of gentle beauty that is peculiarly Japanese. The range is full of memories of feudal times, of fightings and surprises around and over the Hakone pass; and it is also full of hot springs, and therefore of hotels and resorts for invalids and pleasure-seekers, for, wherever there is hot water, there the Japanese are sure to go.

31

It is not a long or a difficult journey, only a matter of three or four hours from Yokohama by train, tram and kuruma successively; and even in Japan, it would be hard to find more varied scenery in the same time and distance. The way is first by the Tokaido, the main line of the railroad southward; passing Ofuna, the junction for Kamakura and the Yokosuka line, and keeping on almost beside the Tokaido post-road, as it runs behind Sagami bay. At first the country is all rice-fields and neat villages; then comes a bit of sandy level, almost like the Jersey barrens, which has been planted with young pine trees, whether for timber or to hold the loose soil I do not know. But, just beyond, in the midst of the sand and beautiful old groves of pine, is the little settlement called Oiso, lying between the sea and a sheltering hill, which has grown of late into a fashionable Japanese watering place; invalids come in winter to breathe the soft air of the pines and take hot salt-baths, and high government officials are very apt to need a run down here about New Year time—of course, it must be for their health, and not, as some naughty people have been known to suggest, to escape New Year's calls. The hotels are all Japanese, but they can provide more or less European food, if desired; and they are arranged on the delightful plan, very common at Japanese resorts, of having a central house and numerous tiny cottages, of two or three to five or six rooms, scattered about picturesquely under the hill. Back a

little in the country there are young peach orchards—
a new thing in Japan; but they flourish well on this
warm, sheltered coast, and on the edge of the low
dunes the gnarled live-oaks are hung with thick
bunches of mistletoe, looking like great green birds'
nests in the branches.

A few miles farther on is Kodzu, where the railroad
leaves the Tokaido and turns inland to make its way
over the Hakone mountains; and here Miyanoshita
people leave the train for the tram. Kodzu is only a
little village, and the people there seem to live chiefly
to receive travelers and send them on their way, whether by the tram to Yumoto and Miyanoshita, or by
kuruma over the coast road to the hot springs of
Atami, twenty miles off. There is a nice little inn
close to the station, where they take you and your
possessions in charge, and buy your ticket and get
your checks, if you will, while you sit comfortably
waiting. As the city trains arrive about noon and
there is all the mountain yet to climb, it is convenient
to bring lunch along and take it at this little station
hotel; you may have a matted room upstairs, or one
below with table and chairs, and you can borrow their
plates, and either drink their pale Japanese tea or tell
the nesan to bring a kettle and pour hot water on
your own leaves in her teapot; and she will wash your
knives and forks and spoons, which the prudent traveler always carries, and repack everything most care--
fully. At the end, a few coppers for her when she has

carried your belongings to the tram, and some small silver for the inn as tea-money, makes every one contented and happy.

Kodzu station stands just back from the edge of a little bluff at the upper end of Odawara bay, famed through Japan for the beauty of its nine-mile curve of smooth sand and the great pines that fringe its line of dunes. They must be centuries old, those pines, and they are of the sort that delights in the buffeting of the wet sea winds; rugged they are, it is true, but not beaten back, only more individual and picturesque for the lifelong struggle. Down on the sand the long, narrow brown sampans are drawn up above the tide, and the nets and fish-baskets are piled about; and under the shadow of the bluff a party of kurumaya are usually found smoking and gambling, not always peaceably, for these coolies of Kodzu are a rather rough set.

A wooded promontory finishes the curve of the beach at its farther end, and looking back the other way, past Oiso and its groves of pine, is Enoshima, Benten's island, scarcely seeming to detach itself from the shore behind. Off on the horizon, a trail of smoke above a faint blue line marks Oshima and its never-quiet volcano; and inland, across the open country, there is a magnificent view of Fuji, looking, as it were, over the shoulders of the foothills of the Hakone group; you see the white cone from the tram during all the first part of the ride, till it is shut out by the nearing mountains.

The Kodzu-Yumoto tram is a most amusingly happy-go-lucky and irresponsible sort of an affair. I do not remember which American car company built its old-fashioned, small, low cars, but they are exceedingly like what used to be known as a "bob-tailed car" in our own part of the world a number of years since. There are usually several of them lying up, so to speak, on the side track under the trees, near the station, and they appear to start whenever they feel inclined. It does not really matter; the nesan always knows when it is time to go and take your place, and there is no connection to make at the other end. They generally start off in bunches of two or three, each drawn by its own pair of shaggy little red horses, which gallop off frantically, bells jangling, windows rattling and car bouncing on the badly-laid track, the driver shouting them on with great enthusiasm. Some cars are marked first and others second-class, the difference being apparently one of empty honor, or possibly of the number of packages per passenger permitted without extra charge.

The track lies along the old Tokaido, which runs for a long way just behind the low sand dunes and the pines, its own avenue of evergreen trees still standing, though not unbroken. After a time the pines cease, and you begin to go through Odawara, a forlorn, ill-kept town, strung out for a mile or more along the highway, looking as if it ought to be big enough and old enough to make itself more tidy, though it may very probably have pleasanter parts farther back toward the hills.

In the midst of Odawara the tram pulls up with a jerk and a jarring of brakes; the second edition behind clatters up and checks likewise, and conductor, driver and half the passengers get off to superintend changing the horses, assisted, as the French would say, by several policemen and what one would take for a quarter of the population. Just here by the tram depot, on the other side of the road, rise some green terraces and foundation walls built of great blocks of stone. It is all there is left of Odawara Castle, formerly one of the strongest fortresses on the Tokaido, which practically controlled the gateway of the Hakone pass. It belonged to a younger branch of the Hojo, the family of Yoritomo's clever wife, Masako, who, though they could not obtain the Shogunate, yet contrived to have the office of Regent of Kamakura handed from father to son in their own house; and by appointing boy Shoguns, and deposing them when they grew troublesome, they ruled both Kamakura and Kyoto for several generations—all in the name of the unwilling emperors.

Yoritomo's dealings with his future father-in-law, Hojo Tokimasa, began during the lifetime of Kiyomori, the Taira chief who had killed Yoritomo's father and nearly all his house. Hojo was a retainer of the Taira, but his family had been often allied with the Minamoto, and when forced to escape from a

Children Carrying Babies

neighboring lord whom he had offended, Yoritomo took refuge with his family's former friend. He was well received, and presently proposed for the hand of Hojo's daughter. Now there were two daughters; the elder, Masako, was more beautiful and clever, but the younger and gentler was her father's favorite, and moreover, the only child of the second wife, and for her Yoritomo intended to ask; but his message was altered through a mistake, and the name of the elder substituted. Meanwhile, on the previous night the younger girl had dreamed of a bird which brought her a little golden box. She told the dream to her sister Masako, who offered her mirror in exchange for the dream; and the younger girl accepted, hoping therewith to win some of her sister's beauty. When Yoritomo's request followed immediately after, Masako believed the gift had truly come to her, and that it was the will of the gods.

But Hojo had already betrothed his daughter to a neighboring lord, and the ceremony was partly accomplished, when on the very wedding-day Yoritomo stole the bride away—doubtless with her connivance, perhaps with her father's also. At any rate, Hojo continued to help him, and Masako's clever scheming is credited with not a little of their final success.

After Yoritomo's death, such a woman was not to be lightly set aside; though she became a nun, it was merely for the sake of appearances, and in point of fact she was the power behind the throne for many years. The young Shogun resisted her ; he was killed in his bath by unknown assassins ; and when the second son succeeded, Masako made him powerless by having her brother appointed Regent. This second Shogun was murdered, on his way to worship at the shrine of Yoritomo at Kamakura, by a son of that elder brother who had been murdered in the bath ; and the guards cut down the youth on the spot, so ending Yoritomo's line. The nun and the Regent chose a child of two as successor to the Shogunate ; the Emperor and the Kuge nobles tried to take the opportunity to throw off the yoke, but the Hojo defeated the imperial forces, deposed the Emperor, and confiscated the estates of the Kuge who had taken part, and made the office of Regent hereditary in the family.

The succeeding rulers were able and successful ; order was maintained and the country prospered greatly. But their usurpation of power and disloyal treatment of the imperial house made them always disliked and distrusted ; and the Mongol invasion of Kublai Khan did much to increase their unpopularity. It was then that the ex-Emperor Go-Daigo plotted against them, was defeated and exiled, escaped, and plotted again, and that finally the faithful generals, Nitta and Masashige, succeeded in taking Kamakura and overthrowing the Hojo—only to substitute King Stork for King Log, the Ashikaga Shoguns for the Hojo Regents. However, the cadet branch of Hojo maintained itself at Odawara, and remained in very considerable power till that wonderful monkey-faced adventurer, the Taiko Hideyoshi, conquered them in a great battle. Even then they retired to the castle and shut themselves up, disputing among the councilors of the clan whether to wear out the enemy by remaining still, or to attempt a sally—till one day, while they were arguing, the Taiko attacked and took the castle from their hands. But it was not destroyed then; that was done only in 1868, when there was hot fighting along the pass between the Imperial and the Tokugawa partisans, and the castle was finally demolished. The small, crowded houses and poor surroundings make the ruin of its fine walls even more impressive.

There is another contrast at Odawara, too, if you are clever enough to find it—a most charming little inn, standing back not a block behind the street, but as sheltered and still in its walled enclosure as if it were miles from another habitation. There is one main building, and a half-circle of tiny cottages in a pine wood looking toward the bay, which is only a few hundred yards off. For a yen or two a day you may have a thatched houselet of two or three rooms and a bath, furnished with spotless tatami and a cushion or two, and a neat nesan to wait on you and serve your rice—all in Japanese, of course, for the little nest would not long be so pure and quiet if many foreign residents frequented it.

Just beyond Odawara the tram line crosses the Hayakawa, the river which drains lake Hakone, and which, like all Japanese rivers, has an immense stony bed, much too wide for it to occupy except in flood time, and then not always wide enough. The farmers try to keep it out of mischief by banking up the sides with neat rows of bamboo baskets filled with stones—a contrivance often used in other places also.

The road leaves the bay now, and goes straight away towards the mountains, which come down suddenly, almost like a wall, into the plain. The river breaks suddenly from a narrow valley, and just here is Yumoto village—the end of the tram line, huddling, as it were, at the very gate. Just beyond Yumoto a pretty waterfall comes into the river, which is already swift and like a mountain stream in the deepening gorge; a quarter of a mile farther, at Tonozawa, you cross by an unsteady bridge to the left bank, and keep it all the rest of the way. Here at Tonozawa there is another pleasant little inn, a little more modernized than the Shoto-En at Odawara, but still fresh, quiet and unspoiled. It has one of the amusing contrasts of new Japan in its electric lights from the large plant on the river near by, which are set in rooms guiltless of chairs and heated by hibachi. It is only another proof that Japan can and will adopt what she cares for in our Western life, and leave the rest untouched.

So far we have been following the Tokaido ; here,

after crossing the river, the highroad kept on to the left and climbed straight up into the Hakone pass. This road now is very rough and almost disused, and the newer way to Miyanoshita keeps instead along the gorge of the Hayakawa. It is a beautiful wooded valley, cleft almost like a V between the mountains. In May it is like a garden of azaleas and single red and white camelias, and purple bunches of Wistaria blossoms, and spireas and laburnums and scarlet pirus Japonica—half the flowering shrubs of an American lawn, flung helter-skelter up and down the hillsides. The road is none too good, and it is a stiff four-mile pull for the kuruma men, who toil up to a sort of grunting chant—*in-saka hoi! in-saka hoi!* The wonder is that they have any breath left to pull. When it comes to the return journey, the runners like to dash down headlong at a pace that is not only alarming, but actually dangerous, besides shaking you almost to pieces over the rough stones; so that unless one prefers to walk and be rid of them entirely, it is well to contract beforehand that they shall go at a walk whenever the road is steep or rough, under penalty of forfeiting all chance of chinsen ("tip") at the bottom. Even in going up, when the weather is fine, it is not too far for a good walker, and there are little paths and short cuts between the zigzags, and you can enjoy the flowers and the changing views to your heart's content.

The Fujiya hotel at Miyanoshita is one of the best

hotels in Japan, if it is not the very best of all; its but-
ter, milk and fresh fruit and vegetables are brought from
an excellent farm in the Hakone country, and everything about it is clean and well managed. The bathing arrangements are particularly delightful; there is
a big, detached bath-house, containing a dozen or
more rooms, each with a deep wooden tub sunk below
the level of the slatted floor, the favorite Japanese
arrangement. Into each come two pipes of mountain
water, one scalding hot and the other as deliciously
cold, and you may draw it, and waste it, and paddle
in it without stint, for there is always an overflow
from the springs far up in the hills. The hot water
is only slightly impregnated with sulphur, and any
one may bathe in it as freely as in any ordinary water,
without waiting to consult physicians.

The Fujiya stands against a steep hillside, facing
directly down the valley, and on clear days across the
V-shaped cleft you can trace the faint blue horizon of
the Pacific beyond Odawara bay. One thinks invol-
untarily of that "Vale in Ida:"

> "Lovelier
> Than all the valleys of Ionian hills."

Here, too,

> "The swimming vapour floats athwart the glen,
> Puts forth an arm, and creeps from pine to pine,
> And loiters, slowly drawn. On either hand
> The lawns and meadow-ledges, midway down,
> Hang rich in flowers, and far below them roars
> The long brook, falling through the cloven ravine
> In cataract after cataract to the sea."

Miyanoshita village lies partly below and partly above the hotel, and, like all the rest in this region, is given over to the making and selling of inlaid boxes, frames, toys, and every other conceivable article that can be made of wood. Many of the things are exceedingly pretty, but it is well to remember that American furnace-heated houses are apt to make sad work of the larger pieces. A peculiar reddish, mottled effect, seen in some of the wood, is obtained by cutting it in spring, when the sap is in the trunks, and laying it out of doors all summer; the sap settles in spots and mildews, discoloring the grain in irregular patches, which come out effectively when the wood is turned and polished.

There are two or three other little villages about, picturesque enough at a distance, but really poor and tumble-down. The one called Kiga is a little way up the road, just by an exceedingly high and well-built bridge across the ravine; the houses hang almost over the edge of the cliff, looking as if a very small shake would send them crashing into the tree-tops two or three hundred feet below, where the stream calls all night and the uguisu—warblers—are singing all day long. A pretty Japanese inn is perched among the little houses at Kiga, said to be well kept and pleasant.

A *dépendence* of the Fujiya stands a little below the main house, overhanging this same ravine; it used to be a separate hotel—Naraya's—and the building is still known by the old name, though it has long since

been absorbed by the larger establishment. Many of
the rooms are exceedingly pleasant, especially those
which are on the ravine side among the warblers ; but
in other ways the house is less pleasant to stay in.
Moreover, in showery weather, the walk · to one's
dinner seems considerable—across the village street by
the post-office, where blue-black swallows dart over
the puddles, and all up the steep garden of the main
house.

The walks around Miyanoshita are uncommonly
pretty, and there are plenty of easy ones for those who
cannot climb far. There is Fujitai, overlooking the
right wing of the hotel, up which a narrow path winds
in steep zigzags for some six hundred feet, giving at
last a splendid view of Fuji, half-way down to its
base ; and there are rambles up the gorge and down,
and straight down by a path, which is almost a flight
of steps, to a pretty waterfall in the side of the ravine,
just a little way below Naraya's. Quite at the bottom
of the gorge, below this waterfall, is the forlorn little
village called Dogashima, where the men always seem
to be off cutting wood on the hills, and where dirty
beggar children follow you with whining cries, pitched
in a shrill crescendo—*chisai chabu-chabu kudasai*—
"something to eat—a *little* something to eat, condescend !"

Beyond the stream and up over the hills there are
beautiful views of the gorge and the far-off blue bay ;
but it is not very safe to wander off there without a

guide, or at least a compass and a pretty clear knowledge of the lay of the land; the narrow footpaths wind and fork and double among the slopes, and in many places the bamboo grass is so tall that for long distances you cannot see over it to get your bearings. A party of students from the Naval School in Tokyo once started to walk up from Gotemba to Hakone, and lost their way among these moors; they roamed about for hours, till it grew quite dark, and they had just made up their minds to make a night of it, supperless and without blankets, when they saw a light a long way off, and, after some difficulty, reached the stock-farm, where they were fed and set on the right road.

For a long time Miyanoshita was the only place in these mountains where there was a foreign hotel, but now several of the bathing places provide beds and European food, more or less good, and there is a capital hotel at Kowakidani, seven hundred feet higher up. Miyanoshita is very lovely in the early summer and autumn, and in the early spring, too, and even in winter, on account of its sheltered situation; but, for the same reason, the summer is undeniably hot and close, and Kowakidani, the " Valley of the Little Boiling," is very much more bracing.

A charm of these moors in summer is the wonderful quantity and variety of the wild flowers; from the first spring violets and irises to the small late autumn chrysanthemums, the grass is full of them, and all so like our wild flowers of the Atlantic coast, that one

need be very little of a botanist to pick out most of
the sixty genera said to be common to the two sides of
the world.

Japanese art and poetry takes little account of these
wild flowers; the only ones it condescends to notice
at all are the little delicate uncurling fronds of fern,
which suggest spring, and the yellow ranunculus which
pushes up before the leaves come out, and which they
call fukujiso—flower of happiness; and the " seven
flowers of autumn," which may really be accounted
favorites with the painters, at least.   They are the
eupatorium, a little like our boneset; the wild pink,
wild convolvulus, *hagi*, a graceful bush, with small
purple papilionaceous flowers; the tall, feathery knot-
grass, called suzuki; a purple flower, which I believe
is pueraria, and the delicate yellow umbelliferous
patrina.   These are the special flowers for the month
of September, and, like our own golden rod, are asso-
ciated with thoughts of the turning year, and at the
same time they bear suggestions of solitude.   It is
proper to depict with them wild horses, or deer, or
the wild boar.

One other flower, often grown in their gardens as
well as ours, is nevertheless considered to be a wild
plant—the deep yellow cocorus, which they call
yamabuki and " mountain rose."   At any rate, it has
a wild-flower story, which concerns Ota Dokwan, the
founder of Yedo and builder of the first castle there.
This knight was one day out hunting in the hilly

region near his new fortress, when he was caught in a
smart shower, and, seeing a cottage, he went to the
door and asked for a straw rain-coat—such as peasants wear now and knights used to put on for journeys afoot, or hunting expeditions. The pretty girl
who received him listened and bowed, but said no
word; then she ran away, and presently came back,
blushing, and handed him no coat, but only a yellow
yamabuki flower. Decidedly disgusted, Sir Ota
walked off in the rain, and not till he was half-way
home did he remember a poem by a famous poet,
"The yellow mountain rose has many pretty petals,
but alas, it has no seed." Now *mino* is a seed, and *mino*
is also a straw rain-coat, and the young man perceived
that, like a true daughter of Japan, his pretty wood-
nymph had expressed both her refusal and her regret
in a poetic pun.

CHAPTER III.

HAKONE AND ATAMI.

MIYANOSHITA is situated in what is known as the "Hakone district," which is a general name to include all the heaped-up mass of mountains lying at the base of the Izu peninsula, between the "skirts" of Fuji San and the sea. There is one little village called Hakone on the side of the Hakone lake, or, rather, two little villages of the same name and close together. The lake lies over the passes towards Fuji, a thousand feet higher than Miyanoshita, and the Tokaido came over by it on the way down to the plain. The old name of the lake was Ashi-no-Umi, Sea of Reeds, which does not seem remarkably well suited to a deep body of water, surrounded as this is by high hills and shores nearly everywhere rocky and steep. But the old name is still used in poetry, much as Byron talked of "clear, placid Leman," lying beside Chillon's walls.

In summer lake Hakone is much cooler than Miyanoshita, and many foreigners come up from Yokohama and Tokyo to stay there, but, rather strangely, there is no European hotel; only a pretty little tea-house overlooking the lake, very pleasant for rest and lunch in the course of a day's excursion, but not very comfortable to stay in long. What the people do is to rent cottages in the village, and bring up servants and such household goods as are absolutely necessary, and keep house for a few months in a more or less free and easy fashion. The boating on the lake is a great attraction, and the walks and longer excursions are very delightful.

The easiest way of getting to lake Hakone is by going to Miyanoshita and spending the night there, and going on over the hills next day; but it is shorter and quite possible to go by kuruma from Yumoto directly over the old Tokaido and the Hakone pass, though the road is rougher than the Miyanoshita way and less apt to be promptly repaired after a storm, and the ride is longer. From Miyanoshita to Hakone there is only a footpath over the moors, and all who are not prepared to walk the eight miles must be carried in chairs or *kago*.

Now the chairs are all very well; they are like Swiss ones, or the kind used by everybody in Hong Kong—an ordinary wicker arm-chair slung on bamboo poles; and you are merely warned to sit still, for fear of overbalancing the men, who carry high, with the poles on their shoulders. But about the charms of kago riding there is diversity of opinion. Some maintain that whereas the kago in use at Miyanoshita are higher and longer than the common kind found

elsewhere, even a European can curl up a little and
lie on the cushions comfortably, not to say luxuriously ;
but others call it an instrument of torture and will
have none of it. The thing is simply a very short
litter, with a low roof, slung on a bamboo pole ; the
bearers take each an end on his shoulder and a long
staff in his hand, and trot off at a good speed with a
fairly pleasant motion. In old times kago were the
only mode of conveyance except the ox-cars of the
nobles—the closed norimon being only another and
more luxurious form—and it was the large body of
trained kago bearers who made the jinrikisha possible ;
as soon as the little carriage was invented they simply
dropped the pole and picked up the shafts, and went
on running without any real change in their manner
of life.

The path to Hakone starts up through the woods,
then out over a rolling moor covered with coarse grass
and innumerable field flowers—violets, orchids, blue-
bells, buttercups and lilies—or dense thickets of wild
bamboo higher than a man's head. The moor is really
a pass, reaching three thousand feet at the highest
point, where you turn from the path a little and climb
the hill called Benten Yama, to look over all the Izu
peninsula and even to Yedo bay. The village of
Ashi-no-yu lies in a rather steamy hollow just below,
probably an extinct volcano—*yu*, " hot water," because
of the sulphur springs, and *ashi*, reeds—a name
which seems much more appropriate here than at

Kago (Traveling Chair)

Hakone, because the springs really do come from a swampy part of the hollow. The water here is much more heavily charged with sulphur than at Miyano-shita, and many invalids come to take the baths for rheumatism and such things; one of the hotels gives very fair European accommodation. Ashi-no-yu lies higher than any of the rest of the resorts in the Hakone region, nearly three thousand feet in all, and is consequently cooler even than the lake; but the air is apt to be less pleasant, because the moisture from the springs seems to hang in the air and seldom rises fully over the edge of the hollow in which it lies. This high, rolling, treeless region is often compared to the English lake country, and it is really strikingly like the wilder and more desolate parts, say toward Buttermere and on some of the passes.

From here the bearers swing along at an easy trot over another two or three miles of rolling moor, nearly all gently down hill, towards the lake. There are two little pools on the way, hardly worthy of the name of lakes, each filling the crater of an extinct volcano—more reminders of the way things have been made, which make one feel as if Japan had been occupied before it was altogether finished, geologically speaking, as people go into a new house before the carpenters are quite out of it, taking their chances of pitfalls and fresh paint.

Near the path there are a few little shrines and monuments, and especially a fine image of Jizo, friend

of travelers and protector of little children; it is life-
sized, and carved in high relief out of the gray rock
against which he sits.   Tradition attributes both this
and another work, a rock-cut group of Buddhist saints,
to that wonderful artist-priest, Kobo Daishi, of the
eighth century; but it is nearly certain that both
belong to the latter part of the thirteenth—the century of the Kamakura Daibutsu, which the Jizo
greatly resembles in general style.

His lap is always piled full of pebbles, laid there
by bereaved mothers, who pray the compassionate god
to help their little ones in the other world.   For they
say that the spirits of little children wander forlornly
in the dry bed of the River of Souls, crying after
father and mother, and heaping little prayer-towers of
the stones in the bed of the river ; and wicked demons
come and frighten the children, and throw down their
piles of stones.   But Jizo comes and drives away the
bad demons, and the children run and hide themselves
in his sleeves, and he comforts them and helps them
to build their towers up again.

Suddenly the lake appears below in a nest of hills,
and the path drops steeply to it, meeting the Tokaido
at the first little village, which is called Moto Hakone.
Here is the Matsuzakiya inn, looking out over the
lake and its picturesque windings, and over to the far
hills, which are all wooded with pines and beautiful
deciduous trees, making a variety of tints in the foliage, even when all are green with the full summer.

From the inn there is a fine view of Hakone's greatest boast, *Hakone no saka Fuji*, the pure white cone of Fuji rising above the nearer mountains which conceal its base, and reflecting in the blue water of the lake. It must be just the right weather to see this—the still maple weather of October or November, when the sky is clear and there is no wind to break the image on the smooth surface. Perched on the cliff a little farther on there is a summer palace where the Crown Prince often stays, and beyond this, the second and rather larger village, where most of the foreigners spend the summer.

All about this part of the shore there are tokens of the past; a fine stone torii stands across the road near the village, flanked by two weather-worn stone lanterns, and up the steep hillside another torii, of wood and colored red, marks one of Yoritomo's haunts when he used to come here hunting; in a shed close by they show the iron pots in which tradition says the rice was boiled for his camping parties, and in another place his sword and other relics. A village in the plain below is still called Gotemba, the August Camp.

Another shrine a little farther up is dedicated to the Soga brothers, whose small stone monuments are beside the path on the way from Ashi-no-yu; and whose virtue was that they fulfilled the law of Confucius, which said, "Thou shalt not live under the same heaven with the slayer of thy father." It must be remembered that when a Samurai paid such pious debts, he did it knowing that his life was inevitably forfeit, whether his attempt was successful or not. The civil law said, "Thou shalt do no murder;" the Samurai broke the civil to keep the moral law, and bent to the punishment.

"On the 28th of May in the fourth year of Kenkiu (1293)," says a Japanese chronicle, "the Shogun Yoritomo ordered a great hunting expedition at the foot of Mount Fuji. The two orphan sons of Kawazu Sukeyasu, Soga Juro and Soga Goro, thought to profit by this occasion to avenge their father, by slaying his murderer, the Lord Kudo. Therefore, watching for a favorable moment, they appeared at the chase with the rest.

"Now about noon of this day rain began to fall, and the chase was suspended, every man retiring to his own shelter and amusing himself as best he could. So Lord Kudo sent for dancers, that he might make a feast and entertain his friends. And going out for some purpose, he found at his door Soga Juro, who had come to spy out the position of Kudo's camp. Therefore he asked the young man to enter, and offered him a cup of wine, and spoke plausibly, saying that it was not·he but another who had done to death the father of Soga. And Soga Juro feigned to believe him, and sat and drank wine with Lord Kudo and his son; and afterwards he excused himself and went away. And Kudo saw that he was no mean man, and he set guards about his camp, for he knew that the youth was not deceived."

Meanwhile the younger brother waited with the retainers at an inn, and when Juro returned they completed their preparations, meaning to act that night; for they were helped by one Tora Gozen, a beautiful girl from the town of Oiso, who had given her heart to the younger brother. She it was who got into Kudo's camp in disguise, and opened the door for the brothers, so that they entered and killed their enemy before the guards were aroused. Then, when a band of knights sprang out upon them, they cried their names and station, as Samurai should, and fought bravely, till the elder was killed and the younger overpowered and taken before Yoritomo. There the young man calmly related what they had done, and why, adding that it had been part of their intention to slay Minamoto no Yoritomo himself, as the enemy of their grandfather. Yoritomo, who loved bravery above all things, would gladly have spared the outspoken youth, but he had no choice but to condemn him by the laws he himself had made. The two brothers were buried together on the mountain, and a third monument is raised to the beautiful Tora, who, when her lover was put to death, cut her hair and became a nun, spending her life in prayers for Goro's soul.

The story has been powerfully dramatized — the secret preparations, the farewells and last charges to the faithful retainers, who pray in vain to share; the night attack and the great fight, which, on the stage, becomes a series of wonderful rhythmic poses, only one step removed from those historical Nô dances from which the Japanese drama sprang; all leading up to the closing scene, when Yoritomo sits in judgment in the hunting camp, and the head of the elder brother is brought in and laid before the younger, and the boy, already on his way to execution, makes the gray thing a Samurai's farewell. As Danjuro renders the part, the one moment of overmastering emotion, instantly suppressed, is not only intensely Japanese in feeling, but a masterpiece of suggestive acting.

A prettier bit of history belongs on the post road just beyond the other village, where a few foundation stones mark the site of the famous barrier on the Hakone pass, the point at which, till a generation ago, every one was carefully examined before being allowed to approach Yedo. Here then Yoritomo thought to catch his fugitive brother Yoshitsune, who was known to be escaping northward in disguise, with a few followers and his faithful henchman Benkei, ex-temple-porter and all-round scamp; and the guards had orders of the strictest to let no suspicious persons by. Therefore when a party of Yamabushi (begging monks) one day appeared, headed by a tall fellow none too monastic looking, the captain was for giving them all in charge. Monks, forsooth! he declared, they were no Yamabushi, but knights in disguise; if they were begging for their order, what credentials had they? What, indeed? Without the slightest hesitation Ben-

kei, the audacious, plucks out a roll—now may these
men of the sword be bravely unlearned!—and in de-
voutest sing-song intones a lengthy *Kanjincho,* or Buddhist contribution register, beautifully conceived and
worded, evolved upon the instant from his own fertile
brain; an exhortation to all pious persons to give according to their ability for the rebuilding of a certain
temple.

"The Emperor Shomu had a wife, to whom he gave
his whole heart; and when she departed from this
world he caused a temple to be built on the spot where
she died. Some time later this temple was burnt
down; in order to rebuild it contributions are asked.
Those who contribute even a penny shall enjoy perfect
peace in this world, and shall sit upon thousands of
lotus leaves in the world to come.[1]

The company listen reverently; it is enough, quite
enough, declares the captain; the good priest must
pardon the erring zeal of an ignorant soldier; only—
there is one young fellow in the company, who does
look strangely like the man they are after; perhaps it
may be well to detain him for a little. This will never
do! Round turns Benkei, and deals his master a
sounding thwack, crying, "Down on your knees, you
lout; don't you know any better than to stand gaping
at the gentleman?" And then to the captain, "Pardon, honorable; shall I kill the stupid? In truth it
is but a lump just from the rice-fields, and knows no

[1] "Benkei, the Quick-witted Loyalist." Translated by Y. Negishi.

better." And so they pass safely by, only to die in the north; but history neglects to mention what became of that captain when the story came to Yoritomo's ears.

Just as he was, save in his dealings with his brother, Yoritomo cannot have been a pleasant person to meet in anger. In effigies and records he appears as a tall, spare man, with piercing eyes, and thin lips under a small moustache. When he could not be fighting, he loved to go hunting, on horseback, with his favorite hawk on his wrist, and surrounded by the gentlemen whom he thus encouraged to hardy pastimes. These mountains, but a few miles from his capital at Kamakura, must have been the delight of such a prince; the wild boar and the bears are gone now, and even the monkeys and deer, but there are miles and miles of moor and forest, uncleared and unplanted even yet.

There is another way back from Hakone to Miyanoshita, which bears the rather startling name of Ojigoku, the Big Hell; or, if you prefer, Owakidani, Valley of the Great Boiling. The place deserves an emphatic name; it is what the Italians call a solfatara, a place less violent than a volcano, but of the same nature. It is a rather narrow, open valley, perhaps a half mile long, filled from end to end with scalding springs and outbursts of sulphurous smoke, like Yellowstone Park in miniature; a place rather unpleasantly suggestive, in this shaky country, which seems to have such a thin crust at the best. The valley is reached from Hakone by taking a boat to the other

end of the lake—they put in chairs or kago and all—
and then following a steep path a mile or so through
a mossy wood, which ends as suddenly as if it had
been cut off at the top of the solfatara. Looking back
from this point, there is a beautiful view of Fuji San
and the nearer mountains, making the keenest of contrasts with the dreary inferno at your feet. However
fine the day may be outside, a whirl of steam and
smoke always sweeps through the valley from end to
end, half-hiding, half-showing the ghastly expanse of
lumpy gray and yellow mud through which a slippery
ridge of a path winds down. You marvel why there
should be so well trodden a track through such a
place, till you see a party of laborers following along
it in single file, carrying loads of sulphur, which has
been deposited by the water and steam. The reek is
horrible, and the trees and blossoming shrubs, creeping to the very edge, make the desolation only the
more complete ; one hardly needs the warning not to
venture from the path onto the treacherous crust. It
is a relief to climb out into the safe woods, and presently enter the litters again and be carried at a swinging trot over the long home-stretch of grassy moor
back to Miyanoshita.

From Hakone lake three chief roads go down—
none of them fit for anything but men's feet. They
are the old Tokaido, to Mishima and the coast ; the
Ten Province pass, with its wonderful sweep of view,
leading down to the sheltered hot springs of Atami, on

Sagami bay; and the Maiden's pass, Otomo Toge, from the farther end of the lake to Gotemba, at the foot of Mount Fuji. People coming to Miyanoshita from Kobe and other southern points, often get off at Gotemba and ride by kuruma nearly to the top of the Maiden's pass, and walk or take chairs the rest of the way. The fine cattle farm at Sengokuhara lies to the left, soon after crossing the summit, between the mountains and the valley of the Hayakawa, which you follow the rest of the way back to Miyanoshita, much as in returning from the Ojigoku. To reach Hakone from the Maiden's pass, it is needful to turn off at the farm and follow a rough trail to the end of the lake.

From the Gotemba side the view of Fuji is unbroken. You see the whole green plain between the Hakone side and the base of the great mountain, and the perfect cone sweeping up its twelve thousand three hundred and ninety-five feet, flanked at a respectful distance by Ashitakayama to the left and the spurs of Oyama to the right, while far around to the south there is a glimpse of the blue Suruga bay.

The Ten Province pass, as its name suggests, overlooks the whole region round about, from Tokyo and the Musashi plain all along the coast and past the rocky Izu peninsula to Suruga bay, and across to Fuji and the Koshu mountains behind. The Taiko Hideyoshi left his mark upon this part of the region, in the name of the mountain called Taiko-yama, which

Hakone

is part of the ridge lying behind Hakone village, and completing the circle of mountains on its southeastern side. Here, they say, Hideyoshi marched over, when he assembled his army to attack the Hojo at Odawara. The Hakone pass was held against him, but a hunter showed a pass across the wall of mountains, and the Taiko went over and reached the slope of Ishikake-yama, which is next to the Sagami plain, and won there a decisive battle.

From the "Ten Province Stone," at the top of the pass, it is a steep descent of about three miles to Sagami bay and the cliff road, which follows all along the coast from one little village to another; and just here, where the two meet, is the little village of Atami, built about its famous geyser. Hot springs are plenty enough in Japan—there must be scores in this Hakone region alone; but geysers are not at all common, and this one is accounted a great curiosity, as well as most beneficial to the sick. A remarkable feature of it is the situation—almost on the beach. The water contains a good deal of salt, and even the steam is perceptibly salty. They have built a house around the spring now, so that invalids may inhale the steam, which is found to be very helpful to the throat and lungs.

There are plenty of good hotels at Atami, one at least furnishing European accommodation; but tourists seldom find their way here, perhaps because it is rather out of the way. The most convenient road is not by Hakone and the pass, but from Odawara by a curious combination of tram and jinrikisha—a series of small, roofed hand-cars, pushed by men along a narrow railroad. As the line is not much graded, when it was first opened the men's carelessness caused a number of accidents; but the authorities required improvements, and it seems to be safe enough now. This " Riviera of Japan," as Chamberlain calls it, is one of the most beautiful parts of the coast; to the right are the mountains, sending down little spurs which break the shore into picturesque nooks and coves, and on the left the deep blue of the bay; and all about the rich vegetation, the palms and the orange groves and daphnes, which flourish in the soft air. The mountains keep off all but the warm sea-winds from the " Black Current," and Atami knows even less about winter than Nice or Mentone.

Besides the pleasant Japanese visitors who frequent Atami for their health, the villages near by are picturesque and entertaining, especially when a school of bonito comes in and a keen-sighted man stands high on the cliff, where he can see the dark mass of fish through the clear water, and signals to the fleet of little boats which way to go. There are many attractive walks, both along the shore and inland, and the flowers on the hills in early spring remind one afresh of northern Italy.

Near the geyser there is a villa belonging to the Crown Prince, where he was often sent for part of the winter during his childhood, for the sake of the warm, sheltered climate. He has been a delicate boy, but happily seems to be much stronger since he has grown up. A photograph taken when he was about nine years old shows a thoughtful, sensitive little face, rather overpowered by the big military cap which he wore as a pupil of the Noble's School. The well-cut chin, and firm, sweet mouth, promise well for the future of the nation. Visitors at Atami used to tell pretty stories of his activity and sprightliness and his eager curiosity about everything new; he particularly wanted to know exactly why the water lay quiet for just four hours, and then ran half an hour and subsided again, until time for another outburst. There are pleasant accounts, too, from those around him of his thoughtfulness and winning disposition, and his warm friendships with his companions and teachers; and, just now, of the pretty little princess, whom he married a couple of years ago. The young couple drive out together quite frequently—something the Emperor and Empress do only on rare and important occasions—and in other respects conduct their household much as European royalties might do.

CHAPTER IV.

THE TOKAIDO.

"Toward the far northern land
Wild geese are flying,
'Mid their sky journeyings
Mournfully crying.
Ah! It must be that sore
Is their fond yearning
For one that hither came,
Now unreturning;
Here on this alien shore
Lost to them evermore!"

"Log of a Japanese Journey" (Tosa Nikki). Translated by Mrs. Harris.

THE same glamor of romantic association that gathers for us around the Appian Way and the passes over the Alps, or the old Roman roads in England, clings for a Japanese to each mile of his Tokaido, the scene of so many great events, so many historic journeys. It was probably the oldest road to the north, certainly the most famous even before the Tokugawa period of Yedo residence and the Daimyo's periodic migrations.

One of the most charming bits of Miss Scidmore's "Jinrikisha Days" tells how their party rode over the Tokaido just before the railroad was built, making a

64

sort of farewell trip, before the old character of the road should be quite taken away. Happily, it is still quite possible to make all or part of the trip by jin-rikisha if one so desires, for the highway is kept up in good condition, and the inns, if less elegant than in the days of Daimyo, are still comfortable and pleasant enough for anybody. And certainly if there is a place in the world where one resents even the moderate speed of a Japanese railroad, it is on the Tokaido line between Kodzu and Nagoya; there is no lovelier scenery in the empire, and none in the world, perhaps, so infinitely varied, so crowded with picturesque life, with alternations of mountain and coast and richly cultivated plain. Kipling indeed complains that it is quite too various to be comfortably appreciated. "We came into the Hakone mountains by way of some Irish scenery, a Scotch trout stream, a Devonshire combe, and an Indian river running masterless over half a mile of pebbles. This was only the prelude to a set of geological illustrations, including the terraces formed by ancient river beds, denudation, and half a dozen other ations. . . . Anybody can keep pace with Indian scenery, arranged as it is in reaches of five hundred miles, but this blinding alternation of field, mountain, sea-beach, bamboo grove and rolling moor covered with azalea blossoms was too much for me."

The name of Eastern Sea road is well deserved. Starting at Sanjo-bashi (Third Street Bridge), in Kyoto, and ending at Nihonbashi, in Yedo, the

Tokaido is seldom many miles out of sight of the sea; and the railway follows it through most of its course, except where it turns aside to find an easier if longer route over the mountains, and later again from Gifu on, where it strikes on to the other, the Nakasendo or Central Mountain road, coming over by way of Karui-zawa. Thus, while the post-road went up to Odawara, and entering the gate of the mountains, climbed boldly across the neck of the Izu peninsula by the Hakone pass, the railroad just touches Odawara bay, at Kodzu, and sweeping round in a great curve to the right plunges into the rocky valley of the Sakakawa river, which drains lake Yamanaka high up in the Kofu range; and climbing over passes and through tunnels, comes out suddenly on a high level plain, with Fuji San sweeping up in the midst of it, not twenty miles away. The railroad's nearest point to the mountain is Gotemba, Yoritomo's hunting camp, which lies against the foot of the Hakone range five miles across the rice-fields from "the skirts" of Fuji, as the Japanese call its spreading base. After that the line draws away again, running down the valley of another little river till it meets the highway again at Numazu, on Suruga bay. Thence the two keep together for half a day, always across rice-fields, and through villages, and past shrines, marked far off by their graceful groups of trees; crossing rivers, touching picturesque coves, and running for miles along the shore, the blue peaks always in sight, and Fuji floating above them all.

The first place of importance south of the mountains is Shizuoka, famous for two wealthy monasteries, and because, when Prince Tokugawa resigned the Shogunate, he retired to a family seat here and settled down quietly as a country gentleman; but most of all celebrated because it was here that Ieyasu withdrew during his last years, to work out his policy of administration at leisure from the cares of active rule; and here that he prepared his political "Testament," for the guidance of his son and grandson.

From Shizuoka the road and railroad run a long way close to the shore, which is here low and unsheltered, receiving the full beat of the Pacific, till, after crossing a wide inlet—it was a lake, until the fifteenth century, when an earthquake broke down the sandbar which shut out the sea—the line makes a sudden turn to the west and north, to sweep around the deep pocket of Owari bay. At the head of this bay is Nagoya, much the largest and most important city of the Tokaido, which was once a castle-town and is now the capital of a prefecture. It is a flourishing place, quite semi-modern, owning an enterprising new European hotel, besides good Japanese inns, and the old (and uncommonly poor) half-breed one, which has been there for a couple of decades. The castle, with its golden dolphins on the gable ends, is visible on its hill for miles around.

Leaving both Owari bay and the old Tokaido, the

train now strikes across to Gifu, three hours beyond; a pleasant little town, which got itself unpleasant fame by its share in a terrible earthquake that devastated this part of the country a few years ago. Gifu is the last large town before reaching Kyoto; fifteen miles beyond it, the line crosses Ieyasu's great battle-field, Sekigahara; then climbs through a mountain range and drops on the other side to lake Biwa, which it skirts for a couple of hours through some beautiful scenery; and so, by a last tunnel, arrives at Kyoto and the end of the Eastern Sea road.

From first to last, the Tokaido provinces have an air of abundance and prosperity that recalls the rich meadows of Holland and the Belgian coast; they are all well watered (which means everything in Japan), and the warm, sheltered parts near the foot of Fuji produce small Chinese sugar-cane of good quality, and on the hill-slopes excellent tea, second only to what is grown in the region near Nara and the head of the Inland Sea. Everywhere cultivation is carried out over every foot of ground, till you feel that the farmer must know every stalk of his rice crop, so carefully he tends it, weeding and re-weeding and stirring up the well-fertilized soil. In the midst of the fields delightful scarecrows, in faded blue garments and huge straw hats, wave frantic arms at the crows and sparrows, who settle and pick unabashed by their gestures or their fluttering rags. Passers-by may be not less bold, to judge from the verse which

Hearn quotes, attributing it to some cheerful, philosophic, half-starved tramp of a student:

" Heavily falls the rain on the hat which I stole from the scare-
    crow."

Probably much of the prosperity of these provinces
is due to the fact that in recent times they belonged
either to branches of the Tokugawa family—Tokugawa
proper, or those who bore the name Matsudaira, which
was Ieyasu's own family name—or to *Fudai* Daimyo,
those who were near to the Shogun and enjoyed his
favor. And, besides, the road itself must have brought
traffic and profit to those who were fortunate enough
to be within its reach. In the old days, inns and
booths and villages stood so thickly along it that in
some places they made almost a continuous street.
Ieyasu, with his unfailing wisdom, caused the Tokaido
to be greatly improved; bridges were built or strength-
ened, ferries marked, and wide, open spaces arranged
for on the banks at the landings, so that everybody
might have room for his preparations and for the
necessary delay while waiting for ferrymen. The
width of the road itself was set at thirty-six feet—
narrow enough we should think it—while the cross
roads were to be eighteen feet, and paths across the
fields three—these last for men's feet only. The road-
bed was not paved, but laid on a foundation of small
stones, well packed down and raised like a dike above

the surrounding fields. Thus water drained quickly off, and though after a rain it might be gloriously muddy at first, the light, dry soil of Japan would soon be quite dusty again. Ieyasu also had the distances marked off in *ri*, which is a little less than two miles and a half, and established fifty-three relay houses, or post-stations, where bearers and pack-horses had to be always in waiting, to convey any official person. It was the duty of the prince, in whose province any part of the road lay, to keep it in order, maintain the bridges, and see that the post-houses were well kept and met all regulations of traffic, or whatever. And, finally, it was the duty of each prince to forward the mails, whether of the imperial court or of the far more powerful Bakufu government at Yedo. Captain Osborn, R. N., describes graphic-ally how it was done in 1859, when all the ancient customs were still in full force.

"Just as we alighted at the rest-station a bell was heard. 'Out of the way! Out of the way!' shouts a Japanese official, and two men hasten from the house and look expectantly up the road; the crowd divides, as if cleft with a knife, and, at a swinging pace, the carriers are seen approaching—a pair of stalwart, bronze-hued fellows, strong of limb and sound of wind; their garments are few, and those of the official black color, stamped with the imperial crest—a white trefoil. One of the runners has a short bamboo pole over his shoulder, and suspended

Rice Planting

from it a black lacquer dispatch-box, formidable for
its size; and we recognize the strength that has
brought it to our feet so rapidly—no, not to our feet,
for it never touches the ground.   In a second it is
slipped from the tired man's shoulder to that of the
fresh runner, who starts down the road like a hare, his
comrade's bell ringing to warn all travelers to make
way.   Thus the Taikoon's dispatches speed through
the land; for, if one man drops, the other takes up the
burden.   If a bridge is broken down, they must swim
the torrent.   Haste!—post-haste!—must be seen in
Japan to be understood."

What Captain Osborn calls the imperial crest was
evidently that of the Shogun, or the Taikoon, as he
calls him—the three leaves of Tokugawa, which, during their first intercourse, the foreigners naturally took
for the Emperor's.   The nearest representative now
of the running messengers is the letter carrier, who
trots through the city streets, dressed in a neat uniform of dark blue cotton for winter and white for
summer; white mushroom hat on his head and feet
shod in dark cotton *tabi* (toed stockings) and straw
sandals—swift, silent, tireless.

There were many streams to cross, all more or less
liable to floods in summer and autumn; the Oikawa,
near Shizuoka, had always to be forded, because it
was too wide to bridge and too swift to ferry.   Bands
of coolies were always in waiting, ready to take travelers over on small platforms with handles, which

they carried on their shoulders. The rapid current at all times, and the real danger when the river was high, gave these bearers a capital chance to stop in the middle and demand *pour boire*, in excess of the regular fare, which was fixed by law for all stages of the road. As an offset, however, they were held responsible for the lives of the passengers they carried over. The scene at the ford was always a favorite with *genre* artists, especially the moment when some Daimyo's train was about to pass; the lord's norimon had to be set on one of the platforms, and a dozen stout fellows bore the poles, while lesser personages tucked up their garments and sat on the flat boards, and the servants on the bank hastened to tie packages securely and protect the baggage against possible wettings.

But, with the railroad, all these picturesque difficulties have vanished; the lacquered and gilded norimon, with their silken curtains; the retainers clustering about it, their number fixed by the rank of the lord, the standard bearers and the bows and muskets, spears and halberds; the fine cases for the baggage and for the utensils to be used on the journey; and, before all, the runners clearing the road in advance, with the cry of *shita ni iro !*—down on your faces ! So the Emperor went up to Tokyo for the first time in 1868, and so he returned to Kyoto a few months later; but, when he went back to Tokyo in the following year, the *shita ni* was done away forever; all might stand,

in respectful silence, to watch the plain white norimon
and the small band of attendants. Now, when His
Imperial Majesty travels, he goes in a special train,
like other royalties; and when he rides, it is through
streets full of people, all shouting at the top of their
lungs, " Banzai !"—Ten thousand years.

The peasants of the Tokaido, too, were the delight
of Hokusai and his fellow artists of the Ukiyo-ye, or
school of the passing world; Hiroshige, in particular,
made set after set of color prints, chiefly landscapes
with figures, and bridges or distant views of castles.
And always it is the peasant whom they depict, with
the affection of a Millet, but in a far different spirit, a
gayety and subtle humor peculiarly Japanese, whether
he is working in the fields, wielding the great hoe, or
bending under mushroom hat over the sprouting rice,
or bearing piles of straw to be stacked; or with cotton
handkerchief-bundle slung on his shoulders and staff
in hand, setting forth on a visit or pilgrimage—even
as you see him from the windows of the train, in this
latest year of Meiji.

Till the fifteenth century the peasants were practically serfs attached to the soil; during that period they
attained a new degree of freedom, partly through the
breaking down of feudal lines—renewed, however,
even more precisely under the Tokugawa—and partly
through the great number of farmers employed as
soldiers in the new mode of warfare which came with
the use of firearms; some even obtained lands and

rank in consequence of distinguished service and ability, as Hideyoshi himself did.

Agriculture was always accounted an honorable employment, one in which even knights might engage without loss of dignity; several early emperors are on record as encouraging it, by digging ponds and irrigating canals, and building storehouses for rice, millet and other grains. Under the able eleventh Emperor, Suinin, property belonging to the government was mapped out and recorded, and a certain number of farmers told off to cultivate it; while any one was free to take up waste land and reclaim and settle on it. Part of the so-called "Taikwa reforms," made in the eighth century, were directed against abuses of power on the part of governors and local officials, who got possession of lands not properly registered, and used them for their own benefit; and "all lands held by private individuals were confiscated by the State and registered as public property," says the official history. At the same time various rules were laid down for the control of such lands and their distribution among the people; thus every male on attaining the age of six years received two tan of land (about half an acre), and every female one-third of a tan, the areas thus conferred being, however, resumed by the State and redistributed every six years; but this scheme was only carried out for a short time, the land being soon left with a holder till his death, and finally passing from father and son like a real property. Those who did not want to till their land sold it to others, who thus acquired great estates. Yet, throughout, the basis of the national system was the theory that private property in land did not exist; it remained so even down to the regime of Meiji, the reign of the present Emperor, when the right of private ownership was established by law, and all classes allowed to hold real estate. Even under the Tokugawa, though the Shogun and the feudal barons practically owned immense districts, these tracts were still regarded as temporarily rented from the State. In early times, too, it was the custom for the sovereign to bestow grants of land for special merit or service, the ground so bestowed being still theoretically understood to be loaned, not given outright; and certain lords did the same by their followers, with waste lands which they took up, and which had never been registered as belonging to the State.

Taxes under the Taikwa system and the Taiho which followed it were levied in three separate ways, of which the most important was the direct land tax laid on the rice crop; two tan (half an acre) of rice land was considered to bear one hundred sheaves, of which four and a quarter went to the government as its share of the profit. The second was a kind of corvée, each grown man being supposed to do ten days' public work a year; but he might redeem his time if he wished by the payment of a piece of cloth. The third tax was levied (also in kind) on fish, silk, cloth, and other industrial products.

The country was already divided into provinces, Japanese *kuni*, and these again into lesser districts; the Taiho code provided for graded officers to administer them, fixing their salaries according to rank. These officers were to be appointed for their ability, following the Chinese merit system, which is still in vogue in China with all its hideous abuses; but, though there were several attempts to introduce this system in Japan, the thing never worked there long. It would seem that feudalism suited the genius of the Japanese race, and perhaps, too, the broken hill and valley nature of the country, which marked off province from province by sharp natural boundaries; certainly offices always tended to become hereditary, and remain the understood prerogative of this or that family. If the chiefs ruled wisely and justly and with a mighty hand, the family maintained its prestige for generations, even for centuries; if not, the better man took the place by force of arms and established his line instead. As De la Mazelière puts it, "Proprietors assert their freedom on their own domains, and then, menaced on all sides by anarchy, the poorer put themselves under the protection of their rich neighbors; the empire is divided into hundreds of small states, and the result is feudalism"—only, as he goes on to point out, in Japan it was a feudalism differing from that of Europe in having a strongly patriarchal quality—such as the Hebrews, for instance, might have retained, if we can imagine the princes of Israel estab-

lishing a group of petty states under the kingship of
the house of David. The chief of the clan was the
father of all the members, and they were his children,
and owed him the same affection and obedience that
sons owe to a father; the Emperor himself holds the
like paternal relation to all his people. It is the Con-
fucian principle of filial piety as the basis of all law,
the root of every virtue.

Since the governor of a province was to be supported out of the taxes paid in it, these naturally
came to be regarded as the right of the feudal lord,
and in point of fact less and less came to be paid in
to the central government, more and more appropri-
ated to the use of the Daimyo and the local requirements of his territory. The Taiko Hideyoshi, himself
peasant born, made many investigations and reforms
of abuse which had crept into the administration of
estates, causing new surveys to be made, and much
property brought under taxation which had been
unjustly exempted. From his time land was rated
according to its produce in kind, as rice land, wood-
land, ground fit for dry crops (wheat, millet and so
on), or silk, or tea, or lacquer-raising country. On
the lands rated as belonging to the State, the cultivator took about one-third, the government the rest.

The Tokugawa Shoguns made further registrations
and changes, on the whole to the advantage of the
country at large. The "Testament of Ieyasu" declared the yearly revenue of the empire to be twenty-

eight millions nine hundred thousand koku of rice; of this twenty millions were to be divided among the Daimyo and lesser lords, and the rest was to belong to the Shogun, who made from it an appropriation for the support of the court at Kyoto, and discharged the offices of the central government, leaving the care of roads and all expenses of local administration to the Daimyo.

The Tokugawa revived an old division of the people, which classed them in *mura* or villages, theoretically of fifty households, and these again in *kumi* or groups of five families, who were mutually responsible for each other's conduct and welfare. The peasants had their own assemblies, and their own magistrates chosen by themselves; and under the laws of the province in which they belonged they practically governed themselves in all matters of local interest.

This was the proclamation of Lord Yozan of Yonezawa in regard to the association of families and villages:

"The farmer's mission is in tillage and silk raising. Diligent in these, he feeds his father and mother, wife and children, and gives his dues to the government in return for its protection. But all this is possible only by mutual dependence of one upon another, for which purpose associations of some kind are necessary, and we hereby institute anew the Companies of Five and Ten and the Company of Five Villages, as follows:

" The members of the Company of Five should be in constant intercourse with one another, and divide the joys and sorrows of each, as do the members of one and the same family.

" The members of the Company of Ten should have frequent intercourse with one another, and hear to the family affairs of each, as do they who are of blood kin.

" They of one village should be like friends in helping and serving one another.

" The villages which constitute the Company of Five Villages should help one another in time of trouble as befits true neighbors.

" If there is one among you who is old and has no child, or is young and has no parents, or is poor and cannot adopt sons, or is widowed, or is a cripple and cannot support himself, or is sick and has no means of help, or is dead and left without burial, or has met fire and is exposed to rain and dew, or by other calamities his family is in distress—let any such who has no one else to depend upon be taken up by his Company of Five, and be cared for as its own. In case it lies not in the said company's power to succor him, let his Company of Ten lend him its help. If his case needs more than the latter can do, let his village see to it. Should some calamity overtake one village so that its existence is endangered thereby, the four of the Company of Five Villages should give it willing salvation.

" If there is one who neglects his farm, or follows not his calling and runs to other employments, or indulges in banquets, theatres or other laxities, such should have the peremptory admonition, first of his Company of Five, and then of Ten ; and in case he is still refractory, he should be privily reported to the village authorities and receive due treatment."

Unfortunately few districts had before them so wise and unselfish an example as Lord Yozan's. Mazelière thinks that the system of mura, kumi and inalienable homestead, though seductive in theory, was pernicious in practice. "Secure against eviction, yet not allowed to enrich himself, the Japanese peasant showed neither zeal for his work nor desire to improve his methods of culture. In good seasons he thought only of drinking saké, visiting temples, and celebrating the appointed festivals ; in time of scarcity he resigned himself with Oriental fatalism to misery and death, which often he might have avoided."

Further, though the tenant was no longer legally attached to the soil, yet the sharp clan distinctions, together with habits carried over from the period of serfage, made it exceedingly difficult for a farmer to migrate from an over-populous district to a less burdened one ; while the duties laid upon all products in passing from one province to another threw each division back almost on its own resources, even in time of famine. And, last and worst, the peasant was forbidden to change the crop on a given field without

Peasants

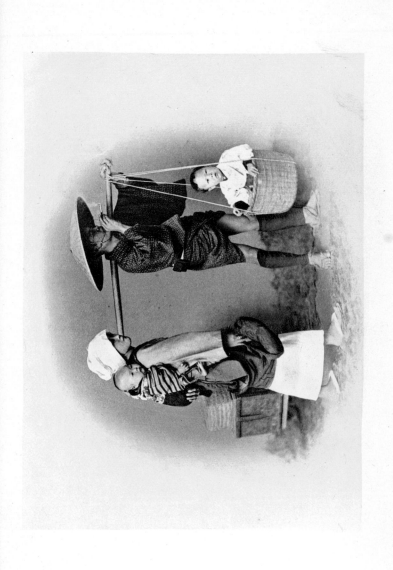

express permission to do so. The authorities fixed for each village the precise number of koku of rice which might be taken from the food supply to distill into saké, and in times of scarcity a whole district might be forbidden to make saké at all, or to plant tobacco for a set term of years.

The philosopher, Kyuso, writing at the beginning of the eighteenth century, declared that the people had far too little access to the authorities, too little opportunity to complain of difficulties and wrongs. He draws a dark picture of the state of things, saying that the towns are full of incendiaries and evil-doers, who have been driven from the country by want, and, finding themselves destitute and far from their villages, in desperation they commit all sorts of crimes. "Pressed by fashion into extravagance and luxury, princes and officials lay burdens upon the people. Their houses are filled with a crowd of servitors who do nothing but drink and gamble. The least wicked stand by and let fire consume their master's house; the rest steal, and then set the place on fire to hide what they have done. The real cause of these crimes is the master's indifference and insensate luxury."

The fact was that the Japanese landlord had almost absolute power to exact rents from his tenants, and the only redress was for the peasants to assemble in a body and present themselves at their lord's gate, setting forth their necessities and entreating relief. Sometimes a prince was merely careless and indifferent, and was thus brought to his senses; sometimes for very shame he granted what was demanded in this public manner; and sometimes the bold petitioners paid for it with their lives; yet perhaps, even so, gained for the rest of the province the needed respite.

Such a case was that of the famous Sogoro, whose story is almost as well known and popular in Japan as the deeds of the Faithful Ronin. Briefly, it is this:

In the days of the third Shogun Iemitsu, a certain lord named Kotsuke succeeded his father in his Daimiate, and, being selfish and careless of his people's good, increased the taxes till the farmers were almost ruined. In vain they besought their overseers to intercede for them; year by year the burden grew heavier, and the villagers became desperate.

The elders of all the villages throughout the territory therefore met and resolved to petition the councilors of their lord; and this they did, but were sent away without any redress. As a last effort they resolved to go up to Yedo, and carry their petition to their prince at his own door. When this was proposed Sogoro, who was head man of a village and one of their number, warned them of the danger of such a step, and said that while it was well to make every effort, he did not think as much attention would be paid in Yedo, where they were not known, as in their own place; and if they went they would do well to set their affairs in order and say farewell to their families before starting. To this proposition all agreed, yet determined to go and do what they could ; but at the last moment Sogoro made some excuse and did not go with them.

As he had predicted, the officials of their lord's household refused to receive their petition, and drove them from the door; so, after repeated attempts, they gave up in despair, and sent for Sogoro in hopes he might have something better to suggest. Sogoro therefore told his wife what was on hand, and gave her careful directions as to all he wished done in case of his death, and went up to join the rest. He told them the next thing was to make an attempt to hand a petition to one of the inner council, the *Gorojiu* (elders), as they were called ; but since their master was a member of the body, he warned them that it would probably be unsuccessful and also cost their lives ; so that he advised all but six to return to their villages, while the rest did what they could for the good of all. This was done, and Sogoro himself contrived to give the petition to one of the elders as he rode in his litter. A few days later Sogoro was summoned to the house of this prince, and the petition returned to him, with a severe reprimand for his audacity, which, however, the prince was graciously pleased to overlook. Sogoro took the opportunity to plead the necessity of the people, but without effect.

There was just one more attempt possible, and that a most difficult and dangerous one : an appeal to the

Shogun himself. Sogoro prepared another paper, and waiting till the Shogun went one day to worship at the shrine of his father at Uyeno temple, hid himself under a bridge, with his writing tied on the end of a bamboo pole, and crying, "I humbly beg to present a petition to your Highness," managed to slip it into Iemitsu's litter. The officers at the same time seized him and put him in prison.

Lord Kotsuke's wrath was directed first of all against his councilors and governors, whom he reproached for having bungled matters in such a fashion that the men had been driven to so desperate a course, by which he might well have been ruined; for he knew very well it was only his high office that saved him from losing his estates. As for Sogoro, he condemned him to death by crucifixion, and not only so, but his wife and children were to be killed also. The retainers were horrified, and tried to induce their lord to punish only the guilty man, but he would not listen; the other six village head men were not put to death, however, but banished from the province, and their goods confiscated.

The sentence was carried out in the presence of a weeping crowd, to whom Sogoro and his wife both declared their willingness to die for the rest, who had been indeed released from the unjust taxation; but Sogoro cried with a loud voice that he denounced his master's cruelty and injustice in putting to death his wife and the innocent children, and declared that he should "pay his thanks to Lord Kotsuke for this day's work." They should see it, "so that it shall be talked of for generations to come. As a sign, when I am dead, my head shall turn and face toward the castle. When you see this, doubt not that my words shall come true." [1]

And it was even so, as he had said. Then, when the retainers who had charge of the execution saw how the dead face looked toward the castle, they were frightened, and came and bowed before the corpse, making apology on the part of their lord; praising Sogoro's self-sacrifice and acknowledging that, though his own doom was deserved, it was wrong to punish the innocent. But when Lord Kotsuke heard it he only laughed at the notion of fearing a dead peasant.

However, a few months later, the Lady Kotsuke began to fall ill, and to have strange visions and hear terrible sounds at night; and her ladies heard them, too; and when Lord Kotsuke himself kept watch in her room, he, too, heard the noises and saw the ghosts of Sogoro and his wife, tied to the crossed poles, floating in the air before him. In vain he sent for all sorts of exorcists; the visions would not cease. The lady grew steadily worse, and, after some months, died. Then the ghosts haunted Lord Kotsuke more persistently than ever, and began to attack his young son, so that he became almost mad; nor did the visitations cease till the lord sent to the grave of Sogoro

[1] Mitford: "Tales of Old Japan."

and had a temple built, and sent an embassy to the Emperor himself, making request to have the dead peasant canonized as a saint. Then, at last, his mind became clear and his misfortunes were ended; more, in a few years much prosperity came to him, so that it was evident to all that the saint had forgiven and was helping his former master. Sogoro's shrine, in the level country some forty miles northeast of Tokyo, is a simple one, but most popular with the peasant class, and his grave is seldom without incense burning on it.

Wiser and more careful of his people was the lord of Odawara, who, during the difficulties of the eighteenth century, found among his subjects a peasant philosopher and economist, one Ninomiya, a thinker who based all his political economy upon morality, and, encouraged by his lord, applied his own diligence and force of character so well that he reclaimed almost a whole province from distress. His method was to go and live in the villages which were in difficulties, and working with and among the people, to show them how to help themselves and persuade them back to habits of thrift. Ninomiya also believed in direct help, where help was needed, and had very radical methods of going to work to get it. On one occasion a wide-spread famine involved the province of which he was acting as governor. The lord of Odawara, who was in residence at Yedo, sent him into the district to relieve the distress; he promptly hurried to

Odawara castle and asked for the keys of the granary.
The keepers refused rather curtly, saying they must
have a special order from their lord. "Very well,
gentlemen," said Ninomiya, "we will send to my
lord; but since, before the messenger can return from
Yedo, many of our starving people must die, I think
it is suitable that we, who are their guardians, should
also abstain from food. I will sit here in the guard-
room and fast, and do you do likewise; thus perhaps
we shall be able to understand something of the people's sufferings." The governor was known to be a
man of his word and high in the favor of his lord,
and the keys were presently handed over.

Since the Restoration, the peasant has owned his
land, paying tax to the central government and exercising all the rights of a citizen; and even he, conservative as he is by nature and occupation, is feeling the
changes of the times. He no longer wears chiefly
second-hand clothing, as he once did; he knows much
—at least, along the Tokaido—of what is doing in
the world of Japan; and, most of all, changes come to
him when his son goes off to serve his term in the
army and comes back when his years are up, the wiser
for a good deal of useful schooling, and the worse,
probably, for a sense of knowing a great deal more
than the old folks. Still, the Japanese Tommy Atkins
is a simple-hearted creature, and his few airs are harmless, after all.

One charming little side-trip on the Tokaido can

be made with very little trouble or fatigue, and is more than worth the effort. It is the ride from Shizu-oka to the temple of Kunozan, where the body of Ieyasu was laid till the temples at Nikko were built to receive it. Shizuoka itself is an exceedingly attractive little town, lying on the shore of Suruga bay, and has a very good inn; there are also two very fine temples, the largest and most beautiful belonging to a monastery of the Zen sect. The temples stand back from the town and the shore, almost against the steep hills, which form a half circle around the green little plain. The monastery contains many interesting relics of Ieyasu, and some fine paintings of Kano artists on the sliding screens of the apartments; one beautiful landscape, running all across one side of the room, might be a view from Shizuoka itself—a winding river in a vast stretch of rice-fields; hills to the left and right, and in the middle the white cone and long sweeping lines of Mount Fuji losing itself in the misty plain.

Just such views break on you on the way to Kuno-zan, until you lose the distance behind the high steep hill, at the foot of which the temple lies in a little hamlet, almost on the sea. On the ocean side there are endless green promontories, covered with pictur-esque pines, and the long shore of the Izu peninsula, across the bay. The temple buildings are very fine, much like Nikko in general style, but smaller and less elaborate. Instead of returning to Shizuoka by the same road, one can go on to Ejiri or Okitsu station on the railroad, and take the train back from there; or reverse, and leave the train at Okitsu and ride to Shizuoka by way of Kunozan. Either way is a delightful ride among the country villages; but, going this way, you turn your back upon Fuji San, which it is always a great pity to do.

CHAPTER V.

MOUNT FUJI.

" Where on the one hand is the province of Kai,
  And on the other the land of Suruga,
  Right in the midst between them
  Stands out the high peak of Fuji.
  The very clouds of heaven dread to approach it;
  Even the soaring birds reach not its summit in their flight.
  Its burning fire is quenched by the snow,
  The snow that falls is melted by the fire.
  Of Yamato, the Land of Sunrise,
  It is the Peace-giver, it is the God, it is the Treasure.
  On the peak of Fuji, in the land of Suruga,
  I never weary of gazing."
                —From the " Manyoshiu," Aston's translation.

"Fujiyama is the keynote of Japan. When you understand the
one, you are in a position to learn something of the other."
                —Kipling: "From Sea to Sea."

DESCRIPTIONS are hopeless things. One might as
well try to say why the Hermes of Praxiteles fills us
with delight, or why we stand long before a Raphael
or a Bellini or a great Titian, as to attempt to put
into words the charm of Japan. That it is a mingled
charm goes without saying; that what delights one
leaves another cold; what La Farge perceived and
interpreted with so much sympathy was something

quite different from the dainty prettinesses that roused
Sir Edwin Arnold's enthusiasm. And what is true
of the country at large is even more true of the sacred
mountain; one can tell of its situation, of the level
plain a thousand feet above the sea, and the eleven
thousand feet more rising from the plain in unbroken
sweep, save only where the one little mound breaks
the southeastern side; of the living grace of the lines,
formed by the piling ashes, as snowdrifts are piled by
the wind; the result will be as moving as fair Olivia's
ironical catalogue of her charms—" *Item*, Two lips,
indifferent red ; two eyes, one nose." Even pictures,
photographs, give only the shape and color of the
mountain, not its indefinable effect on the mind ; perhaps the only reproductions which have ever done that
are Hokusai's wonderful " Hundred Views of Fuji,"
and his larger plates of the " Thirty Views ; " and
these owe their success, so far as they do succeed, to
the fact that they are impressions, records of what
one sensitive mind, at least, has felt concerning Fuji
in some of her manifold moods.

There can be little doubt but that the peculiarly
sacro-sanct character of the mountain dates from a
period long before the Japanese occupation of the
country, the period of the Ainu and their hypothetical
predecessors, the Koropuk-guru; as I have said
already, the name is pretty certainly identical with
the Ainu Fuchi, the Fire Goddess of their mythology.
This name, Fuji, may be variously written with either

of three characters, which of itself points to its having been a word kept over from an unknown tongue, and connected with any word of like sound and not impossible meaning.

During all the earlier centuries Fuji San was truly and evidently the abode of fire; till at least the year 1100 the smoke never ceased to hang above the cone, and there were frequent outbursts of ashes and stones. The last great one was in the first years of the eighteenth century, when ashes fell six inches deep in Tokyo, sixty miles away as the crow flies, and the vegetation was killed on all the upper part of the mountain, especially on the eastern side. At this time the little mound was piled, or at least made more noticeable; it is called, from the name of the period in which the shower fell, Hoei-Zan. Since then there has been no smoke or fire, but at one side of the crater even yet the steam pours continually in small jets through the ashes. It may come forth again. Bandaizan in the north had been quiet for eleven centuries, and trees had grown upon the crater, when the inner fires suddenly burst out and flung the whole crest across the valley. Doubtless to the early worshipers it was the awfulness of these hidden forces that gave the charm of terror to the goddess-mountain's beauty.

So sacred was Fuji that in old times no woman was permitted to set foot on it, and even now some conservative ones hold themselves unworthy to go beyond a certain point, the eighth station, as the distances are reckoned off on the climb. They say that the shape of the mountain suggested a pile of rice poured out of the measure, and so they divided it up into so many *go*, like a *sho* of rice; but not all of the ten theoretical divisions have huts for rest or shelter, while others have several. There are six or seven paths by which to ascend, radiating from the cone like spokes from a wheel—two from the Hakone side, one from nearly south, which is most popular with the Japanese, and which they consider the proper or "front entrance;" and the rest from the north and west. All are marked with the ten stations, with or without rest huts at each; and there is said to be comparatively little difference in the time or steepness of the ascent by either one.

The first foreigner to make the ascent was Sir Rutherford Alcock, first British Minister to Japan. It is not recorded that he had any very consuming desire to go, but the idea having been suggested, he pressed it with true British determination, on the ground that as the representative of a friendly power he was entitled by treaty to go anywhere that any lay Japanese might enter. The Shogun's government very naturally feared the effect on the people of what could not but seem to them a gross profanation of the sacred place, and tried hard to persuade the minister to give up or at least postpone his expedition; but he felt that to yield in this was to give up a principle most important to British interests abroad, and insisted on having the permission and full safeguards. It is not for us—who enjoy under the "most favored nation clause" all that England has won—to say that Sir Rutherford was wrong; at least unless we are ready to concede that our own demands by Commodore Perry were wrong also, and that no nation has a right to force treaties of intercourse on an unwilling people. At any rate, Sir Rutherford gained his point, and the goddess of the mountain manifested no displeasure; nor did she seem offended even when Lady Parkes climbed with Sir Rutherford's successor, the bluff, frank Sir Harry Parkes. Lady Parkes was the first woman who ever visited Fuji San; but she has had plenty of successors, for though it is a long and fatiguing trip, there is no danger and no particular difficulty in the climb.

And here be it remarked that I who write know Fuji from many points of its beautiful "skirts"—no farther. Concerning the ascent, I declare what has been told me, no more. Thus, then, they say it is done.

There are a little less than three months during which the mountain is officially "open," and though hardy climbers have occasionally gone at other times, it is for the love of hardship and the unusual. The rest houses are not occupied except during the season, and the guides will not go so long as there is any snow on the path, partly for fear of the anger of the goddess, who should not be approached except at due times. It is cold enough always at night, even down to freezing in the hottest weather, though through the day the sun on the lower part of the slope may be intense. A few years ago a Tokyo meteorologist determined to spend the winter on the top of Fuji, in order to make observations; his friends tried in vain to dissuade him; but he declared it would be no worse than an arctic winter, and made all his preparations to stay through the season, his plucky wife going along, but no one else. But, as it proved, the fearful winds made their situation far worse than in any ordinary trip to the pole; and they would certainly have perished if their friends had not become so uneasy that they sent up a party to investigate. They found Mr. Nonaka almost dead from exposure, and his wife in hardly better condition; the guides of the relief party made improvised litters and carried them down over the snow in safety.

If it were possible to be on Fuji in winter, that would certainly be the best time to enjoy the view; day after day the whole slope stands out clear in the clear winter air, covered with snow nearly to its base, and it must be possible to see not only all the thirteen provinces which tradition declares visible, but even beyond. Indeed, the Rev. Walter Weston declares that in all fine weather you see very much farther than is set down in the usual accounts. The best time for seeing anything is during late July and early

August—July 25th to August 10th Professor Chamberlain says—because at that time the early summer
rains are generally over, and the tremendous storms
of August and September not yet begun. Still, it is
largely a chance, just as in Switzerland, and for that
reason, if no other, it is well to try for two sunrises
and a sunset, since those are the best times of day. By
noon the clouds gather about the cone, or lie in masses
on the sides, affording wonderful effects of shadow
and light, but little distant view, or, rather, little but
the most distant, for sometimes the horizon of the sea
will be visible, or some far-away mountain peak,
when all the nearer earth is blotted out. The wise
ones, therefore, advise starting a couple of hours after
midnight from one of the inns, Gotemba or Subashiri,
and pushing on to a point well up the side before the
sun rises. This also avoids the sun on the hottest part
of the climb. Then they go on slowly, reaching the
rest huts at the summit by noon; take the afternoon
for the crater and the round of shrines, and spend the
night at the top, returning the next day.

In any case, it is safest to take along provisions for
a few days, because travelers have been caught sometimes by sudden storms of sleet and wind, making it
impossible to stir from the sheltering huts, whether to
go up or down. Such an experience Miss Scidmore
had, and it must have been much more unpleasant
than her cheery account of it admits. At most of
the stations where there are rest houses it is possible

Mount Fujiyami

to get cooked rice and hot water; quilts every one brings along, and charcoal is not a bad thing in case of being held some days. The pilgrims carry strings of *waraji*, straw sandals which tie around the ankles, and drop the worn-out ones all along the way, for the sharp cinders quickly cut everything to pieces; foreigners also tie these waraji on over their shoes, and find them a great protection to the leather, as well as a great help in keeping the feet from slipping. Europeans who have done much tramping in Japan often come to discard their own boots entirely, and wear the strong dark-blue cotton *tabi* and *waraji*, like the Japanese pilgrims. The toe strap is uncomfortable at first, but the feeling soon goes off, as every one knows who has tried wearing Japanese dress.

It is possible to ride on horseback not only across the cultivated plain and gradual rise to the point called Uma-gaeshi (horse-turn-back), but for another five miles beyond, over a grassy moor which reaches to the foot of the trees. At what is counted the entrance to the sacred portion there is a little temple, where the priests sell staves, stamped with the temple seal; at the top the staff is stamped again by the priests in charge there, in testimony that the pilgrim has accomplished the ascent.

The trees begin at four thousand feet—a beautiful mossy wood, full of berries and wild flowers; it reaches highest on the west side, something over nine hundred feet, but on the east—the side toward

Gotemba—it is cut off sharply at about five thousand five hundred feet, where the mass of ashes stopped in the last great eruption. Beyond this there is a band of bushy scrub and some few hardy flowers, but only for a little way; all the upper part of the cone is a desolate slope of blackish cinder, through which masses of lava protrude here and there from the blocks below. There is lava underneath to an immense distance — fifteen miles — but very little shows on the surface, and that only where streams have worn away the ashes. Some little distance above the trees another path encircles the mountain, and energetic pilgrims stay over a day and take this, too, in their journey.

A rocky wall of peaks surrounds the crater, which can be entered at just one point by an easy slope; the bottom is nearly flat, and about five hundred feet down. The highest peak is Ken-ga-mine, on the west side, and here it is that Japanese pilgrims go before dawn, reverently to greet the rising sun. They dress in white, these mountain pilgrims, to symbolize the purity of heart needful for the goddess' devotees; and they come by thousands through the short weeks that the shrines are open, peasants nearly all of them, wearing big straw hats, and carrying their provisions and a piece of straw matting, which will serve them for bed or rain-coat as necessity may arise.

As might be expected, the legends concerning Fuji San are endless. As to its origin, tradition has it that there was once no mountain here at all, only a great plain; till one night there was a tremendous earthquake, and Fuji rose to its full height, where now it stands; and at the same time lake Biwa appeared, a hundred miles to the south; the mass which made the mountain had left the hollow where it once was. A Japanese author of some centuries ago gravely discussed this legend, and dismissed it as quite impossible.

The goddess of Fuji was a purely Shinto deity, to begin with, and had a proper Shinto name of nine syllables, but the Buddhist authorities, as usual, adopted her and gave her a Buddhistic appellation, Sengen, and certain Buddhistic attributes. At Shizuoka there is a noble temple in her honor, appropriately placed where the long southeastern slope of the mountain spreads down to the sea, and the view is uninterrupted from cone to plain. This particular temple dates only from early Tokugawa times, having been built under the care of Okubo, Ieyasu's faithful vassal and Iemitsu's counselor. It has a fine hall, supported on red lacquered pillars, and some very beautiful wood carving, part of it by Hidari Jingoro, of Nikko fame. Sengen's father is also honored here; he was a Tengu, or mountain kobold, and the guardian deity of Mount Oyama, which lies northeast of Fuji.

Much of this plain at the southeastern slope of Fuji San is watered from lake Hakone, by an arti-

ficial channel tunneled through the mountains near
one of the lesser passes; it was made many centuries
ago, no one seems to know just when. The water
finally makes its way into the little Kanogawa, and
empties into Suruga bay at Numazu, on the Tokaido.

Much larger and wider than the Kanogawa, and very
swift, is the Fuji river, which rises in the mountains
above Kofu and flows down between two ranges and
out on to the plain to reach Suruga bay. It is
navigable for some thirty miles, the boats having to
be towed up by men, and shooting down through
several small rapids and one great one almost to the
mouth of the river. The number of boats so engaged
is astonishing; at times the stream seems full of them.
A curious bridge crosses the river in one place, made
of bamboo, split and twisted into ropes, suspending a
long series of bundles of bamboo, lashed together to
form the bridge. A single row of planks is laid on
it, and it has one supporting prop part way over. The
whole is a hundred feet long, and from twenty-five to
thirty-five feet above the river; and over this narrow,
swaying affair the peasants walk unconcernedly, carrying their loads of produce or faggots. They say there
are many like it in the mountains.

In the middle ages the Fujikawa just missed being
the scene of a tremendous battle. It was during the
struggle between the Taira and Minamoto, when
Yoritomo had already entrenched himself at Kamakura, but before the death of the old Taira chief,

Kiyomori. Yoritomo had gathered followers from the provinces north of the Hakone mountains; the Taira brought a great army up from the south against them, and the two came at the same moment to the opposite banks of the river. Whichever tried to cross to the attack would be at a terrible disadvantage in that swift stream, and the two armies lay on either side without daring to cross. In the night an alarm arose; it is said that one of the Taira, foreseeing that the rising tide would give an advantage to the Minamoto, scared up a flock of wild fowl, which made a great commotion on the marshy flats near by, and the Taira thought it was an attack and fled. The Minamoto also withdrew, and the decisive battles were fought elsewhere.

In the days of the luxurious Ashikaga Shoguns at Kamakura, picnic parties to the neighborhood of Mount Fuji were much in vogue. The dilettante courtiers no longer hunted and rode as in Yoritomo's time, but amused themselves by composing poems of the most concise and conventional character, full of punning allusions and double meanings, being often a mere naming over of things remotely suggestive, such as—

"Spring-time; a sunny day; rocks on the shore of the sea."

Or this:

"A forest in autumn; the moon; a flight of storks."

Two legends are localized on the shore near the foot of Mount Fuji, both similar in general incidents to stories found in the folk literature of nearly all the world, though naturally they have certain distinct variations. One is the "Robe of Feathers," the other "The Fisher-boy of Urashima." The first is the old tale of the stolen robe, like the mermaid's dress and the fairy ring and the sandal-wood necklace of other lands. A fisherman finds on the shore a beautiful garment woven of feathers, shining in the sun; he is about to carry it home, when a fairy creature appears, and implores him to give it back to her, for without it, she declares, she cannot return to her companions in paradise. In a Norse or a German story, such as we are used to, the mortal would hide the robe and make the maiden his bride, and she would dwell with him happily till some unlucky day she found the dress, grew homesick and departed, with longing, backward looks toward husband and children—

> "For the cold, strange eyes of a little mermaiden,
>   And the gleam of her golden hair."

Not so the Japanese. At first, indeed, he refuses to give up his prize, but at last consents to do so if she will dance for him. This the fairy promises to do; so she dons the shining robe, and begins a wondrous dance. A famous Nô dance took this tale for its subject; while the dancers represent the beautiful fairy, the awed and delighted fisherman, the singers chant a lyric chorus describing the scene:

" Lo, the rising sun, the golden gleam on Mount Fuji,
    On the shadow of Fuji, reflected in the sea.
    Earth and sky mingle in one; the magic form of Fuji rises, glow-
        ing with light.
    Dance, O daughter of the gods ! The garland of thy hair floats in
        the wind."

But, as she dances the divine dance, slowly she be-gins to rise, to float before the fisherman's eyes; up and up, the feather robe wafting her like a bird—

" Over the wooded hill, over Ukushima, and the heights of Ashidaka;
    Even over Fuji and the eternal snows;
    Higher and higher, into the azure sky.
    Now a cloud enwraps her; the heavenly one has vanished from
        mortal sight."

" The Fisher-boy of Urashima " is a story of some-what the same order, and, too, he is a Rip Van Winkle with Pandora's box; his tale is found in different ver-sions in several parts of Japan. One day while he was out in his boat, a sudden storm overtook him, and he was unable to return to the shore. But when he gave up rowing, in despair, a large turtle suddenly appeared in the waves, and said to him, " Get on my back; I will take care of you." The young man obeyed, and the turtle went away with him far into the depths of the sea, even to the Jewel Palace, where everything was beautiful as the day; and there he was welcomed, and the Jewel Princess herself became his bride. And they lived long and happily.

But, after what seemed to him three years, the young man begged his wife to let him go back to the world and visit his old home; for his parents must be unhappy, thinking him dead. With great reluctance the princess consented; and she sent him over the sea on the back of the turtle, first giving him a little casket, which she charged him to keep, if he desired to come back to her; but on no account was he to open it, or he would never, never return or see her more. All of which he faithfully promised to observe.

But when he reached his home, nothing was the same; the village that he knew had vanished, strange houses stood on the familiar shore, strange faces were in the doorways; and though he searched far and near, he could find no trace of his people. Then, in terror and despair, he drew out the little box, and regardless of his wife's monitions, lifted the lid. There was nothing inside except a faint vapor, that floated out and away over the sea toward the Jewel Palace; but as he looked, the young man's knees trembled and grew weak; his hair whitened and his face became wrinkled and drawn; the centuries that had passed as a dream bowed him to the ground, and he sank dead upon the shore.

CHAPTER VI.

NAGOYA.

NAGOYA may be a pleasant town enough to live in, but it is not an attractive or impressive place; it lies too flat, and has too many pretentious modern buildings in "foreign" style—which, indeed, give it an air of progress and prosperity of modern sort. It has, moreover, a population much given to riding bicycles, wonderful rattling structures of the old high-wheel pattern, thin as the skeletons of wheels and unblest with any form of rubber on their tires. After meeting a reckless 'prentice boy on one of these mounts, pack on back and kimono tails flying and straw zori flipflapping on his bare toes, whirling down the street through a crowd of foot-passengers, one marvels how any of the inhabitants survive to make the delicate "egg-shell" lacquer which is a specialty of Nagoya, or the famous Owari porcelain which belongs to the whole district. The term egg-shell, by the way, does not mean thin, but is given because the ware is really made of the inner paper-like membrane of a hen's egg, tiny fragments of which are powdered down on a fresh coat of lacquer, just as gold-leaf is sometimes placed, and then dried in and varnished with transparent lacquer and re-polished, making a cloudy white background for a decoration in gold or silver or color applied in the usual way; the effect is delicate and pretty, and the Japanese prize a good piece quite highly. The work is necessarily very slow, and consequently a box or tray of any size is quite expensive, and this may be one reason why it is seldom sent abroad; indeed, foreigners have never seemed to know or care much about it.

Nagoya has a large Buddhist monastery, the Higashi Hongwanji, surrounded by high stone walls, the remains of an old fortress which formerly stood on its site; the temple is comparatively modern, and everything about it is in the most gorgeous style of Buddhistic art, from the grand two-storied gate, with its elaborate carvings and scrolls and diapers, to the great hall divided into three apartments, and the splendors of the inner shrine. Even the ceiling beams are supported on carved lotus leaves and flowers, and the *ramma* in the spaces above the screens which divide the compartments are decorated with gilded openwork figures of Buddhist angels. The chief image is a figure of Amida, about two-thirds of life size, in a magnificent gilded shrine.

Much less resplendent, but very quaint and interesting, are the figures of the " Five Hundred Rakan " in a shabby little temple not far from the Hongwanji. The Rakan were the " chief companions " or disciples of Buddha, and they are great favorites with Japanese artists, whether in painting or sculpture. These particular images are carved in wood, mostly about two feet high, their garments gorgeously painted; they are of all grades of merit, some dignified and interesting in face and attitude, others clumsy or grotesque or inanely smiling. They are all attributed to one man, but it is quite evident that only a few are really his. However, the variety of pose, feature and expression is the most astonishing thing about them; the Japanese say that every man can find among them a likeness of his own father, and it is not difficult to believe, for every possible type of Japanese face seems to be represented.

But the great glory of Nagoya is its mediæval castle, the finest of all now left standing in Japan. It was built by Kato Kiyomasa, the general who conquered Korea for Hideyoshi; Nobunaga held it, though his own great castle was in Omi province, which borders lake Biwa, and was destroyed soon after his death; while Nagoya, curiously enough, has never been even besieged. When Ieyasu came into power, he gave it to one of his sons, who established the Owari family, one of the Go-San Ke, or Three Great Houses, Kii, Owari and Mito. It remained in their hands till all such property was turned over to the government after the Restoration. The enclosure is used for barracks and officers' quarters, and a special pass obtained beforehand, through one's legation, is the only means of entrance; but it is quite worth a little foresight and trouble to see and touch the wonderful walls, like those of Yedo castle, but even more massive, and the timbers of the great keep, which rises in five stories, diminishing one above another. Each story is gabled and battlemented, and covered outside by an immense thickness of dazzling white plaster; while inside there seems to be almost no space at all, only a kind of gallery around the walls commanding the loophole windows, and a steep stair. All the rest of the space is taken up by the enormous beams, crossed and braced and bracketed together, black with age and hard as iron. The sense of strength, of force immeasurable, is almost overpowering; it gives the impression of a live resistance, as a great piece of machinery does when you see it at rest. Under the castle there is a deep well, called the Golden Water, which never fails; a garrison well provisioned with boiled and dried rice might have held out here for months under the old methods of warfare. Kato Kiyomasa dug the well, and he also had the two golden dolphins cast for the gables of the tower. They will tell you at Nagoya how one of the two was lent to the Vienna Exposition, in 1873, and on the way back the ship which contained it and a number of other treasures was wrecked; but after being sunk for a considerable time, she was raised and the contents rescued, the lacquer and such things in good condition; and the dolphin came back to his perch on the tower, to the good townspeople's great satisfaction.

Nagoya Castle

Gonse calls Nobunaga the inaugurator of a period that may fairly be called modern; "his military dictatorship is the bridge thrown between the vanishing power of the Ashikaga Shoguns and the renovated government of Ieyasu." He has all the qualities of the hero of a transition period—brilliant, penetrating, ambitious, daring to a fault, eager for new things and ready to grasp them at whatever risk. In his dealings with the Portuguese, Nobunaga seems the prototype of the "Meiji statesmen"—the men who have caught hold of Western ideas and made Japan over in our own day. Physically, he was of the North-Asian type of the Buké—the military nobility—tall and slight, with aquiline nose and keen eyes, and long, oval face. His faults are those of the successful fighter—high temper, favoritism and jealousy, and, the monks said, cruelty; but it must be remembered that they had no cause to love Nobunaga, who was their enemy from first to last, and actually broke their power forever.

Ota Nobunaga was of Taira blood, a descendant of Kiyomori himself. When the Taira were annihilated at Dan-no-ura, the wife of one of Kiyomori's grandsons fled with her baby son, and took refuge in a village near lake Biwa, in Omi, where she married the headman of the place. Some years after a Shinto priest from Echizen came that way, on his return from a pilgrimage, and seeing the headman had several sons, asked him to give one for the priesthood. The headman accordingly gave not his own, but his wife's son. The Shinto priests marry, and the priesthood is usually hereditary in a family; young Ota followed the custom, and founded a line which became distinguished, and afterward, as vassals of Shiba, lord of Echizen, acquired wealth and power. When the Shiba family lost Echizen, Nobunaga's grandfather came to Owari, and, like so many others in late Ashikaga times, got possession of large territories. They were ardent Imperialists; Nobunaga's father spent largely from his own means for the repair of the Emperor's palace, and of the sacred Shinto shrine at Ise; and Nobunaga followed the same example of loyalty. He was still quite young when one of the neighboring lords, who already held Suruga and two other provinces, came down with a great army and overran Owari, taking most of the fortified places. Thinking himself safe, he "sat down," as our old Saxon chroniclers used to say, and made a great banquet to celebrate his victories; and while all were drinking at ease, Nobunaga came upon them with a small force and defeated them utterly, killing the chief and destroying the prestige of the family. Nobunaga then made friends with Takeda Shingen, the enemy of the Uyesugi, and also with Ieyasu's family, the Matsudaira; and with the help of his able generals, of whom Hideyoshi and Ieyasu were the chief, he obtained full control over the empire; but had never the title of Shogun, probably because he was a Taira, and the Shoguns had always been of the Minamoto family.

Brilliant himself, the way to Nobunaga's heart was by daring and originality. It is said that one of his retainers greatly desired to rise in his lord's favor, but could find no way to attract his attention. He talked of it with his wife, and she bade him bide his time, and the chance would come. One day he went home and told her of a very fine horse which had been brought for sale, and which he longed to buy, but could not, because the price was very high, and, like all good Samurai, the knight was anything but rich. The wife asked carefully about it, and then said, " You shall buy the horse; my lord Nobunaga loves to see his knights well mounted, and he may notice and praise you." The Samurai answered that he would gladly do so, if he had the means; whereupon the wife rose, and presently brought him a bag of gold-pieces. When she married, she told him, her father had given her this money, bidding her use it as she had need. They had often been in dire poverty, but she would never touch it for less than the most pressing necessity; now she had it ready. The delighted husband bought the horse; the master's quick eye saw the valuable animal, and he thought at once that a man so well equipped must be above the average. The young knight's fortune was made, just as the clever wife had foreseen.

Of Nobunaga's first meeting with Hideyoshi there

are still more remarkable tales. The lad won his
way by audacity and impudence worthy of any city
gamin. A peasant's son, he had become the leader
of a band of thieves; he begged himself out of
Nobunaga's hands by a promise to steal something—I
think it was a certain valuable sword—from the
master's very side. The day when the wager expired
had come, and Nobunaga sat smiling over the lad's
defeat, when the youngster presented himself with the
sword. Rain was falling fast; under cover of the
sound he had crept up and made good his boast.
Nobunaga made the clever boy his groom, then captain, and soon the chief of his generals.

But the great fame of Owari rests not upon princes
or generals, but on Toshiro the potter and his successors, who followed the methods he learned in China
in the middle of the sixteenth century. When
Toshiro came back from his studies there, he settled
at Seto, in Owari, and began to make a new kind
of ware, different from anything hitherto known in
Japan; and from the name of the town all porcelain
came to be called setomono ("Seto ware"). At first
it was only a glazed stone-ware, without ornament,
the form and tint and the laying on of the glaze
being all that was attempted in the way of beauty;
but later an Owari potter learned from the makers of
Karatsu, in the south, certain secrets of color, and the
beautiful blue Owari underglaze was the result. It is
a clear, delicate color, laid on a fine bluish-white

porcelain, often made translucently thin; at times they blend off the blue into an exquisite shade of gray, also laid under the glaze, and particularly suited to the landscape subjects, the ducks flying over the moon and the like, in which Japanese art delights.

The cobalt used for the blue is taken from a black mineral substance rather like clay, found in lumps in deposits of loose gravel near Seto and elsewhere in Owari. The lumps are shaken in a coarse sieve to get rid of the sand and gravel, and then heated till the valuable part becomes peach-red, when the worthless part is separated from it, and the color is ready to be pulverized, washed and precipitated with salt water, and finally rinsed again before being used.

The earliest pottery found in Japan is the much-discussed pre-historic ware of which I have already spoken, which is found in burial mounds, and variously attributed to the Ainu, the Koropuk-guru, and the first Japanese settlers themselves. All the knowledge which they received in historic times the Japanese trace to the Koreans, claiming that after the Empress Jingo's conquest many Korean artisans settled in Japan by her order, and that at other times others followed, making distinct settlements— as, for instance, at Karatsu, in the province of Hizen, where several families are known to have become naturalized about 690. The ware made by these Korean potters was a simple kind of glazed stoneware, gray, brown or greenish, and in no way decorative. The Japanese had to improve much upon their teachers before anything very artistic could be produced.

All the earliest pottery was hand-made. According to Japanese tradition, the inventor of the wheel was one Gyogi, a Buddhist priest; some say that he, too, came from Korea. He is said to have been a great enthusiast for art and industry, and to have gone about the country teaching people improved methods. A number of curious black wheel-made glazed pots and vases are kept at Nara, which are attributed to Gyogi, or at least to his time; but there is good evidence that the wheel was used much earlier than his period, which was the end of the seventh century. In certain parts of southern Japan rude hand-made utensils are still produced, especially for the temple, and no other may be used in the service. In early times the dishes used by the Emperor were broken and thrown away after each meal; to a much later period his clothing was never used twice.

The *cha-no-yu* devotees of Hideyoshi's time and later took great delight in these archaic pieces, and in imitations of them, made by the potters of the time with immense pains and skill. For the tea ceremony, with its rules of strictest simplicity, nothing but these plain pieces would serve; but the devotees made it up by all sorts of shapes and shadings, of greenish glaze running into the gray, of curious blendings on the cloudy ground, such as only the initiated could appreciate.

From the thirteenth century, and particularly after the middle of the sixteenth, Chinese influences predominated; it was just then that so many Chinese refugees came to Japan, and then, too, that there was the most trade intercourse between the two countries. The Japanese always greatly admired Chinese porcelain, and a feast has always been considered incomplete without some unusual and beautiful dishes to serve it in. The Japanese potters frequently imitated Chinese designs, but more often modified them to suit the greater freedom of Japanese line; still they never attained such perfection of material and finish as their more precise neighbors.

In the sixteenth century, too, the Dutch came trading at Nagasaki; and, like wise importers, did not wait to educate their market to enjoy a totally new style of decoration; instead, they brought patterns and caused the Japanese to make articles expressly to their order, in Japanese way it is true, but with the coloring and shapes which best pleased the European public. This ware, known generally as "old Japan," may be seen in perfection in the palaces and museums of Holland, and in other European collections; it was made almost entirely by one or two potteries in Hizen, the province in which Nagasaki lay, and very little of it can have stayed in Japan.

Ninsei, of Kyoto, perfected the making of Japanese porcelain. He lived about the end of the sixteenth century, a generation after Iemitsu and the building of the Nikko temples; and he decorated his ware in colors and gold, on a delicate crackled background. After him came Kenzan, brother of the great lacquer painter Korin; his pottery was less carefully made than Ninsei's, but his color and designs are accounted even finer. Then there was the Kutani ware of Kaga, the earlier pieces of which were done in a curious deep green underglaze, having rather the effect of majolica, and the later work in red and gold; and Satsuma, the last pottery founded in old Japan, being originally a colony of Koreans, who lived quite by themselves, and were forbidden to marry out of their own tribe. It is one of the most pleasing wares, as well as the most individual, with its soft cream-colored ground and fine decoration of flowers just touched with gold. Much of the design imitated the old brocade patterns, and it was sometimes called *nishiki yaki*, brocade ware. As every one knows, real old Satsuma is exceedingly scarce, either in or out of Japan; and the pieces, large and small, of which so many were exported a few years ago, were all made at Ota, or at Shinagawa, the southern suburb of Tokyo. Some of these pieces were very coarse and worthless, but much of it was pretty enough to have stood on its own merits. An exceedingly pretty modern ware is produced at these Ota potteries for Japanese use; it has the warm cream-white ground, and dainty designs of flowers, all restrained and delicate, to suit Japanese taste.

If the truth must be told, Nagoya is responsible for

a very large share of the cheap trash that has deluged the world under the name of "Japanese china," besides a good deal which, though made for the foreign market, is really pretty and tasteful. The very worst of all is the imitation Sèvres and Dresden produced in the last few years, mostly, I am afraid, for the American market. The precise little designs and bright colors are particularly unsuitable for the dashing Japanese brush, and the cheap American gold paint dabbed down here and there adds to the general badness of the effect. But Nagoya thrives and grows wealthy on the proceeds; so they will doubtless continue to make it as long as the Americans will buy.

Fine porcelain has been responsible for many strange things. One literary lady of the Tokugawa period is said to have left her husband because of the family china. They had been entertaining some friends, and the lady herself was carrying the tray with certain fine pieces from the guest room to the lower floor, when she slipped on the staircase and fell. Her husband heard the crash, and called out to ask—not if she was hurt, but if the china was broken; madame was so disgusted at his heartlessness that she declined to live with him any longer.

Another set of plates was so very valuable that the owner left a law for his household that any one who broke a single plate should have a finger cut off. Under these circumstances the descendants had some trouble in getting servants to undertake the dangerous

charge. Now, it happened once that a very charming
young girl took the place, for the sake of the high
wages, because only so could she support her invalid
mother. They were Samurai, who had lost everything on the death of the girl's father, and O Cho
San was good, pretty, and trained in the best of
manners, so that she became a great favorite in the
house.

Now the master had a son, a worthless young fellow,
who presently fell in love with the pretty maid, and
tried to get her to flirt with him; but when she first
avoided, and then, when he pressed her openly, refused
to listen, the youth grew angry and determined to get
her into trouble and force her to turn to him. His
chance came when the master gave a party, as he did
yearly to a few chosen friends, before whom he set the
cherished plates. O Cho San washed them carefully,
counted them and put them away in the store-house;
but when the master came to inspect, the bottom one
was found broken.

There was a great excitement. O Cho San protested her innocence, but only begged that instead of
her hand, her face might be cut, so that she could still
work and care for her mother. Just then one of the
other servants appeared, a big, rough fellow, whom
everybody knew to be honest as the day; this Genzaburo declared that he had broken the plate himself,
because he was in love with O Cho San, and did not
want her to be able to marry anybody else. They

asked him how he had done it, and he said he had been told to mend the box-lid, and as for the rest, he would show how it was done — and with that he lifted up a great rice pestle, and brought it down, smashing the entire set of plates to fragments.

Every one thought he was quite mad; but, begging for a moment's hearing, Genzaburo declared that he had done this thing to prevent any more wrong; that it was monstrous to mutilate a human being for the sake of a piece of china; and that, as the ancestor's command must be respected, the only way to put a stop to it was to break them all at once. This he had done, and he was quite prepared to die. At this the master's son was moved to shame, and confessed his share in the wrong; the master also was convinced by Genzaburo's arguments, and not only forgave, but raised him in his service, and also rewarded O Cho San for her devotion to her mother.

I consider this story typically Japanese; first, in that it is nowhere stated that O Cho San married Genzaburo—whose sudden affection proved to be as much a fiction as his breaking of the first plate—or the master's son, or anybody else—a climax no Western narrator could have spared without intense regret, if compelled by strict accuracy to leave it out; and also because it illustrates what a Japanese writer has lately declared concerning Japanese character: "Scarcely a Japanese, however lowly his origin or humble his

station, lacks the conviction that he carries a natural
mandate to redress wrong in a superior, and that the
method of redress depends upon his own choice, provided that his failure in submission be compensated
by strength of sincerity—the co-ordinates of loyal
obedience."

CHAPTER VII.

GIFU.

ONE of the marvels of Nagoya castle is that it stood almost without a crack through the great earthquake of 1892, which sent the new brick telegraph and post offices and other European buildings crashing like a child's block tower when you shake the table it stands on. It was not one, but a succession of shocks following each other every few minutes for a day or two, some slight, others very violent, and of the sudden "jumping" kind that tries even the stoutest building. This part of the country was the centre of the disturbance, and thousands of houses fell both in Nagoya and Gifu, the only large towns in the district, and in the many lesser places round about. Naturally the buildings that suffered most were the so-called "foreign" houses, with brick chimneys, which crashed through the roofs and wrought destruction in nearly every case. The lesson has been learned, though at grievous cost, and special precautions are taken now to safeguard the deadly chimney, except in the Hokkaido, where so far earthquakes are much less frequent and violent than in the main island or southward.

121

People say that the centre of frequent disturbance is
moving northward; it may be merely a popular
notion, but this much is certain, the great shocks of
the last quarter century have been successively north
of each other—Nagoya, Tokyo, Akita, the tidal wave
on the northeast coast, and at Hakodate, a few years
ago, the heaviest shake on record for the Hokkaido.
Even in the Nagoya earthquake Japanese houses did
not fall, unless they were old and out of repair; then
the supports frequently gave way, and the great roof
came down bodily, imprisoning the inmates, who were
often taken out unhurt. Some broke through the
tiles and made their escape. Fire came to add to
the horror, and the loss of life in both cities was very
great.

Gifu is the capital of what was Mino province, and
is now Gifu prefecture; its specialty is paper, and all
that can be made of paper, particularly lanterns of a
very decorative kind, made of a very thin, tough
tissue, and often beautifully painted. Lanterns are an
absolute essential of Japanese life, from the common
oil paper variety in everyday use to the elaborate
bronze ones of the temples, where the light has become
so small in proportion to the stand that it is merely a
symbol of the Light of Wisdom. At all festivals
lanterns are hung in long chains across the street; not
the many-colored ones which we use for an out-door
fête, but a plain ball of yellowish oiled paper, with
some symbol painted on it in red; most often nowa-

Lantern Makers

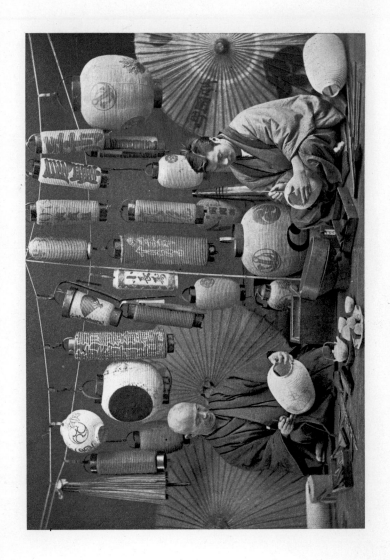

days the red ball of the rising sun, the national emblem. Everybody has a name or *mon* (crest) painted on the side of the one he or she carries in the streets at night. One of the regulations on the passports which used to amuse foreigners was that they were to bind themselves not to go to a fire on horseback nor without a light.

The kurumaya's lantern is an ingenious affair; he needs to fold it up, in order to put it away under the seat of his carriage, and yet it must be stiff enough to fasten to the shafts, and leave his hands free. This is accomplished by a cleverly made handle bent at the two ends, one of which fits into a groove under the wooden bottom of the lantern, and the other is attached by a chain to the top ring when the paper part has been unfolded. The handle is of tough wood, and has to be bent a little like a bow to fasten the chain, so that it holds the lantern stiffly open. The candles are made of vegetable wax, and have a thick wick of twisted paper; the lower end has a hole to stick on a spike in the bottom of the lantern. It is marvelous how even a little candle-end will keep alight in wind and rain, as the man pulls you splashing through the streets.

At one of the temples in the sacred province of Yamato there is a lantern called the Poor Woman's Single Lamp. Its legend is that on some great occasion the people of the neighborhood were all giving lamps to the temple; and a very rich man gave a thousand great ones, making a lavish display of his wealth and piety. But among the common people there was one poor woman who had nothing at all to give; but she cut off her long hair, and by selling that managed to get enough money to buy one poor little light. So on the night of the festival all the lamps were lighted, and the rich man's thousand shone brilliantly, and all the world admired and praised him. But while they were looking a sudden gale of wind rose and swept through the open galleries and blew out every light save only one little forgotten lamp, which shone as never candle shone before. Then they looked and found who had given it; and they knew that the poor woman's sacrifice had been more acceptable than all that the rich man gave of his abundance.

Foreigners often stop at Gifu to see the very curious spectacle of the cormorant fishing at night on the river. The birds are used in this way in other places in Japan, but nowhere to such an extent or so skillfully as on the Kisogawa. It is an exceedingly old custom, for the ancient chronicle, the Kojiki, makes mention of cormorants being kept and used for fishing in the time of the Divine Ancestors. They catch the young birds with limed twigs at their feeding places along the shores of Owari bay, cage them and tame them, and train them to the business while quite young, or, rather, have the old birds train them. They say a good old bird will train a number of young ones at once. They all know their names, which are not strictly names either, but numbers, by which the master addresses them, and they also understand their turns perfectly well; thus the oldest and wisest bird is quite aware that he is Ichi-ban, Number One, and claims all his privileges, making a great fuss if he is not first fed and last to go into the water to work, and first out of it again—and last to enter the pen, too, when they all go home to their cages in the village.

The fishing is all done at night—not on moonlight nights, either, as it would not be dark enough for the lights to draw the fish. The boats start about three miles up the river, above Gifu, and float down with the current, a whole fleet of them together, one man in the stern managing each boat. Visitors who stop at Gifu to see them, take supper at the inn and afterwards hire a boat and lie out in the stream to wait till they come down—often a weary time; for, while it may be nine o'clock, more often it is midnight before they appear.

The first token is a faint red glow far up the stream; gradually it increases and separates into a dozen or more centres of flame, coming from as many great iron baskets filled with blazing pitch-pine, each hung by an iron arm from the bow of the boat. It is a weird scene; the wavering lights flash far out over the river, and the fish gather to it as moths come round a lamp, or catfish to our Pennsylvania boys, when they go out "bobbing" on the pond. In each boat one man stands banging on a bamboo clapper and shouting at the top of his voice, which is intended to encourage the birds; they are held, like dogs in a leash, diving and squattering around the bow of the boat. The master stands forward, handling as many as twelve birds, and a second man behind has three or four more. Each bird has a ring round its neck, just large enough to let through small fish and keep back big ones. As soon as one has stuffed its throat—which requires only a few minutes—the master lifts the great creature out of the water, and, with a quick squeeze, makes it disgorge the fish, and throws it back again; four fish is the usual take each time. As this process is repeated on an average four times a minute, and each cormorant is as big as a goose and plunges about vigorously at the end of its string, it may be supposed that he who handles twelve birds has a lively time of it.

When they get opposite Gifu the work is over for the night; the boats are run ashore and the cormorants are made to stand up, like a row of soldiers, on the gunwale, each in its own place; if they have not had enough supper, the master feeds them in turn with the smaller fish. It is said the birds are kindly treated and well taken care of; even though the season is only five months and the birds must be fed all winter, a well-trained cormorant is very valuable property, and is looked after accordingly. Which leads one to speculate whether economic causes may not some day help matters for the poor, ill-tempered, ill-used horses of Japan—almost the only creatures to whom the Japanese are really cruel.

The province of Mino was one of which Nobunaga got possession, and he built a large castle near the present town of Gifu. Little is left now but the traces, on a hill which commands a beautiful view of the country round. The most noted historical place in the province, however, is Ieyasu's great battle-field, Sekigahara, which lies between the hills a little to the west of Gifu.

The place is called Sekigahara, Moor of the Barrier, because, from old times, one of the outposts stood here; doubtless one of those originally placed against the Ainu, and the clans not yet under the control of the Yamato rulers, and maintained afterward to keep any one from suddenly marching on Kyoto. The great struggle took place in 1600, between Ieyasu, who had already gained all the northern provinces, and Hideyoshi's son, Hideyori, who held Osaka castle and continually plotted against the Tokugawa. The historians give accounts of a tremendous fight, more than eighty thousand men on Ieyasu's side and one hundred and thirty thousand on the other; the plain was red with blood, and the Osaka army retired with a loss of thirty thousand. It is said that the battle was decided by a portion of Hideyori's allies going over to Ieyasu during the fight.

It was Ieyasu's notion to go into this battle without

a helmet. When the victory was won, he sat down on a folding stool, and, ordering his helmet to be brought, put it on and carefully tied the strings. It was doubtless intended as an object-lesson to his followers; and certainly he did indeed tighten, not relax, his vigilance after this battle.

Nearly all the remaining lords now came to him and made submission. Ieyasu proceeded to re-apportion the provinces of the empire, dividing them according to the attitude of the Daimyo toward himself. He classed them all as Fudai and Tozama; the first were those who had been allied with him before Sekigahara; the latter those who joined him afterwards; and the first class had a number of privileges denied to the Tozama barons. Under the Shogun's direct sway were the provinces of the Kwanto, around and north of Yedo (Tokyo); Kyoto likewise was guarded by a ring of nobles faithful to the Tokugawa house, and finally the Tozama were so placed that they could not command the lines of intercourse between the two capitals. Thus, although the Fudai nobles were often possessed of smaller fiefs than the Tozama, they held far more influential positions. By his new distribution of the country, there were two hundred and thirty-seven Daimyo—the number was afterwards raised to a little over three hundred—and of these, one hundred and fifteen were direct vassals of the Tokugawa family. As a Japanese writer points out, it was not like planning a house or a garden; the interests of each had to be consulted, rewards and punishments meted out with at least a show of justice; the powerful conciliated, the weak overawed. The process took years to complete.

It is recorded that when Ieyasu's grandson, Iemitsu, came to the Shogunate, he summoned to the palace at Yedo all the Tozama lords and declared to them that henceforth he proposed to place them on the same footing as the Fudai nobles. "My ancestor," he told them, "having been originally of the same rank as yourselves, and having been enabled to pacify the country through your assistance, was prompted by a sentiment of deference from classing you with the Fudai barons. But I differ from my ancestor, in the fact that I was born to the position which he acquired, and I am under no obligation to preserve any distinction. Should this resolve be displeasing to any of you, an interval of three years will be given you to consider the matter quietly on your own estates; during that time you will be expected to come to a final decision." To this speech, which amounted to a request for a fresh declaration of fealty, the Shogun added the gift of a sword to each Daimyo, reminding them of the creed of the Samurai, that they should guard with weapons of war what was taken by that means. Both Fudai and Tozama acquiesced quietly to this proposal, and the work of consolidation was done.

CHAPTER VIII.

THE SHRINES OF ISE.

" What it is
　　That dwelleth here
　　I know not;
　　Yet my heart is full of gratitude,
　　And the tears trickle down."
　　　　　　Saigo, Priest of Ise.　Aston's translation.

"Think not that God is something afar off, but seek for him in your own heart; for the heart is the abode of God."
　　　　　　Kiuso.　Aston's translation.

" Pay no heed to the praise or blame of fellow-men; but so act that you need not be ashamed before the Gods of the Unseen. . . . If you desire to practice true virtue, learn to stand in awe of the Unseen; it will prevent you from doing wrong. Make a vow to the God who rules over the Unseen, and cultivate the conscience implanted in you, and thus you will never wander from the Way."
　　　　　　Hirata Atsutane.　Japanese translation, Anon.

IT will hardly be safe to compare Ise with Delphi, and yet the Shrine of the Sun Goddess in Yamato has had something of the same unifying influence on the nation that Apollo's had over Greece—the same in kind, though by no means in degree; to note only one difference, in Japan the political side of religion, so to speak, was altogether usurped by the imported

Buddhism. Nevertheless, this temple, which is held to be the oldest in Japan, was so very sacred that Buddhism, with all its prestige, scarcely touched any of its rites or traditions; for it goes back to the very Age of the Gods, and the mirror of the Sun Goddess herself is kept in the innermost shrine.

Concerning this mirror, tradition relates that when Amaterasu sent her grandson Ninigi, ancestor of the first Emperor Jimmu Tenno, to make peace on the earth and conquer the demons and evil spirits, she gave him "the Jewel, the Mirror, and the Sword" (the one that her brother Susa-no-o took from the body of the eight-headed dragon), saying, "This mirror is my spirit; regard it as myself." Therefore it is that these precious things are the insignia of her descendants; but, as has been already noted, in the second century the Emperor Sujin, fearing they might be accidentally polluted, sent them to a certain shrine, after having fac-similes made to preserve in the palace as the tokens of the imperial rule; and from that shrine they were afterwards removed to Ise, where the mirror remains, the sword having been sent on to Atsuta, near Nagoya, where it now is. The mirror probably signifies the female, and the sword the male principle, much as some American Indians represent a woman by a water-jar and a man by a knife or an arrow.

The temple of the mirror is called the Naiku, or Inner temple; the other is the Geku, or Outer, and is thought less sacred than that of the Sun Goddess; but this, too, belongs to one of the earliest cults—the worship of earth and the creator of food. They stand at a considerable distance apart, surrounded by beautiful trees, and approached through wooden torii of the plainest early shape, the supports resting on the ground and not in sockets, and the single cross-beam perfectly straight. These two temples only their special priests may approach, or the descendants of the gods, the members of the imperial family. Till the fourteenth century a virgin priestess of the house was always in charge of the " eight-petaled " mirror of the sun, but since then the rule has been less rigidly enforced.

The custom, however, is not a little suggestive of the virgin priestesses of Vesta and the Roman fire rites. And just as Lanciani has traced back the temple of Vesta at Rome to the round straw huts of the half-nomad Latins, Sir Ernest Satow carries these temples at Ise back to a pre-historic Japanese house, raised a little on posts, thatch-roofed and wattled, its floor of bare, beaten earth, partly surrounded by a low platform, where doubtless the members of the family sat. In the temples the platform has already spread over the whole space, but it may be in memory of the primitive type of dwelling that at certain times the Emperor must worship his ancestors " standing upon the earth " — a necessity that was cleverly provided for at the imperial palace in Kyoto by cementing one corner of the great hall and strewing it daily with fresh sand for the morning invocations. In a series of drawings of peasant houses owned by Dr. Nitobé, a good slice of the bare ground often remains not floored over; but in most houses all that is left is the small vestibule where shoes are taken off—a rudiment, as the anatomists would say, of the original state of the house. It is most probable, too, that another prototype may be found in the rude dwellings of a Malay *campong* (East English, " compound "), which are rough straw huts, raised on piles above the side of some bay or river, no doubt for better defence from animals and hostile tribes, as you see them, for instance, at Singapore. The superficial resemblance is certainly strong, and becomes closer in the case of the temples than of ordinary Japanese houses, because, as Sir Ernest Satow points out, the earliest temples had their supports set into the ground, not merely on it, as is done at the present day.

One of the unique and curious customs at Ise is that the two chief temples, the Naiku and the Geku, must be pulled down and rebuilt at the end of every twenty years, " that our Fatherland may be happy, and that the five fruits of the field may prosper." It would seem that the underlying thought was that of keeping away any touch of decay or imperfection from the sacred place. Each temple has therefore a pair of sites, and goes from one to the other alternately. When the old building is pulled down, the wood is broken up into little pieces and sold in tiny packets as charms against disease and misfortune. Every smallest detail of the old temple is copied in the most minute way, and always has been, so far back as our knowledge goes; so that these—say, seven-thousandth descendants of the original temples —are probably very close fac-similes of what stood here some fifteen hundred years ago. The builders, while at work on such temples, must follow a certain rule of life; they must go to their work "washen, barefoot and in white," and there are rules, too, for the use of tools and materials. Ieyasu decreed that the Daimyo of Owari and of Kiushiu should provide the *hinoki* wood used to rebuild the Ise temples.

All of which would be highly interesting and instructive if one were allowed to see it—if it were not all so supremely sacred as to be hidden away behind a series of palisades and groups of trees, through which only the priests may pass, and which allow you merely a tantalizing glimpse of thatched roof and the crossed ends of the gable rafters projecting through it—suggestion of the time when these supports were tied together, as the Ainu tie them now. Even the Japanese pilgrim must be content to gaze only on the outside of his holy of holies, and enjoy instead the very beautiful landscape through which he journeys to the shrine. The way there is by rail from Kyoto, or by a little steamer across Owari bay, and then by

kuruma to Yamada, the town which exists solely by
and for Ise and the pilgrims thither.   All about here
the coast is most picturesque, the groves of camphor
and cryptomeria wonderful, even in this country of
beautiful forests.

We are used to the myth of Chronos and the birth
of Athene, and many another tale whose grossness has
been transformed or overlaid by the beauty of Greek
art and poetry; but the Japanese account of the creation of things has come down to us in all its crudity,
bald and grotesque almost as the beliefs of the North
American Indians.   At first, say the Kojiki and the
Nihongi, all the world was chaos, a dreary waste of
half-liquid mud, till the gods above sent down the
creator pair, Isanagi and Isanami, to make the earth.
Then Isanagi and Isanami came down and stood on
the Bridge of Heaven, and thrust down a jeweled
spear into the mud, and flung out the half-liquid
drops that clung to it; and the drops became the
islands of reed-growing Japan.

After this various and wonderful things happened;
several gods and goddesses were born, and last of all
the Fire God, at whose birth Isanami died.   Her husband made a journey, Orpheus-like, to bring her back
from the under world, and found, and was in the act
of returning with her, when, like Orpheus, he dis-
obeyed orders and turned to look at what he carried;
and seeing the horrible corpse, he dropped it in terror
and fled.   Being thus unclean, he bathed in a river

to purify himself, and as he did so various divinities were born from the touch of the water. The Sun Goddess Amaterasu sprang from his right eye, the Moon God from his left, and the very troublesome and unruly Wind God Susa-no-o from his nose or breath.

Later there were other gods and demi-gods created, such as Prince Fire Shine and Prince Fire Fade, and Ninigi, the grandson of Amaterasu, who married the daughter of an earth god and became the ancestor of Jimmu Tenno; and the food goddess, an uncouth Demeter, who made rice and fish and game to entertain the Moon God, only to be slain by the ungrateful guest, because he said she gave him unclean food; whereat the Sun Goddess was very wroth, and punished the Moon God; but " from the body of the murdered Earth sprang cattle and horses, millet, silkworms, rice, barley and beans." So says Chamberlain, quoting from the Kojiki and Nihongi.

The story of Prince Fire Shine and Prince Fire Fade is one into which wise people read a great many things, such as the conflict between the hill tribes and the coast tribes, the hunting and the fishing population; it also concerns the palace of the Dragon King under the sea, which appears in so many Japanese legends.

The two princes were brothers, sons of Ninigi and the daughter of the earth god. Prince Fire Shine was a fisherman, and possessed many fine hooks and caught much fish; his brother was a hunter, who killed beasts and birds upon the mountains.

One day Prince Fire Fade said to his brother, " I am minded to go a-fishing; do thou lend me thy hooks, and I will lend thee my bow and spear, wherewith to hunt things large and small." So Prince Fire Shine consented, and took the bow and spear and went to the mountains, and killed much game. But Prince Fire Fade fished and fished, yet he caught nothing; and at last he lost one of the hooks in the sea.

When Prince Fire Shine returned, and Prince Fire Fade told him what he had done, he was very angry. Then Prince Fire Fade took his spear, and beat it out, and made many hooks for his brother; but Prince Fire Shine would not be appeased, and demanded his own hook again. And seeing there was nothing else to be done, Prince Fire Fade plunged into the sea to look for it.

He sank down and down into the waves, but suddenly a sea monster came to him and bore him up, and took him to the Jewel Palace, where the Dragon King received him kindly; and when he heard the Prince's story, he sent to all the fishes (who were his subjects) and asked if any of them had seen the fish-hook; and by and by a large fish came and brought it.

Then Prince Fire Fade was glad, and would have gone back to his brother; but the Dragon King invited him to stay, and offered him his daughter, the

Jewel Princess. So Prince Fire Fade married her, and lived happily under the sea.

Then, when he wished to return, the Dragon King gave him the two jewels that control the tide, the ebb-tide jewel and the flood-tide jewel; and the sea monster bore him on its back through the waves to the earth again.

But when Prince Fire Shine saw his brother returning he was again angry, and threatened to kill him. Then Prince Fire Fade raised the flood-tide jewel; and as he held it up the water came flowing up over the shore, higher and higher, and Prince Fire Shine cried out in terror, and begged Prince Fire Fade to spare him. So the Prince lifted up the ebb-tide jewel, and the sea went back to its own place. And Prince Fire Shine saw that his brother was stronger, and he made submission to him. After that Prince Fire Fade built a little hut on the shore, and lived there with the Jewel Princess; but when Prince Fire Shine peeped into the hut one day all that he saw was a sea monster, which crawled out of the hut and went into the sea. Nevertheless the monster was the Jewel Princess in disguise; and her son was Jimmu Tenno, the first Emperor of Japan.

Instead of dismissing these elder gods to devildom, Buddhism quietly absorbed them, by the simple process of recognizing them as Avatars or Gongen, temporary manifestations or incarnations of Buddha, like Shaka (Gautama) himself. Thus came about the

Ryobu Shinto, a strange fusion of Buddhas and Kami, so blended at last that no one can say of certain elements whether they came from this side or from that. The recent "purifying" movement has drawn lines as best it could, turning out priests and pagodas and incense, and a hundred picturesque accessories, by which Buddhism had "defiled" the worship of the Kami; leaving only the mirror and the gohei, which are regarded as emblems of truth and purity of heart, and of self knowledge and obedience to that innate sense of right that Shinto claims for man. For the rest, the grosser forms of nature-worship have been suppressed or eliminated, and ancestor worship has become with many a sort of passion of enthusiasm for the great departed; so that modern Pure Shinto may be allowed to cover almost anything, from a belief in deities innumerable to a vague acknowledgment of a power over all—a belief not far from Matthew Arnold's "Something, not ourselves, that makes for righteousness."

An interesting example of the way in which these Shinto nature deities were taken over into the Buddhist pantheon is quoted by Chamberlain. In the early centuries there was a devout Buddhist priest, who was troubled with questionings about these matters. He therefore went on a pilgrimage to Ise, and, praying for many days at the shrine, besought the Sun Goddess Amaterasu-no-kami to show herself to him in her true form—for, it must be remembered, at Ise there is no

image, nor any representation of the divinity whatso-
ever. It is needful to take on faith even the mirror
of the goddess herself, in its silken cover, which is
never taken off, but, when it might decay, is covered
with a new one on top of the layers of old ones which
have hidden it for centuries.

On the last night of his hundred days' pilgrimage,
the goddess appeared to the priest in a dream (under
what form is not stated), and told him to go to the
seashore at a certain place, and there she would mani-
fest herself to him. Full of joy, the priest went to
the spot to which he had been directed by the heavenly
vision; but to his dismay and disappointment there
appeared only a great serpent, ten feet long and of a
bright golden color, floating on the waves. This, he
felt sure, was but a delusion of the goddess, meant to
try his faith, and, crying, " Monster! show thyself in
thy true form," he took off his scarf, a part of his
sacerdotal vestments, and flung it at the serpent, which
did not change its appearance, but slowly sank into
the sea.

Three nights later the faithful priest had another
vision, in which the goddess told him that he had indeed seen only another appearance, and not the reality;
but as a reward he should go to a certain little temple
in Yamato, and there he should find her as in very
truth she was. The priest joyfully obeyed; but when
he reached the place, the image proved to be so holy
that the monks in charge of the temple at first refused

to show it. When at last they consented to open the shrine, to their astonishment they found that the very scarf which the pilgrim had thrown at the serpent was twisted around the image of Amida. Then the priest knew that the goddess had indeed condescended to enlighten him, and he worshiped Amaterasu in the Buddha of Light and Wisdom.

At the World's Parliament of Religions at Chicago, in 1893, the Right Rev. R. Shibata explained the meaning of the name Shinto as used to signify the ancient religion of Japan. " The word Shinto or Kami-no-michi comes from the two words *Shin* or *Kami* (they are the Chinese and Japanese pronunciation of the same character) meaning deity, and *to* or *michi*, a way; and it designates the Way transmitted to us from our Divine Ancestors, in which every Japanese is bound to walk.

" According to our ancient scriptures there was a generation of Kami or Deities, who created the heavens and the earth, together with all things, and became the ancestors of the Japanese. And, as every child of the Heavenly Deity came into the world with a soul separated from the one original soul of Deity, he ought to be just as the Deity ordered; he must be plain and simple as the form of the sacred mountain Fuji, and make his mind and body pure as the serenity thereof."

Purity, actual and ceremonial, is the one law of Shinto; and a large share of the rites are directed to

purification. Twice yearly from the earliest times the
Emperor, as head of the national family, has performed the office of purification for himself and his
people, whereby they are "purged from offences and pol-
lutions, and saved from possible calamities." According to one authority, it is the custom for each Shinto
household to have in the Kamidana—the shelf where
the name-tablets of the ancestors are kept—an amulet
made of a bit of the sacred wand used by the priestess
of his temple who dances the sacred dance at the festival of purification; this amulet is renewed at each
half-yearly feast, and the old ones are to be used to
kindle the fire for the bath, which the priestess takes
before the dance.

In early times it is recorded that fear of pollution
sometimes led to neglect of the sick and the dead;
corpses were left by the roadside because no one would
care for them, and laws had to be enacted enjoining
decency in these things. The custom of moving the
palace after the death of an Emperor rose from the
same kind of superstitious dread of defilement. In
early times, if a traveler died upon the way, his comrades
were obliged to pay a sum of money to the people of
the district in which he died, to defray the expense of
the rites of purification and sacrifice necessary to protect them from the defilement; and even in case of
sickness the same rule was held. Moreover, when a
man went out of his own part of the country, he had
to take with him food and a vessel to cook it in; and

he might not cook it beside the road without permission from the neighbors, lest by some act of his the place should be made unclean; if he failed to do this, he might be required to pay for rites of purification for their houses. If he borrowed a pot, and accidentally let it touch anything unclean, he was required to pay for the purification sacrifice. Naturally, this sort of thing was afterwards discontinued — and yet it was probably no more than the Hindus practice to the present time. But it is really true, as their own writers have said, that the Japanese have an instinctive horror of uncleanliness; and their "causes of defilement" are often curiously like those of the ancient Hebrews; while their ways are quite as astonishingly unlike those of any of their neighbors nearer than the Malay, who seem to have an equal passion for the water.

Shinto is likewise sharply distinct from Chinese ideas in the position it gives to women. As at Ise, in all Shinto shrines an important part of the temple service belongs to virgin priestesses; it is they who dance the sacred dances, they who clean the sacred shrine. At the great Kasuga temple at Nara, young girls and women rode on horseback in the procession at the most important festivals; and when a temple was to be erected, girls cleared the ground and dug the holes for the corner posts, and a virgin took the axe and made the first cut in the wood for the timbers.

Like the vestal virgins, the Shinto priestesses

were to remain virgins only during the term of their service at the temple; celibacy was no part of the doctrine, rather the underlying idea was that of a family, in which the head of the house acted as priest, assisted by his virgin daughters. The sacred hymns were long handed down orally, without being committed to writing. There are twenty-seven greater rituals, nearly all of them invocations for peace and plenty; one only for protection against evil spirits. But without these rituals properly performed, it is thought that the Kami might be angry, and send or permit evil to befall the crops or the houses. Naturally the most important of all were the harvest rites, the prayers for a plentiful crop.

"Harken all ye, for I speak in the presence of the gods who rule over the harvest. If they render bountiful the harvest we have sown, that for which our hands have toiled and our feet have trodden the soil of the rice-field, then will I offer of the first-fruits of rice a thousand heads, and saké in the wide cups ranged duly in line." And duly are the thanksgivings offered still, on the day of the First-fruits, which falls now in October, and on the festival of the later harvest, now held in November.

The offerings in kind have been long since discontinued in the Shinto ritual, except the daily offerings of food and water paid both at the temples and before the Kamidana at home. The ancient chronicles record the gifts of "bright cloth and glittering cloth, fine cloth and coarse cloth, saké jars and sweet herbs and bitter, things wide of fin and narrow of fin, piled up like the ranges of the hills." For all these, the strips of paper fastened to a wand, called gohei, are supposed to be the representatives and substitutes. They are nearly always pure white, and cut in a particular way, and they are certainly used as an indication of divine presence in the widest sense.

Here is a Japanese description of the ceremony of "Earth worship" on the estate of a Daimyo; it was, however, a special occasion, to invoke an increase from the land, not the regular yearly service.

"The lord, governor, county officers and village officers, all dressed in sacerdotal robes, proceeded first to the temple of Kasuga, to inform the god of their aim and purpose. The procession then marched to a piece of ground recently opened, and there, with all solemnity, the chief first took up a hoe and struck it three times into the ground. After him the governor struck nine times, the county officers twenty-seven times, and so on down to the very tiller of the soil. The whole was a public acknowledgment that the soil was sacred and to be sacredly handled, and that all blessings of life were drawn from it."

Not only the great deities, who are forces of nature or spirits of the departed, found a place in the system of Kami worship; like the Latins, the Japanese finds a divinity for almost every article of daily use, and one to watch over all his actions; there was one who guarded the rice pot, and for every part of the house, as well as the god of the spring and the god of the thunder. Yet for all these many deities the true Shinto had no images; that was left for Buddhism to introduce, along with the many other foreign elements of Japanese religion as it stands to-day. The only outward tokens are the mirror of the Sun Goddess in her temple, and the *ihai*, the name-tablets of the dead, which stand to their people almost as the living presence of the departed.

There is a touching little story—one of many illustrating the universal sense of the nearness of the beloved dead—which is based on this idea of the ihai as representing the very person whose name it bears, and, too, of the possibility of their return in bodily form to our world. Many years ago, says this legend, a young Samurai was betrothed to a beautiful girl; they were about to be married, when suddenly the young knight was summoned to follow his lord to battle. In those days there was little communication between one part of the country and another; the war was long, and for months nothing was heard of the knight. The little bride began to droop; then she fell sick, and at last she died. The distracted parents set up a tablet at her tomb, closed their house, and departed on a long pilgrimage.

At last the Samurai returned, and reaching the village, learned for the first time what had taken place; and he went to the tomb of his bride, meaning to kill himself there. But as he drew the dagger, a soft voice called to him to stay; and before him stood the young girl, beautiful as he had left her. "I did not die," she told him; "I only disappeared for a little while." Together they returned to the deserted house, and, calling in the neighbors, the marriage rite was celebrated.

For a year they lived together in perfect happiness, and a son was born to them, whom the young wife cherished with a tender sadness. Then one day her parents returned from their pilgrimage, and as they drew near their own part of the country they heard that the man who was to have been their son-in-law was married and living in the village; and they sought him out, and loaded him with reproaches for his unfaithfulness to their daughter. But he told them he had done no wrong, for his wife was no other than their own daughter, whom they supposed to be dead; and leading them to the house, he bade them enter and see. So they entered, and in her chamber, wrapped in a quilt, lay the rosy baby; but the wife was no longer there. Beside the child lay the ihai, inscribed with her name, which the parents had placed over her tomb.

In regard to the assertion so often made that Shinto is too vague to be considered a religion at all, the writer of the unsigned paper in "Japan Illustrated" says: "It is hardly necessary to point out that the intuitive system of morality receives its fullest recognition when ethical sanctions are not coded. If a man derives the first principle of his duties from intuition, and if he be so constituted that the notion of right carries with it a sense of obligation, then a schedule of rules and regulations for the direction of every-day conduct becomes not only superfluous, but illogical. That was the moral basis of Shinto. If the feet were kept firmly in the path of right, the guardianship of the gods was assured, without even praying for it."

Of this, which may be called the higher Shinto, the common people probably comprehend no single word, though the devout among them unquestionably find a real comfort in their visits to the shrines. Indeed, this same writer declares that " not a peasant believes that his farm can be productive, not a merchant that his business can thrive, unless he pays, or honestly resolves to pay, at least one visit to Ise during his lifetime." Further, if to us most of the visitors seem to give themselves up to a mere unthinking festivity, it may be consoling to remember that the unlettered children of the East are really much more of children than we can easily imagine ; and, like children, they can pass very quickly from a state of religious awe to a very different condition, without spiritual shipwreck.

As a large part of the pilgrims are peasant farmers, their best time to come is in the winter, when there is least doing in the fields ; but the favorite season is early spring, when the cherries are in blossom. Then the town is more than ever gay with flags, and the three hundred or more inns packed to overflowing with pilgrims, most of them bent on merry-making, like those Homeric youths who, after the sacrifice, "ate and drank, and pleased the god all day with dance and song." The pilgrim societies furnish a large part of the contingent — those curious clubs which flourish in all parts of Japan, and send a certain number of representatives each year to this or that shrine or sacred mountain. All pay certain yearly dues, and the pilgrims for the year are chosen by lot from among the members, their expenses being paid out of the general fund. They mark their favorite inns all along the way, putting up little banners stamped with the device of their club, and the inns naturally are delighted with such good advertisement. One member, usually the most experienced, acts as the head of the party, and "personally conducts" them from shrine to shrine, explaining and exhorting, for all the world like a tourist agent with a party of zealous sight-seers.

The temples are quite outside of the town, and the crowd ebbs back and forth under the torii and through the great wood, "a natural nave of cryptomeria," as Percival Lowell calls it. Here and there among the trees are glimpses of the plain, unpainted buildings, and the curious projecting rafters seeming to push through the deep velvet-brown thatch ; for on these temples are no tiled roofs, as on the Buddhist or even the Ryobu Shinto shrines. There are many buildings

besides the Naiku and the Geku, such as the one for
the sacred dance, and that where the members of the
imperial family or their representatives change their
garments before entering the shrine of the Food Goddess on the festival of the "Divine Tasting"—the
thanksgiving of the first-fruits.   Among the camphor
and cryptomerias and other tall trees are clumps of
the sacred sakaki (*cleyera Japonica*), whose touch
purifies.   The wood of the sakaki is used for the
wand on which the gohei are hung for the purification
rites, and two vases containing sprigs of sakaki are
generally placed in Shinto temples, with the mirror
and gohei.   This, too, it is that is used at Shinto
funerals, when at the end of the rites those nearest
akin go one by one and lay a sprig of sakaki on the
bier.   It is a last sign of separation, the token that
now they are purified from the touch of death and
may approach no more.

The Naiku is far away over the hills at another
little village, reached by a picturesque road, which
winds along the shore and across a long bridge, giving
beautiful views of the near mountains, and even of
Fuji, they say, in certain very favorable weather.
One of the curiosities on the way is the pair of rocks
in the sea, a few yards out, called the "conjugal
rocks," which are united by a straw rope—sure sign
of some legend of sanctity.   One version is that the
sacred rope wards off contagious disease, and that the
god Susa-no-o taught this to a peasant and his wife

in the neighborhood.   At the Naiku itself there is
even less to see than at the Geku—only torii and
fences and the tops of thatched roofs through the
trees.

Beyond the wood leading to the Geku there is a
little fenced court, and on the far side a third torii
leads to a flight of wide stone steps, ending in another
high fence or palisade, smooth and unpainted, which
surrounds the temples of the Food Goddess.   In the
middle of this fence is a thatched gate, not closed, but
hung across by a white curtain, like a great sheet,
quite concealing the inner court.   Before the gate and
the curtain there is a mat, on which the worshipers
throw their offerings of thin copper rin, and now and
then a bigger coin ; and before the mat the pilgrims
put off their shoes, believing they have reached the
very threshold of the gods.   The thing is all the more
solemn because the people firmly believe that any
irreverence, even unintentional, may bring the wrath
of the deity upon the whole country; and they
instance the case, centuries ago, when an offering of
food on its way from the temple of the Food Goddess
to the other was unwittingly carried past some unclean
thing.   The Emperor fell sick, and all sorts of dire
things happened, till the cause was discovered and
expiation made.   Since then they have taken no risks;
the offerings for both divinities are made in the temple
of the Food Goddess, and are not carried across to the
Naiku.

A tragic proof of the intense popular feeling on this subject was given in 1885, by the assassination of Viscount Mori, one of the best and ablest men in the country. He had been much abroad, in negotiations at Peking, in America, and as Minister to England; and after returning home, as Minister of Education, he practically created the present educational system in Japan. A progressive of the progressives, he lived at the top of the pro-European wave, and was almost ready to drop everything national if only Japan might be brought immediately in line with the rest of the world. Prof. Max Müller, not long before his death, gave an amusing account of the impression made on him by the way in which Viscount Mori rushed down to call, between trains as it were, to consult the professor as a specialist on the best religion to introduce for the common people of Japan. Educated men, he considered, did very well on philosophy; but the lower classes needed a religion; their own cults, he said, were obsolete, Christianity "had proved a failure," and what would the professor recommend? Max Müller seems to have intimated that religions could not be served to nations by order, and to have declined to propose anything by way of substitute for the beliefs the Viscount had proposed to reject; and Mori hurried back to catch his steamer for home.

Evidently it was in this mood of indifference, if not actual disdain, that he visited the Ise shrines late in 1884; for he not only failed to make the usual offering, but even pushed aside the white curtain with his walking-stick. Some say that when warned he apologized, others that he was haughty and overbearing. This much is certain, that a young man of the place became greatly excited, and brooded over the act and its possible effects on the Emperor and the nation, till he resolved to kill the evil-doer and save the country from the awful consequences of such sacrilege. So he wrote a letter declaring his purpose, and went up to Tokyo and stabbed Viscount Mori in his own house, just as he was about to go to the palace on the morning the Constitution was signed. The fanatic was cut down on the spot, and unhappily became at once a hero and a martyr in the people's eyes.

CHAPTER IX.

KYOTO — THE PALACES.

Tokyo, the Japanese say, is the brain of new Japan, but Kyoto is its heart. Though deserted by the Court since 1868, the old imperial city is still dear to the people as the centre of heroic and sacred associations, and still the centre, too, of art, all the schools and guilds of the capital notwithstanding. Naturally aristocratic and conservative, the departure of the Court took away that progressive modernizing element which was so valuable to the nation as a whole, but so dangerous to its relics of antiquity, and left Kyoto to cultivate its arts and preserve its monuments and traditions in peace; wherefore the old capital remains to-day the most thoroughly Japanese of all the large cities in the empire, and far the most interesting to Western visitors.

Not that Kyoto is without the touch of modern life; an imperial university, a Christian college and an electric tram are side by side with a very bewilderment of temples and palaces and curio shops, a jumble of works of art old and new, good and bad, together. Most of the town now crowds close around the bridges,

154

but there are long rides through streets far too wide for their shrunken traffic, and out to monasteries once in the city and now surrounded by yellow rape and paddy-fields. For when the Court moved here from Nara at the end of the eighth century, closing, so, the brilliant "Nara period" and beginning "Heian," the Peace, the Emperor was still a power and not a name, and he laid out his new capital generously. A great palace enclosure stood at the north end, and a space for the dwellings of the Court nobles; then wide streets numbered off from this, one, two, three—Ichi-jo, Ni-jo, San-jo—crossed by still wider Tera-machi running straight down from the palace gate. The whole city space was three miles wide and a little longer, enclosed by a wall and a ditch, and provided with bridges and water-gates at the end of each street. The situation was wisely chosen, in a beautiful little plain crossed by the Kamogawa, and circled by wooded mountains. Even so Florence lies in the Tuscan hills; but there comparison ceases, for the view from Yaami's or Maru-yama shows no Duomo, no Palazzo Vecchio, only a sea of low, black-tiled roofs, and here and there a mass of trees, or a high red temple, "shouldering up," as La Farge says, among the lesser houses.

Venerable as some of them look, none of the buildings actually date very far back; a purely timber architecture would preclude that, even if the city had not been besieged and defended, sacked and rebuilt, over and over again during those long, stormy centuries.

But many of the temples were founded in the thirteenth century by the luxurious Ashikaga Shoguns,
who patronized the arts and plunged the country into a
chaos of misrule ; and others by the Tokugawa, builders of Nikko and Yedo, who, whatever their faults, at
least brought in two centuries of peace and order and
cultivation.

The first European hotel in Kyoto was Yaami's,
which rambles delightfully up a pine-clad hillside east
of the town ; it was originally a famous tea-house
called Ichi-ri-ki—the very one where Oishi, chief of
the Forty-seven Ronin, drank and played the fool to
such deep purpose. A pretty Japanese garden slopes
down the hill below the house, and from the balconies
you look over the gray city, and the misty fields
spreading away to the mountains. The Yaami is
cool and pleasant in summer ; but the Kyoto hotel,
across the river in the town, which is under the same
management, has the advantage of being more central,
and sparing the extra half-mile of jinrikisha ride ;—
which is a consideration, for Kyoto jinrikishas are
execrable old rattletraps, and Kyoto streets are fanged
with murderous stones, and the temples are very
many and a weariness to the flesh.

Then there are hours to be spent in the curio shops,
which some are thought to find more interesting than
too many temples. Whether interesting or not, at
least no one is allowed to forget them. Not half an
hour does the stranger remain at his hotel before there

comes a soft knock at the door, and a gentle person, deprecating, but by no means obsequious, asks permission just to inform you of his establishment, where he will be most pleased to exhibit his unworthy goods—fans, cloisonné, bronze, old swords, embroidery, porcelain and "genuine old" Satsuma, as the case may be. Probably he has a small package, done up in a green cotton *furoshiki* (wrapping handkerchief) stamped with the ideograph of his house—*goran kudasai*, beholding condescend! A courteous bow, and the little catching of the breath that expresses so much deference in Japan. It is not at all necessary to be rude to these people; a polite refusal dismisses them at once; and the truth is, four tourists in five find their cards, or a private view of their wares, a real convenience and saving of precious time. Nor are the goods they show to be entirely despised. Of course, they are modern, and of course, too, Kyoto puts out yearly an enormous amount of hasty, flashy stuff, solely for export to foreign markets—it sells as the other does not; but, happily, not all the nation is utterly corrupted, and there is good work still, bearing much of the dainty charm, the exquisite refinement, belonging to things genuinely Japanese. As for antiques, everybody knows the time for bargains and wonderful finds is long gone by; it belonged to the unsettlement following the opening of the country and the cruel Satsuma rebellion, when heirlooms were sold for a little rice, and when it was the fashion to run after Progress with a very large P, and exchange priceless lacquers for American "Pre-Centennial" carpets. Mercifully, there was a reaction that saved the country much beside art; and nowadays, if good things find their way to second-hand shops—as from time to time they undoubtedly do—there are plenty of dealers who very well know their value, and Japanese collectors ready to give full prices; so that the fascinating chase is no longer an inexpensive amusement.

Doubtless it was the famous bleaching powers of the Kamogawa that made Kyoto early foremost in the dyers' arts, as the neighboring clay-banks drew to her the makers of fine porcelains. For the human element the crafts probably owed far less to the patronage of the Court than the Church—that elaborate Buddhist ritual, which called forth a gorgeous art to supply its needs. Yet the Court was not without influence; it represented a taste, a tendency, that seems always at war with the Buddhistic element; a national impulse of restraint and severity, which acts as a check, or balance-wheel, to the rather florid inclinations of the other.

Thus it happens that there are here in Kyoto two sharply-contrasting buildings — the imperial palace (the "Gosho") and the so-called Nijo palace of the Tokugawa Shoguns; each an almost typical example of these two diametrically opposed tendencies; the one simple, reserved, delighting in wide, restful spaces and delicate tones; the other rich, splendid, full of

Nijo Palace, Kyoto

brilliant color and exuberance of crowding fancy. The one original, Shintoist, strictly national; the other, offspring of Buddhism, which, coming from India through China, brought with it all the sumptuous, half-barbaric glitter of its home. In considering them it is needful to remember continually what each one stands for; to remember that the imperial palace goes back for its model to the remotest past, that it is consciously, intentionally conservative; intentionally simple, too, in accordance with those Shinto precepts which enjoin purity of heart and life, comparable to the snow-crowned Fuji; an expression of the Yamato Spirit, *Yamato Damashii*, the *Volksgeist* of old Japan. On the other hand, the Tokugawa Shoguns, patrons of Buddhism and inheritors of the Chinese influences of the Middle Ages, holding a military power, won by sheer energy and military genius from scarcely less gifted rivals—these Tokugawa not only surrounded themselves with whatever tended to increase their own power and dignity, but with deliberate purpose sought to weaken their rivals through luxury and self-indulgence, encouraging to that very end all the splendid arts of peace.

Both the palaces are now imperial residences, and not open to the public, but foreign visitors can obtain permits beforehand through their proper legations. Visiting cards are handed to the gentleman in charge —who is an officer of the imperial household, and *not* a hall porter—and names are to be signed in the visit-

ors' book before beginning the round. The same form-
ality is repeated at each palace.

The two are alike in general plan, except that the
Gosho (imperial) seems more strictly a group of dwellings in a garden ; the Nijo, a castle. The long, yellowish white, enclosing wall of the Gosho is little
higher than a man, built of earth, and plastered and
roofed with tiles like a temple wall—a screen and not
a defence ; while the Shogun surrounded himself with
a moat and a mass of cyclopean masonry, set with
heavy gates and towers. Vivid enough tokens, these,
of the real relation between the Emperor and his
nominally obedient vassal, under the Tokugawa Shogunate. In fact, for many years before the Restoration, the Court revenues were disgracefully insufficient
for its needs, and Yamato reserve in matters of taste
was too often cruelly enforced by necessity.

The large space next to the palace, which used to
be enclosed and occupied by the nobles' houses, is now
thrown open as a kind of park, giving an effect of
solitude to the long, straight wall and carved gates.
Within the wall there are fine trees and open levels,
not grassed, but strewn with small pebbles, and in the
innermost recesses, behind the palace, is hidden the
choicest of Japanese gardens, rocks and streams and
lake, trees and shrubbery, all imitating to perfection
some bit of wild forest scenery. The palace garden
at Tokyo has nothing half so lovely.

The closed storm-shutters make the place look desolate, as all unused dwellings must, but cannot spoil its beauty of proportion, or the magnificent sweeping roofs, with their upward tent-curves and wide over-hang, thatched two feet deep with gray bark, fine and close as velvet. Within, the sense of chilly empti-ness is not lessened by the white brocade hangings of the throne, the only piece of furniture, in a European sense, in the vast "Clear and Pure Hall," which is first entered; nor are the broad masses of intense cobalt-blue dashed across the sliding screens altogether satisfactory in decorative effect, however symbolically correct as the clear color of the sky. But it is im-possible to judge rightly of an effect planned for the presence of a brilliant court, clad in those beautiful robes of ceremony which have vanished before the latest Berlin fashions; and elsewhere the color is be-yond praise, the drawing of bird and beast and flower so masterly that it is difficult to believe they were all produced since the middle of the nineteenth century —copies of copies, made when the palace was rebuilt, after being burned in 1854. All is of the most exqui-site simplicity; the woodwork beautifully grained *keyaki* or *hinoki*, perfectly polished, unspoiled by paint or varnish. The only decoration is on the sliding paper screens which divide the rooms—here chrysanthe-mums, there graceful branches of yellow *yamabuki*; again, flights of wild fowl, all in low-toned browns and gold. One long room has figures of Chinese sages, copies from originals of the ninth century, stiff, slant-eyed, long-moustached worthies, whose presence must surely have had a solemnizing influence on the company before them. In other rooms there are delicate landscapes, in the Tosa style, and more saints and sages, and everywhere glimpses, through opened shutters, of the sunny garden and the blue hills. No wonder that, when the Emperor and Empress visit Kyoto, they are apt to linger long; they must have gone from it as from a little paradise.

The Nijo palace was built by Tokugawa Ieyasu, who needed a foothold in Kyoto while governing from Yedo; it is therefore nearly contemporary with Nikko, but in a stronger, bolder style, as befitted the palace-fortress. An earlier castle stood here, built by Ota Nobunaga, which was pulled down to make way for Ieyasu's. The first entrance is by a gorgeous gateway in the heavy stone wall, admitting to a court and another great gate, carved, painted, overlaid with lacquer and gold. This came from the wonderful palace which Ieyasu's predecessor, Hideyoshi, built at Fushimi, near Kyoto, and is a dozen years older than the rest. The peonies and phœnixes are so like those at Nikko that it is no surprise to find they are by the same master carver, Jingoro *Hidari*, the Left-Handed. There are more wonderful carvings of his in the *ramma*, or spaces above the sliding screens; openwork panels of peacocks and phœnixes, peony and pine, so cleverly cut that the two sides are quite different— peacocks, perhaps, in this room, flowers in that. On the screens majestic eagles soar or rest on twisted pine trees, and tigers stalk in bamboo jungles, all life-sized and startlingly bold, painted on wide backgrounds of dull gold, giving to the great empty rooms a marvelous air of stately magnificence.　The metal fastenings on beam ends and the sunk handles of screens are exquisitely chased or inlaid, and wooden doors and panels of corridors decorated with paintings of smaller birds and flowers, much of it modeled up with chalk under the color, and all toning in with the grain of the polished brown wood.　One room contains a sad relic of vandalism in a half-effaced drawing of a beautiful white heron, resting on the side of a boat, known as the Wet Heron.　When the palace was used for the offices of the Prefecture—for some years after 1868—this precious panel served as a bulletin board for posting up notices.

Yet this building was also the scene of an "epoch-making" assembly—the first meeting of the present Emperor with his council, just after his accession to the throne and the resignation of the Shogun.　He promised them to create a deliberative assembly, and submit all questions to the will of the people ; and the Constitution and the Diet are the result of that promise, made in the Nijo palace in 1867, by a youth of sixteen, who, before, had seldom left his own palace walls.　It was not a little significant that he should come to the Shogun's palace to do it, though the choice may have been a matter of necessity on account of room.

The most magnificent room of all is the great audience hall, where the Shogun used to receive homage from the Daimyos. The upper end is raised for his Highness to sit on, while the lesser princes occupied the lower level. The mats are still here, thick, close, finely woven, covering all the floor to the glossy-black lacquer sills; the metal fastenings are gilded bronze, delicately wrought, the three asarum leaves of Tokugawa appearing on the beam-ends, though elsewhere in the castle they are usually replaced by the imperial chrysanthemum. The wall decoration of the audience hall is great pine trees, broadly painted, which here, as in the other rooms, do not dwarf, but rather add to the sense of space. A second great hall, quite at the other end of the palace, was intended for imperial ambassadors, and this, too, has rich decoration, a ceiling coffered and lacquered, and walls of lavish gold, adorned with maples and blossoming fruit trees. By each room are small reception-rooms for the great lords, all gorgeous and all different, having screens of heron and wild fowl, clouds of pink cherry blossoms, Chinese scenes in sepia and dull gold; everywhere the same abandon of splendor, yet nowhere—and this is the abiding wonder—nowhere in it all is there anything heavy, anything oppressive or overwrought. The instinct of restraint has been here also, keeping decoration in its place and holding fancy in check, as with an inexorable Greek μηδὲν ἄγαν, Nothing in excess.

Not far from the Nijo palace there used to be a famous gate, where one of the ancestors of the Minamoto had lively dealings with a particularly obnoxious ogre. This unpleasant being was the leader of a band of his kind, who lived in the mountains, and had a way of breaking into the city at night and devouring any one who was unlucky enough to be found on the streets. Raiko, the grandfather of Yoshiiye, conqueror of the Ainu, determined to put a stop to these doings; so he set his men-at-arms to watch with him by turns at the gate Rashomon.

One night the turn fell to a young man named Tsuna. As it drew toward dawn, while all was still, suddenly the knight felt something clutch him by the head; a frightful creature was reaching down from the roof, trying to drag him up on to it. Tsuna grasped at the ogre and tried to pull him down, but in vain, and he was being slowly lifted off his feet, when he managed to free one hand, draw his sword and cut off the monster's arm. It dropped him with a howl and fled, and much delighted, Tsuna presented himself at the master's castle.

As it was an affair of the supernatural, Raiko sent the young man to consult with a famous wizard, who bade him place the arm in a chest and seal it tight, and pass seven days and nights in fasting and vigil, or worse would come of it. So Tsuna made a strong box for the arm, and shut himself up in his house, and passed the time devoutly in prayer.

When the seven days were nearly done, one night there came a great knocking at the gate. Tsuna called out to know who was there, and a voice answered that it was his old aunt, who had come from the country to congratulate him. Tsuna explained that he was under a vow to talk to no one till the seven days were accomplished; but the old lady wept and pleaded, and at last he consented to let her in. Then nothing would do but she must see the arm—the wonderful arm; she never saw an ogre in her life, and she was getting old and might never have another chance; and altogether she took it so to heart that Tsuna finally undid the cords and opened the lid just a little way; when, with a yell of delight, the old lady suddenly grasped the arm and shot through the roof, in the true form of a huge, hairy ogre. Poor Tsuna had nothing to do but report to his lord, and Raiko proceeded to get up an expedition to chase the monsters to their den, where he finally subdued and slew them.

Meanwhile, however, Raiko himself had an adventure. He had ridden quite far from the city one day, unattended, and had lost his way; when night came, he found himself in a dreary place on the bank of a little river, in which was reflected the faint light of a young moon. Beside the river stood a ruined temple, under an enormous pine tree, and under the pine tree was a toothless old hag, dressed in white—the color of death. Alighting from his horse, Raiko politely asked for shelter for the night. The old woman told him he had best go elsewhere, for the temple was haunted by demons, who had made her their slave. Demons being quite in Raiko's line, he requested to be announced; and after some persuasion the hag took him within. Here he found a brilliant hall, and in it a lovely damsel, "with eyes like stars and teeth like pearls, and lips that seemed the flower of the peach." This lovely being smiled upon him, and Raiko gave himself up to her charms; but presently the bright eyes began to glare, the mouth to grin hideously. Raiko reached for his sword, and found his arms caught in a monster spider's web, while the beautiful woman slowly grew before his eyes into a demon spider. With a mighty effort, Raiko wrenched his hands free and drew his sword, and keeping the creature at bay, strove to cut himself loose from the toils. The lights went out; he struck wildly about the hall, and suddenly his sword clashed against something hard as iron. Just then day broke, and web, demon, all disappeared; but in the ruined temple he found a monster spider, cleft in two; and by the gray blood that dripped upon the floor he knew her for a demon of the most diabolical kind.

In those days Kyoto was full of palaces; every noble's residence was a cluster of buildings surrounded by high walls and gates, within which were spaces for the ox-cars, and then walls again and more gates, and finally the master's dwelling, flanked by the kitchens and outhouses and the lodgings for the retainers, much as in a Yedo yashiki of six or eight hundred years later. But as the troubles of the Court increased, the houses of the Kugé nobles diminished, and under the disloyal Ashikaga Shoguns the imperial palace even was often greatly in need of repair. After so many disasters, the wonder is not that there should be little left of Kyoto's past grandeur, but that there is anything left at all.

Besides the two great palaces, there are a few minor ones still standing about Kyoto, most of them originally intended for retired emperors, such as the Awata palace, on the east side of the river, not far from Yaami's hotel; this was built for the Emperor Seiwa, who came to the throne at nine years and left it at thirty—not necessarily, however, to resign the real power; but he died at Awata the following year. Seiwa's grandfather was one of the Fujiwara family, and acted as Regent during the young Emperor's minority, and in this way gained the ascendency which the Fujiwara exercised for so long. Some quite old buildings stood here, but were burnt down some ten years ago, and a beautiful little palace has been built on the old site, the sliding screens and other portions of it being decorated with fine paintings of the Tosa and Kano schools. The place is kept as a sort of art gallery, and in the grounds beyond two buildings are still standing which were left over from the National Exhibition in 1895; they are used for industrial and

fine arts exhibitions.   Just beyond is another piece of
art education, a restoration on a small scale of the imperial palace, as it is supposed to have been in the time
of the Emperor Kwammu, founder of Kyoto.   It is
very Chinese, and very curious; the roofs are covered
with green glazed tiles, and end in turrets turning up
at the corners, and there are doors instead of sliding
screens, and gorgeous red lacquered pillars of *hinoki*
wood resting on stone floors.   Certainly the Court was
under Chinese influence, indeed, to have housed itself in
such a building.   It is another evidence of the strength
of Japanese individuality, that they should have so
entirely thrown off or modified these influences after
once adopting them.

Quite on the other side of Kyoto, and a good distance out as the city stands now, is another monastery
palace, called Omuro Gosho, founded for ex-emperors
and used chiefly for members of the imperial family,
who resided there as prince abbots.   The ex-Emperor
Uda lived here for thirty years as a Ho-o, or imperial
devotee, doubtless exercising a great deal of control
over the affairs of the empire, for after reigning five
years he had retired in favor of a son only thirteen
years old.   Uda was an able man, but his greatest
claim to admiration was his wise choice of a prime
minister, Sugiwara Michizane, one of the noblest men
of old Japan, as well as one of the greatest statesmen.

It may be no particular virtue on the part of a ruler
to have able officers; but in Uda's case the choice at

least implied some force of character, for he went out of the established order of things to make it, since during two or three generations the prime ministers had all been chosen from the Fujiwara family, who practically controlled the throne, and had come to look on the office as their hereditary right. The Sugiwara were their greatest rivals, and part of Michizane's efforts went toward lessening the Fujiwara power. Besides the office of prime minister, Michizane held that of tutor to the young Emperor Daigo, and served him also as prime minister after Uda's retirement.

One of Michizane's wise strokes of policy was to discontinue the gifts to the Emperor of China, which Japan had been sending for several generations. The reason given was that the Chinese dynasty being unsettled, there was no knowing who might be on the throne when the messengers arrived; but the real reason probably was that China was beginning to regard the gifts as tribute, and as an acknowledgment of her suzerainty—something Japan by no means intended.

But the Fujiwara plotted against him and accused him to Daigo, saying that Michizane was intriguing to get Daigo deposed and make his younger brother Emperor in his place, this brother being the son-in-law of Michizane. The ex-Emperor did all that he could to save Michizane; but Daigo believed the story and took his high office from him, appointing him "Governor of Dazaifu," a little place in northern

Kiushiu, to which it was the custom to banish political offenders. Had he been so minded, Michizane might easily have rebelled against his master—perhaps have done what he was accused of plotting; but no temptation could induce him to show the least disloyalty. Popular fancy has added many picturesque details of the hardships which he is supposed to have suffered in that half-barbarous country; in pictures he is represented riding about the country on a cow—the only means of conveyance possible. And legends describe him, ragged and starving, and dying at last of exposure and homesickness, his eyes turned ever toward the land of Yamato, his last words in honor of his ungrateful master. All nature loved and cared for him. One day, as he looked on the spring flowers, he cried out in longing for the plum tree of his own garden in Kyoto, and, even while he spoke, the tree flew over the sea and the mountains and planted itself at his feet.

When he was dead all the people mourned bitterly for him, and dire misfortunes began to befall the country, which were popularly attributed to the anger of the gods on account of the injustice wrought against him. Presently a number of the followers of the Fujiwara, who had compassed his ruin, died one by one, and the Emperor became convinced that he had been deceived, and in sorrow and repentance raised Michizane to posthumous honors; afterward he was deified under the name of Tenjin. The Kameido temple, in Tokyo, which is dedicated to him, is copied from the one at Dazaifu, in Kiushiu, where he lived during his exile, and where he died. It is he who is the patron saint of all who wish to write well, because he added to his other accomplishments the art of forming most beautiful letters, even more beautiful and wonderful than those of Kobo Daishi, the Nara saint.

Two other palaces there are in the neighborhood of Kyoto—or, rather, two gardens, for the buildings are of minor importance ; they are both used as villas by the Emperor, and cannot be seen without special permit. One, the Shugaku-in, has a charming situation, quite away in the country, on the lower slope of Mount Hiezan ; the other is nearer the city, on the side toward the hills beyond the Katsura river ; it is called Katsura no Rikyu (summer palace of Katsura), because it belonged to the Katsura branch of the imperial family. The charm here is an exceedingly pretty garden, in the most exact style of the *cha-no-yu*, or tea-ceremony gardens—a place of trees and little hills and rocks, of lakes and streams, and bridges and plain little summer-houses, all typifying that serenity of mind a true devotee should strive to cultivate.

But the cradle of cha-no-yu in Japan is over on the other side of the city, a little way out toward the hills now, though in the palmy days it must have been almost in the town. It is the Ginkakuji, or Silver Pavilion, so called in imitation of the Golden Pavilion (Kinkakuji), built about a hundred years earlier.

Both were the work of the Ashikaga Shoguns, and both were intended for the same purpose—pretended retirement from the world and actual indulgence in all its delights.

The Kinkakuji lies north of the city, and well out of it now, reached by a long ride through pretty lanes, where you hear the clatter of looms and silk reels all day long. The place was, and still is, a monastery of the Zen sect, the one which lays stress on mystic contemplation, and was naturally a favorite with the cultivated upper class, as the "Nembutsu" was with the illiterate. Here the Shogun Ashikaga Yoshimitsu retired after fifteen years of actual rule, and ten before that, when he was still a boy and the nominal Shogun, after his father had retired. With all his extravagance and self-indulgence, Yoshimitsu was a really able ruler, as well as a clever politician; he made the country peaceful, and encouraged trade, industry and all the arts.

The Golden Pavilion stands beside a little lake, dotted with tiny islands, among magnificent old pine trees, and surrounded by a dainty garden laid out in the usual picturesque style. It is a large, three-story building, with galleries running all around and roofs turning up a little at the corners; the topmost story is a good deal smaller than the two below, and is crowned by a bronze phœnix, with wings spread. It was built with the finest timbers that could be found, which the feudal lords were required to furnish for the purpose; and dull and shabby as it looks to-day, there are traces left to prove the truth of the story that it was gilded all over, from bottom to top—walls, ceilings, woodwork, even the projecting beams and the railings of the galleries, covered with gold-dust, thickly laid on a lacquer ground. Here Yoshimitsu mingled his plans for the administration of the empire and his meditations on the Zen doctrine with banquets and poetical contests, and exhibitions of music and dancing—those choruses and pantomime dances from which lyric drama afterwards sprang.

Yoshimasa, the builder of the Ginkakuji, seems to have had neither ability nor virtue of any kind. Even before he retired, he left the whole care of the administration to the Regent, and taxed the people past endurance to get money with which to gratify his extravagant tastes. The inevitable consequences followed in due course: revolts among the people, open theft and plundering, and among the nobility feuds and plots and counterplots. "Yoshimasa lived to see Kyoto an eleven years' battle-field. The Muramachi Shoguns had lived on the principle, *après moi le déluge;* and the deluge duly came, reducing Kyoto to a heap of ruins and burying the debauched dynasty under the débris."[1]

The pavilion does not seem to have been really covered with silver, but in it and the apartments of the palace-monastery he gathered rare pictures and por-

[1] "Japan Illustrated."

celain and other works of art, both native and
Chinese, some of which are said to be those still preserved by the monks.   In the garden is a heap of
sand, called the Silver Sand Platform, and beyond
that the Mound Facing the Moon, where Yoshimasa
and his chosen spirits would sit and enjoy esthetic
contemplation; and near by is a small separate building, which was the first tea-house of the prescribed
four-and-a-half mats ever built in Japan.

How shall I describe a tea ceremony ?   The mys-
terious virtue and charm thereof is one of the things
that puzzle a Western mind almost as much as some
of our habits—for instance, that of doing our own
dancing—surprises and bothers the Eastern.   Why
do they like to do it ?   What is there in it beyond
what meets the eye ?   For something there certainly
must be, and that something not utterly childish,
either, to attract the men who have practiced it, both
in the past and the present.   If the *cha-jin*—tea-
devotee—whom you see performing the rites, happens
to be an ex-Daimyo, like the courtly old prince who
unfolds the mysteries to the daughters of the nobility
at the Kazoku school, the thing seems to have a certain old-world appropriateness; he seems to be per-
petuating the leisurely fashion of his former days, and
fashion is always a law to itself.   But if your host is
a distinguished scientist, a man posted on the last
results of European thought and experiment, the
fashion theory breaks down ; men of that stamp do

not go in for mysteries, just because it is the "correct thing." There must be something deeper about this strange cha-no-yu, which everybody talks about and few attempt to describe.

The truth is that description fails to give any clear sense of the impression of it. Its essence is an affair of mental atmosphere, as of a religious exercise; and it must be remembered that in its origin the rite actually was religious, being practiced chiefly as an aid to meditation. The very origin of tea has a religious legend. There was once a holy priest who had vowed to spend a certain number of days and nights, fasting and without sleep, in devout meditation; but being overcome with fatigue, he gave way and slept before the time was over. Waking, in dismay over the breaking of his vow, he plucked off his eyelids and flung them from him; and where they fell there sprang up a little plant of aromatic leaves, whose virtue was such that they drove away all temptation to slumber. Henceforth the raising and brewing of tea was a part of every monastery service.

Both the plant and the use of it originated in China, and spread east and west from there. It is a species of camelia, and looks not unlike the plants of our green-houses, except that the leaves are smaller, thinner and less leathery, and the flowers are single, as in the wild camelia; they are white and rather wax-like, and about an inch across, looking not unlike a wild rose. The plants are trimmed low, in round, compact bushes,

Tea Picking

and plantations of them have a very pretty effect on the hillsides, where they are generally set out, the dark glossy green making a pretty contrast with the vivid tones of the rice in the fields just below.   In some places—for instance, around Kyoto and Nara, where the best tea is raised—the bushes are planted on the level plain; but when this is done there must be great care to secure under drainage.   Their favorite situation is on a gentle slope, where water will drain off without carrying away the soil, for they need a great deal of enrichment and deep working.   Much of the Hokkaido oil-cakes and fish guano go to manure the tea plantations, and a great deal of seaweed from all along the coast.

The finest quality of tea is raised around Uji, near Nara, and a great deal is also produced on the foot-hills near Mount Fuji, and, indeed, all along the Tokaido; a large part of this goes up to Yokohama to be refired and packed for export.   There are two pickings, the first in May, when the young leaves have just put out, and this is the smaller quantity, but finer quality; the second comes five or six weeks later, after the June rains, when the leaves are more fully grown and less tender.   The more quickly they are dried, the better the flavor.   Women and girls do the picking, and their bright sashes and red petticoats and plump arms, bared by the tied-back sleeves, make a picturesque sight.   They pick into large, flat baskets, bringing them back to be weighed at a central shed; four pounds of fresh leaves go to a pound of tea.

Naturally there is a great difference in the quality of the leaf, which depends both on the seed planted and the care used in cultivating, and, too, on the climate in which the bush is grown. Thus, on the west coast of Japan, around Niigata for instance, no amount of protecting with mats will save the leaf from being affected by the cold winter and the spring frosts; it becomes coarse and bitter. It is a very common thing through the country for people to raise a little tea for their own use; just a few bushes, planted perhaps like a hedge along their fields, as European peasants often raise their own grapes and make their own wine.

The difference between green and black tea is simply a matter of preparation; leaves taken from the same bush will produce either kind, according to the way they are dried. As the Japanese themselves use it, the tea is nearly sage-color before the water goes on it, and the decoction is of a pale golden tint—the better the tea, the lighter the color, except only the ceremonial tea, which is differently treated.

The first process is steaming, which is done in a sieve set over an iron pan half full of water, which is kept boiling by a steady charcoal fire. This takes only a few minutes, the object being to make the leaves soft and pliable. As soon as they give out a strong scent of tea, they are tossed out on flat pans and quickly cooled, when they are ready for the more important process of firing. For this the leaves are put into a frame covered with strong paper, set over a gentle fire on a kind of hearth; the bottom does not come nearer than half a yard to the coals, else it would scorch and also heat the tea too much. While they are in this frame a man works over them for several hours, rolling them with his hands, forming them into balls and pressing them against the sides of the frame, breaking the balls and rolling again, till all the leaves are curled and twisted up. Then he spreads them out on warmed frames, and lets them dry for several hours, when they are quite brittle and ready to sort and pack. A good many flower buds, bits of twig, old seed pods and so on get in among the leaves, and these are now picked out, and the leaves also sorted into sizes, fine and large, so that the tea shall look evenly graded and attractive. This is work for the girls and women, and their light fingers do it marvelously fast.

Treated in this way the tea will keep for years in tight glazed jars of pottery or porcelain, such as the Japanese themselves use, but it will not bear transportation. Therefore, the tea merchants in Yokohama and Kobe build their large tea go-downs, and when the crop comes in they have it refired until it is entirely dry, and can be packed down in the chests lined with lead which come to us in the West. Naturally this adds much to the cost of the tea, but there seems to be no other way to make it fit for export.

As might be expected, it was the Buddhist priests who first introduced tea in Japan. Tradition has it that about the beginning of the ninth century a priest named Yeisei went on a mission to China, and when he returned he brought with him some tea seeds which he planted on a mountain in the western part of the country, and raised therefrom a good crop of bushes; whereupon he presented some of the choicest leaves to a distinguished friend, " who relished them as a rare tonic against headache." Another priest then transplanted some of the bushes to Mount Togano, near Kyoto, where they flourished, and spread through the country. This abbot is considered the founder of tea culture, and at Uji they hold a service in his memory every spring.

The ceremonial observance—the cha-no-yu—was not brought to Japan till much later, about the middle of the thirteenth century, when a set of utensils were sent over from China; and at first it was a semi-religious pastime of the cloistered priests. Later this tea service fell into the hands of the first Ashikaga Shogun, Takauji, he who was so disloyal to the Emperor Go-Daigo; and from that time it became a favorite excuse for displays of extravagance, till reformed and laid under the most stringent rules of simplicity by the great masters of Hideyoshi's time.

There is a little story told about Rikyu, the most

famous of these cha-jin, and the one who gave most of the rules of the art. It seems some one tried to run Rikyu a little on the occult secrets of his cult, to which Rikyu replied, " Well, there is no particular secret in the ceremony, save in making tea agreeable to the taste, in piling charcoal on the brazier so as to make a good fire for boiling the water, in arranging flowers in a vase in a natural way, and in making things look cool in summer and warm in winter." The questioner answered rather contemptuously, " Who doesn't know how to do all that?" To which Rikyu answered, " Very well; if you know, let us see you do it."

That is all there is of it really; a series of very simple actions reduced to a fine art, each several act and movement made in the easiest way, and therefore the most graceful. All that is on the outside, that is; for the real object is no more the making and drinking of tea than the drill of a body of soldiers or the exercises of a gymnasium are an end in themselves. The true secret of cha-no-yu is that it is meant to be an exercise, a means of discipline and training, for the body, indeed, outwardly, but most of all for the mind, which must be absolutely withdrawn from all worldly cares and excitements, and tuned to a perfect serenity. " Not upon utensils or external environment, but upon the minds of the participants, depends the success of the ceremony," says Professor Takashima; and he quotes from Rikyu: " It is ridiculous to make ado about costly utensils when all that is required in cha-no-yu is a kettle."

Professor Takashima quotes a pretty story to illus-trate this point. "It happened over sixty years ago that one day the famous poet, Arikoto, in a walk through a street in Kyoto, came across a little hut by the roadside, with a little patch of ground about it and two or three trees, thoroughly sprinkled with water and looking very refreshing." (It must be remem-bered that such a Japanese garden would be strewn with pebbles among the shrubbery, so that the sprink-ling they are so fond of implies no mud or draggled grass.) "He saw inside this humble cottage a man practicing cha-no-yu all by himself. He was seated in a little space of not more than six feet by three, scrupulously clean, and on the wall was hung a screen with a rare autograph poem by a famous poet."

Arikoto was so surprised that he made some excuse to enter, and talked to the man about cha-no-yu; finally the unknown invited the poet to become his guest at cha-no-yu early the next morning—the proper time for such meetings—in the forest near by.

"This strange invitation was at once accepted. Next morning, upon coming to the appointed place, Arikoto found three stools beneath a shady tree. The old re-cluse, in a coarse but clean dress, received his distin-guished guest most cordially, and went through the tea ceremony in a masterly way, the utensils employed being of the humblest description, such as may be found any day in the kitchen. As the guest was about to drink, they heard overhead the sweet tones of a nightingale, much to the delight of the host. It is said that when a messenger was dispatched next day with a bounteous present for the hermit, he had disappeared no one knew where."

Stripped of all non-essentials, the requirements of a cha-no-yu meeting are these :

A small room, perfectly clean and retired from all disturbance; one picture or autograph verse, one flower.

A clean, fresh fire.

Kettle, teapot, tea-jar, cups; bamboo dipper and whisk. (Ceremonial tea is not only of very choice quality, but it must be ground to a fine powder; it mixes with the water, and the host whips it to a pale green froth.)

Finally, a select party of friends, all prepared to withdraw their minds from care and excitement, and centre them on moral and esthetic ideas.

Everything about the ceremony is simply a carrying out of these principles. Thus the tea-room should be apart from the rest of the house; it should be small, and it should be perfectly plain, that there may be nothing to distract the eye; spotlessly pure it must be, and the woodwork and mats should be of the best possible quality. I know of just one thing in the world that gave the same kind of impression as these cha-no-yu rooms, and that was the parlor of an old-fashioned Quaker house, in its summer dress of white matting, the green Venetian blinds at the windows, and the spotless linen covers on the plain mahogany furniture. There was just that same impression of purity and restraint—and costly simplicity, too; for the very best material suited our Philadelphia Quakers, as well as the cha-no-yu masters. Alas! such rooms are no more.

It was this desire for things that looked perfectly plain and cost enormously that led to the unearthing of old Korean pottery, and the efforts of Japanese potters to imitate their styles. The cha-no-yu cup is much larger than the ordinary one, and to the unlearned eye it looks like any old kitchen bowl, but the wise know by the shape and glaze and color just which province produced it, and how many years it has spent in the soft brocade bag in which such things are wrapped; perhaps even the ideograph of the famous potter who fashioned it to serve the Taiko Hideyoshi and his clique. The kettle and tea-jar, too, are often pieces of great antiquity and beauty. There is a certain stage in the proceedings at which it is proper for the guests to ask to look at and admire these things.

When a cha-no-yu party has been invited, the host himself sees to it that not only the room, but the garden is in order; in summer the ground should be spread with pine needles and sprinkled with water, and in winter, if there is snow (which will delight his heart), the stepping stones only must be carefully swept. All the necessary articles must be in place, from the screen in the tokonoma (alcove) to the cushions for the guests and the kettle and charcoal basket. When his guests arrive, he meets them and asks them to enter the tea-room, which they do one by one, stooping their heads to its purposely low entrance; the last guest shuts the door with a little click, to announce to the host that they are all in. He then appears from another room, and welcomes them; the chief guest should make some remark about the neatness of the garden. The host now builds the fire, and if there is a meal, it is served then, and the guests afterwards retire to another room while he arranges fresh flowers, hangs a suitable picture, places all the appliances in readiness on the floor, and summons them to return.

All the actions which now take place are, as Rikyu said, merely making tea; but each movement is according to set rule, and is performed with a deliberation beside which a mass at St. Peter's would be galloping haste. Possibly some one trained in the Swedish system of physical culture might learn to move as slowly and smoothly; certainly no ordinary American could. The tea is taken out of the jar, the water poured on it, the mixture whipped and passed round, each guest drinking in turn, wiping the cup and passing it to his neighbor. When the cup returns to the host, he washes it, and makes a fresh supply of what is called usucha, weak tea; at this moment the guests may examine and comment upon the utensils.

The tea ceremony is said to have been encouraged by Hideyoshi, Ieyasu and other rulers for the purpose of quieting the unruly spirits of the Samurai; and though no doubt such meetings were often used as opportunities for political scheming, in theory nothing of the sort was to be mentioned; all was to be ethical, esthetic, uplifting. One important rule was that no arms were to be brought into the enclosure; swords must be left in the sword-rack outside. There is a story that Hideyoshi's general, Kato Kiyomasa, the conqueror of Korea—he who built the keep of Nagoya castle—insisted on entering the room with his sword on, taking it off and laying it by his side, on the ground that it was unseemly not to be equipped and ready for his master's service in any emergency. Rikyu said nothing, but bided his time. One day, when the doughty knight came to a party and sat down as usual, the tea-master suddenly upset the kettle over the brazier, filling the room with a cloud of ashes, and Kiyomasa fled outside, quite forgetting his sword. Rikyu quietly hung it on the rack, swept up the room and invited the guests to return, whereupon Kiyomasa missed his sword and rushed to the cha-jin in great dismay, only to be politely referred to the sword-rack, where, said the host, he would find it ready for any sudden need. It is said that from that time Kiyomasa obeyed the laws of the tea-room.

Sorting Tea

CHAPTER X.

KYOTO—THE TEMPLES.

"It is almost ubiquitous, this perfume of incense. It makes one element of the faint, but complex and never-to-be-forgotten odor of the Far East. It haunts the dwelling-house no less than the temple, the home of the peasant not less than the yashiki of the prince. Shinto shrines, indeed, are free from it, incense being an abomination to the elder gods. But wherever Buddhism is, there is incense. In every house containing a Buddhist shrine, or Buddhist tablets, incense is burned at certain times; and even in rude country districts you will find incense smouldering before wayside images—little stone figures of Fudo, Jizo, or Kwannon."

—Hearn, "Ghostly Japan."

KYOTO, the stronghold of Buddhism, is the natural home of the incense-maker; and you may know his shop as you pass by the mingled odor wafted from it. For the most part it is an exceedingly delicate perfume, this Japanese kô, and it seems even more so, perhaps, because so often it is burned in the open air, or in house or temple closed only by openwork screens. One of the esthetic delights of the luxurious used to be an incense party—an occasion for proving the keenness of your perceptions by distinguishing among half a dozen or so of these subtle perfumes, as we might undertake to judge, for instance, between

Jockey Club and millefleurs and all the other varieties of sachet, except that the composition and variations of kô are far more complex and evanescent. Invitations to such an occasion were sent out some time ahead, in order that the guests might prepare themselves, by avoiding any kind of strongly-scented food for days beforehand. The party took the form of a game, and it was not only a question of discrimination, but of memory, each kind being smelled once, and then each person given a set of packages marked with a private sign, which he or she was to burn singly, and write on the package the name guessed. It was for these parties that many of the beautiful bronze or porcelain incense-burners were made that are the delight of the curio collector. Kyoto produced these, too, in almost every shape and material. The typical form seems to be of Chinese origin; it has three straight legs, small ear-like handles, and a Chinese lion-monster on the pierced lid. It is incense, too, that gives the indefinable, lingering odor that clings to old silks and embroideries in Japan, hangings or vestments, it may be, steeped as it were for years in the smoke of the altar.

City of temples though it is, Kyoto has none now standing that can compare with the Tokugawa's golden palace, or with the elaborate adornment of Nikko. But there are many very noble buildings, rich in masterpieces of art; three especially which go to show, among other things, how much power and mass and dignity are possible to a timber architecture, without so much as a stone foundation. These three are the Chion-in monastery, and the Higashi (Eastern) and Nishi (Western) Hongwanji.

Of the three the Chion-in has all the advantage to be had from situation; it stands on a pine-covered hillside, not far from the Yaami hotel, approached by an avenue of cherry trees leading up to the great two-story entrance gate, which is red-lacquered, carved and decorated from end to end. The main temple stands on a stone terrace, well up the slope above the gate, reached by two flights of those wide stone steps Japanese architects understand the value of so well. Close by in a little tower is a bell, nine feet across and nearly eleven feet high, one of the three great bells of Japan; a second, almost the same size, is at the Daibutsu temple here in Kyoto; and a third, rather smaller, at Nara. They ring it by smiting with a huge swinging beam—no bell in Japan ever has a tongue—which strikes the gilded chrysanthemum on its lip, and sends a tide of sound throbbing through the air and the sky and the ground under foot—a deep, shuddering boom that seems to roll from every quarter of the compass, and dies away after long moments as a wave dies on the sand. It does not ring often; but they say those who have once heard it never forget the sound of Chion-in's great bell.

The temple is not, like Nikko, a shrine in a grove,

but a true assembly hall, part of the large monastery, and planned for the presence of a congregation, as well as a considerable body of officiating priests. The great, curving, black-tiled roof rests on dull-red porches, and these again on a tremendous foundation of interlacing beams; within, the spacious hall shuts itself away in a warm twilight, through which a forest of polished golden-brown pillars rise up and are lost among the heavy rafters, fifty feet above; far back the altar lamps throw a soft glow on gold and bronze and rich embroidered hangings, the only ornaments in the hall, except those on the lesser shrines on either side. Then at the hour of service come the priests, vested in silk, crape, brocade, of every color and every conceivable shade, glowing, blending, wavering together as the chanting line files over the noiseless mats and spreads and settles before the altar, each in his place at his roll and lacquered reading stand. They use no instrumental music; only the antiphonal chant, and from time to time a slow, pausing stroke on drum or gong; the seated figures bow and rise, incense dims the lamps and curls into the dusky roof; little groups of worshipers sit or move to and fro behind the priests, while beyond, in the open porches, swallows dart and children romp and chatter unrestrained.

Chion-in's greatest art treasure is not the image of Amida or of Kwannon, nor the life-sized figure of Monju, Incarnation of Wisdom, in the garb of a priest,

Nishi Hongwanji

but a set of sliding screens in the detached apartments used as reception-rooms for the Emperor or the Prince High Priest, or other dignitaries. The apartments were built by Iemitsu, the third Tokugawa Shogun, and artists of the Kano school adorned it—Kano Tanyu, Naonobu, painter of the Wet Heron at the Nijo palace, Eitoku, Nobunasa; a noble quartette, and worthy to be called Kano. Of course, they were not necessarily lineal descendants of the first great fifteenth century Kano Motonobu. If there were no son of sufficient ability to carry on the family tradition, according to Japanese custom, a relative or pupil might be adopted into sonship and bear forward the art and the name. A formal tradition, perhaps, and a cramping conventionalism; but, after all, the conventions were more than half necessities of material, of brush-mark in unchangeable ink on a smooth surface; and within these limits, self-imposed or not, there is all the breadth and freshness of a Pompeiian fresco, all the marvelous sureness of touch that only a brush-trained hand can know. Rein was one of the first authors to draw attention to the effect of writing on Japanese painting; Chamberlain alludes to it; Gonse grows eloquent over the contrast between the pen, most rigid of instruments, and the brush, most supple and delicate; over the position, too, hand in air, fist closed and wrist bent, bringing the point of the brush vertically to the paper. " Thence comes that astounding pliancy of the stroke, those broadenings and attenuations, those brusque turns, which are the delight of a Japanese eye," says Gonse—qualities all here, in Naonobu's crows and pine, plum and bamboo, the summer landscapes and snow scenes, or the sparrow which, they say, flew through to the other side of the paper, and the pine trees that dropped resin from their painted trunks.

Not less valuable Kano paintings are in the State apartments of the Nishi Hongwanji, which is likewise a great monastery, and one of the richest and most influential. The main hall is a little smaller than Chion-in, but not less massive and noble, the plain white-plastered walls and *keyaki* pillars of the nave contrasting effectively with the gilded chancel and its ornate flanking chambers, the gold of the front, the painted doors and screens, and the rich openwork *ramma* above them. The light is dim, as always in these halls, and scarcely shows the delicate carvings of the altar and the shrine upon it, which holds a wooden image of the founder, Shinran. "Faith, not works," was the special doctrine of this thirteenth century saint, based on Amida's vow, "that he would not accept Buddhahood unless salvation should be made attainable for all who should sincerely desire to be born into his kingdom." Shinran's was an offshoot of the Jodo sect, to which Chion-in belongs, and it split again in Ieyasu's time into the Western (Nishi) and Eastern (Higashi) Hongwanji—that is to say, Monastery of the True Vow.

Amida's shrine is in the smaller hall, Amida-do; the gilt-wood statuette behind the gilded columns is black with age. The hall is arranged like the other, with a plain nave and a highly decorated chamber on either side of the chancel; the *ramma* over the screens are peonies, and above them are angels, carved in high relief—a somewhat unusual feature. On a sliding screen near the chancel, a beautiful peacock and pea-hen stand on a white blossoming peach tree, against a gold background, the work of a Kano; and on the way to the state apartments are more panels by Kano Eitoku, grandson of Motonobu. The apartments themselves are resplendent with gold, with *ramma* carved by Jingoro, with wild geese on dull gold back-grounds—fragments, many of these, of Hideyoshi's renowned palace at Fushimi, the same that furnished the Nijo palace gate.

The hall of the Higashi Hongwanji is the largest of these three temples—indeed, the largest in Japan; and it is absolutely new, finished only in 1889, to replace one burned in 1864. The *keyaki* wood pillars and rafters are fresh, instead of time-browned; the carvings less masterly than Jingoro's; otherwise, none but an expert would guess that it differed from six-teenth century originals. There are the same mighty beams supporting the tiled roof, the same dim interior, the wooden pillars four and five feet thick, the glow-ing altar, chanting priests, and to and fro of humble worshipers. The Higashi Hongwanji is of all things a popular temple. It was built by offerings from all over the country, contributions of material as well as money, and, among the rest, great ropes of hair, from glossy black to thin, pathetic strands of gray, the gift of women who had nothing else to give.

One thinks of these three temples together, because they are alike in all essentials—alike as three Roman basilicas might be. Kiyomidzu-dera, not less famous, is a complete contrast to their rather formal, stately elegance; its floor is bare, the rough-hewn pillars set in bronze sockets, the exterior much weather-beaten, yet unusually picturesque and striking. A long, steep street climbs to it between rows of china-shops—Teapot Hill, Miss Scidmore calls it—where they sell, besides teapots, immense numbers of grotesque little pottery *ningyo*, "Fushimi dolls," some comic, some rather frightful. At festival times the street is crowded with a lively throng, but at other times almost deserted, except for the ever-present children.

Reaching the court and terrace of Kiyomidzu, you are among trees and tea-booths, the main temple and a group of minor shrines dropped, as it were, casually here and there; at the back the hill falls suddenly into a little ravine, and on the farther side a second temple perches, like a swallow's nest, above a gulf of swaying foliage. The main temple was founded in Ashikaga times—say about the middle of the fourteenth century; the interior is a strange, dim confusion of shapes, figures of the Twenty-eight Companions of Kwannon ranged about her closed shrine, which holds an image so sacred that it is only opened once in thirty-three years. Beside these, there are two of the Heavenly Kings, guardians of the four quarters; Bishamon, god of good fortune in war, and Jizo, friend of little children, helper of all who are in trouble. Half the space in front is filled by a high scaffolding, which supports a dancing stage and side-platforms for the musicians, fronting a long hall filled with strange votive pictures; the whole effect has something almost uncanny about it, due perhaps to the broken spaces, so unusual in a Japanese temple, and the crowding of images and symbols, lamps, vases, incense burners and swinging banners, all jumbled together in the flickering light. It is pleasant to come out again to the trees and the sound of running water, coming from the little cascade in the gorge, flowing from five miraculous springs, where women come to drink. Beside these springs, tradition says, the founder saint waited years for help to fulfill Kwannon's command, received in a vision, to carve his image out of a mighty log, which lay by the stream. The wood should have been well seasoned, and surely the saint's character no less.

Older still, and even more crowded with strange images, is the San-jiu-san-gen-do, the temple of the Thirty-three Thousand Statues of Kwannon the Compassionate, the Eleven-faced and Thousand-handed. The hall is filled with them, row after row, stretching out innumerable hands, holding each an emblem—a lotus, an ox, a cord, a diamond, the Wheel of the Law, or an open palm, to succor all who need. Each head is crowned with a sort of tiara of little faces; a pair of hands fold on the breast, a pair are lifted, as if in blessing; others hold little images of the god, which must be numbered in to make up the full count of 33,333. In the midst sits a large figure of the Compassionate One, and around this stand the Twenty-eight Companions — mystic personifications of the stars. In the gilded confusion it would not be hard to persuade oneself that arms waved, glittering heads might turn or bow, eyes look down kindly or threateningly from the strange throng.

Close by, in a rickety, dusty building, is the Daibutsu, a gilt-wood image dating from 1801, and testifying much more to the piety than the taste of the age. There would seem to be some ill-luck about placing a great image at this spot; first, Hideyoshi built a temple, but died before it was complete; his widow ordered a bronze figure made, but in the final casting it set fire to the frame-work and destroyed temple and image together. Then that clever person, Tokugawa Ieyasu, put it into the widow's mind to try again on a greater scale, that she and her son might weaken themselves by a ruinous outlay; all of which was accomplished, including a disastrous riot over a delay in the consecration—this, too, provoked by the wily old Tokugawa, who pretended to be insulted by an ideograph in the inscription, and ordered the rites to be stopped in the midst. Fifty years later temple and image were again destroyed, this time by an earthquake. A wooden figure replaced the bronze, and was struck by lightning; a second one met with the same fate. The present figure has stood the century, and perhaps broken the spell; it is certainly unlovely enough to escape the envy of the gods. The thing is fifty feet of head and shoulders, without a body—colossal, lumpish, not spirited enough to be even grotesque. The best one can say is, that it is thoroughly in keeping with its tawdry surroundings, with the dust and the bare planking, and the worthless ex-voto pictures on the wall. The great, calm Buddha of Kamakura is not to be thought of with this wretched travesty.

All these are Buddhist temples, and so, too, is Kori-uji—interesting for a curious collection of wooden statues, many of them Korean, or made under Korean influences in the early centuries of Japanese art. Another collection of statues is at Toji-in—these not gods or saints, but portrait effigies of Ashikaga Shoguns, in gorgeous court robes. There are fine screens and kakemono here, too, by Kano Tanyu and his fellow artists; and again at Daito-kuji, Tanyu's famous Man with a Dancing Monkey, peacocks by Okiyo, and a roomful of people working at various trades, by Kano Tanshiu; and here, too, a collection of kakemono, said to be the finest in Japan, hidden away in fireproof storehouses and never visible. The Daito-kuji is a fine building, and its carved gate is one of the wonders of Kyoto. A portrait bust of Ota Nobunaga gives a certain personal interest to the rather faded magnificence of the place.

At yet another monastery, Ko-daiji, there are relics of Hideyoshi, " Monkey " Hideyoshi, who began life as Nobunaga's groom and ended it Taiko Sama, high lord and Regent of Japan, would-be conqueror of Korea. To him is due the " Ear Mound " on the other side of the city, where they buried the ghastly trophies of that Korean campaign. Hideyoshi's effigy sits in the chapel, in full robes and wearing a tall hat given by the Emperor of China as a token of rank ; his wife is near by, dressed as a Buddhist nun. In the chapel there is much lacquer and gold and gorgeous trappings, and masterpieces of painting by the Kano, much of it ornament taken from Hideyoshi's palace and from his war-ship and his wife's sedan chair.

The Korean affair seems to have been pure Napoleonic ambition. There was no particular reason for the attack, though it is true there were plenty of standing grievances, such as failure to pay tribute for a century or two, and the fact that the Koreans sided with the Mongols in any conflict of pirates, as well as in the great invasion of Kublai Khan. But the real cause was that Hideyoshi, having subdued all Japan and attained the highest post possible for him to hold, desired new worlds; and he even conceived the idea of conquering China itself. The first step was an invitation to the King of Korea to visit Japan and have an audience with the Emperor, which, of course, meant to make submission to him. This was followed by a demand for gifts both from China and Korea; the Koreans, as Chinese tributaries, were ordered to inform China and convey her gifts; directions which Korea not unnaturally declined to comply with.

Hideyoshi then proceeded with the invasion. He had been already building vessels, and when the army sailed "the ships were so many they seemed to cover the sea." There were said to be one hundred and thirty thousand men under the generals Kato Kiyomasa and Konishi, and they divided into two sections, overrunning different parts of the country. The suddenness of their attack at first swept everything before them; Korean generals were captured, the King fled, and the capital fell into Kiyomasa's hands. In the meantime the Koreans sent urgent messages to China asking for help, and an army was sent, and defeated by the Japanese; a second detachment made better resistance, and when pestilence began to reinforce them, Hideyoshi was willing to make peace.

His demands were not modest. A Chinese princess was to be given him for a wife; the Crown Prince of Korea and several nobles were to be sent as hostages; half of Korea should belong to Japan, and there were to be treaties of commerce with both China and Korea.

32425

The envoys refused the princess and the partition of Korea; and Hideyoshi prepared for another invasion. Meantime the envoy returned to China and suggested to his Emperor that Hideyoshi would probably be satisfied with a title and seal and an official hat; and he was sent back to Japan therewith. Hideyoshi received the envoy in great state at his palace at Fushimi, in the outskirts of Kyoto; but when the document was read conferring on him the title of "King of Japan," he flew into a great rage, flung the hat and the papers on the floor, and said he would be King of China and no tributary of hers.

Another invasion of Korea followed, and this time a large Chinese force besieged Kato Kiyomasa in a Korean stronghold, where his army suffered much from cold and lack of food. Two Japanese generals marched to their relief, and were again victorious, when news came that Hideyoshi had died, and left orders for the return of the army. It was withdrawn, and shortly after Korea sent gifts and envoys, who concluded peace.

Kurodani is a large and fine monastery on a hill a little way out of the city; it was the first foundation of the Jodo sect, the place where Honen, the first teacher of the doctrine, retired when he left the great Tendai monastery on Hiezan. The architecture and decoration is full of dignity and reserve, and the apartments are unusually rich in paintings and carvings, and there is a very splendid altar in the main temple.

Winding Silk From Cocoons

The great renown of the place, however, comes from the hero Kumagai, who here put off his armor and exchanged sword for rosary, and prayed and sorrowed all his life for Atsumori, the fair young knight whom he unwillingly slew.

It is a pathetic story. Kumagai was a famous warrior who fought on the Minamoto side in the great struggle between the two clans; in one of the fiercest battles he met in single combat—as the custom then was—a knight of the Taira, whom he grappled and bore to the ground. "The etiquette of war required that on such occasions no blood should be shed unless the weaker party proved to be a man of rank or ability equal to that of the stronger." Kumagai would have the name of his foe; the other would not answer, and the grim knight snatched off the helmet, revealing the smooth, fair face of a lad only just grown, just the age of Kumagai's own young son, who that day fought in battle for the first time. "Helping the youth to his feet, in paternal tones he bade the stripling go. 'Off, young prince, to thy mother's side! The sword of Kumagai shall never be tarnished by a drop of thy blood!' The young warrior refused to go, and begged Kumagai for the honor of both to despatch him on the spot." The knight, who had never trembled, hesitated now. Again he besought the boy to fly, but hearing his companions coming up, he exclaimed, "If thou art overtaken, perchance thou mayest fall by a more ignoble hand than mine. O, thou In-

finite, receive his soul!" The sword fell, but after
that day Kumagai never fought again. He retired to
Kurodani and hung his armor on a pine tree in the
court-yard, shaved his head, and took monastic vows,
and "devotes the rest of his days to holy pilgrimage,
never turning his back to the west, where lies the
paradise, whence salvation comes and whither the sun
hastes daily for his rest."

"Critics may point out flaws in this story," continues Dr. Nitobé. "It is casuistically vulnerable.
Let it be; all the same it shows that tenderness, pity
and love were traits which adorned the most sangui-
nary exploits of a Samurai."[1]

This is by no means the end of the temples, even
of the famous ones; indeed, Kyoto reminds one of
Cologne, in Heine's poem:

> "Koeln, die viele hundert
> Kapelen und Kirchen hat."

Gion, the most popular, has a curiously tumble-
down air; the Higashi Otani possesses a wonderful
gate carved by Hidari Jingoro, and an exquisite little
chapel all in gold; and there are at least a dozen
others, none without some point of interest, divided
among as many sects and sections of sects, Zen, Jodo,
Nichiren and the rest, differing among themselves
much as denominations differ in Protestant Christen-
dom, and appealing some to the philosophic, some to

[1] Nitobé: "Bushido, the Soul of Japan."

the popular mind, for Buddhism well knew how to be all things to all men.

There are Shinto temples, too, not so many as Buddhist, nor of course so magnificent, but much frequented of the common people. Not only Kyoto folk, but pilgrims from all over the country flock to visit the Inari Sama, on the road to Fushimi, which is said to be the most popular shrine of that most popular deity. Probably the old nature-gods have kept most of their original character, however overlaid with later symbols, and the universal fox worship would seem to have scarcely changed at all.

The legend goes that Inari Sama, Goddess of Rice, here manifested herself to Saint Kobo Daishi as a little old man carrying a sheaf, and she is frequently worshiped under that form; but to the common people Inari is actually the fox-god, the true primitive animal deity, crafty and uncertain of temper, delighting in mischief, yet on the whole well disposed toward the well-doing and siding with justice and fair play. Therefore, the many fox holes are undisturbed among the "sacred boulders" on the hill behind the temple; and at the door of every Inari shrine throughout the land sit a pair of stone foxes, rigid, sharp-nosed beasts, their tails curled stiffly over their backs; baldly formal figures, yet at the same time livingly, intensely alert. This pair are huge ones, standing by the great gate at the end of a long flight of steps, which leads up from the red entrance torii. Most of the walls and pillars here are red, and the strangest feature of all is a double row of small red torii, two hundred on each side, crowded close together like a double colonnade, which leads up to a pilgrimage way, winding in and out up the hill among the shrines and boulders and fox holes. The slope is famous for fine mushrooms, and here in the gay Middle Ages the Court used to come mushroom gathering, just as the gentles of Queen Elizabeth's day went a-Maying in the spring.

The Ainu have a legend of the origin of fox-worship, which may have a Japanese folk-story behind it, though it sounds like their usual style of accounting for facts by making up something to fit. They say that a man was once near a fox hole, when he saw a fox come up and call to the one within, "Come with me to-morrow and I will show you a splendid way for us to get many good things." "How is that?" asked the second. "This," said the first. "I will turn into a man, and do you turn into a horse, and I will ride you to the next village and sell you to some one for plenty of good things. Then afterwards I will come and let you loose, and we can run away." "All right," said the other fox. "Come for me to-morrow about noon." So the first fox ran away.

The next morning, a little before noon, the man came to the hole, and imitating the voice of the fox said, "Come out quickly; I have changed into a man, so do you become a horse as we agreed." At this the fox came out of his hole, and turned into a very fine chestnut-colored horse, with a fine, long tail; and the man rode him to the village; and because he was such a very fine horse, everybody wanted to buy, and the man got a great price for him, and bought many fine things, and went away.

But the man who had bought the horse did not put him out in the field, because he was such a fine horse; he shut him up in the house, and fastened the window, and tied him with a strong rope. Then he brought plenty of grass for him to eat; but the fox, not being a real horse, could not eat it at all; he wanted fish and good things such as foxes eat, and he was almost starved. But after several days, he took a chance when no one was looking, and got away. Then he ran to his friend, and reproached him for not coming to help him; and so they found out that it was the man who had played the trick, and they determined to go together and kill him.

But the man, when he saw them coming, bowed very humbly, and said, "It is true I have done very wrong, and you ought to kill me; but if you do that it will do you no good, whereas if you let me go I will promise to worship you from this time forth; and when I take fish, I will offer some to you; and I will give you millet cakes, and part of all that I have." Then the foxes accepted his offer and let him go, and that is why men worship foxes even until now.

Just one more fox legend, which belongs to Kyoto. In the reign of the Emperor Konoye, a fox took the form of a beautiful lady and became an inhabitant of the palace. Her real character was discovered by means of a magical mirror, and she fled to the mountains in her true shape. Two valiant knights were sent to hunt and destroy her; but they could not succeed till, after praying to the gods, one of them dreamed that the only way to catch the fox was to get a helmet, a suit of armor, and a bridle, made by a certain famous swordsmith of a neighboring province. This was done, and the fox was caught and killed. The Emperor was so delighted with the beauty of the smith's work that he gave him the title "best and unequaled." This armorer was one of the early members of the Miochin family, who were Court armorers for six hundred years.

It was out this way, near the village of Fushimi, that the Satsuma and Choshu and the Tokugawa partisans had the first battle of the War of the Restoration. Prince Tokugawa had been summoned by the Emperor to come to Kyoto, and was marching up from Osaka with a large following, when he heard that some of the Satsuma men had attacked his followers in Yedo, and that there had been a sharp fight, which ended in the Satsuma men being driven from their lord's yashiki, at Shinagawa, to a warship in the bay. Enraged at this insult, the Tokugawa ordered his followers and the Aidzu men to attack Choshu and Satsuma at Fushimi; there was a bloody battle, and Prince Tokugawa was defeated and fled to Osaka, where he fired the castle and escaped on a ship to Yedo.

In this battle General Saigo commanded the Imperialist forces, and his coolness saved the day for them. In the early part of the fight, a messenger came to him where he waited with part of the army, and asked for a reinforcement. "I will send one," said Saigo, "when every one of you is dead on the field." The messenger returned, and the Tokugawa were driven back.

Almost as popular as Inari is the temple of Tenjin Sama, nearer the city, whose simple massive stone torii looks strangely out of place before the confusion of objects that crowd the enclosure — stone lanterns, swinging lanterns, grinning monsters, bulls, stone or bronze, gaudy carved and painted gateways, tea-sheds spread with coarse red blankets, ex-votos, and woven pictures after the new manner of the Kyoto looms, which produce so much they had better not. The cheap accumulation is most unworthy of the hero deity, who in life was Sugiwara Michizane, the great prime minister, who was honored after death by his too late repentant master. His caligraphy being as famous as his wisdom and devotion, he is the patron saint of school-boys, who offer to him their worn-out writing brushes—perhaps as a proof of diligence.

Not far away from the Tenjin shrine is a modern temple of Pure Shinto, made charming in spring by a garden of lovely cherry trees, which seem highly appropriate to this somewhat archaistic piece of Early Yamato. There is a modern Shinto shrine to Nobunaga, too, near the Buddhist Daitokuji, which holds his portrait bust.

An interesting bit of history belonging to the modern era is at the temple called Shimo-Gamo. This is a long panel picture of the last Emperor, Komei, and his train, coming to worship at this, which is one of the oldest Shinto shrines. The remarkable thing about it is that it was the first imperial expedition outside the palace walls in many a year, since the Tokugawa Shoguns succeeded in making hard and fast the rule of absolute sacred seclusion. The heavens did not fall, nor were the people rendered disloyal by the act; and this effort of Komei Tenno's probably made the present Emperor's innovations less difficult. Shimo-Gamo is a pretty place—a group of little buildings, hardly more than sheds, in a grove of beautiful cryptomeria and maple and evergreen oak. An avenue of pines leads from it by the Kamogawa ("Wild-duck river") to Kami-Gamo, another rather ruinous shrine of the same goddess-maiden, who wedded an arrow winged with wild-duck feathers, and afterward flew away to heaven with her son in a clap of thunder.

Though Kyoto people have a Parisian reputation for frugalities, *petites économies*—learned, poor things, in the days when the Yedo had all the revenues, the Court and Kugé almost none—in spite of this frugal mind, they are often enough on pleasure bent, and have plenty of famous spots for flower-viewing and verse-making. Besides the many places outside, on the Katsura river and lake Biwa and the hills, there is the bed of the Kamogawa, in the heart of the city itself, which, after all, is the most popular and characteristic playground of Kyoto. The Kamogawa, like all Japanese rivers, has an unconscionably wide bed, which it seldom occupies more than a fraction of, an expanse of pebbles, little and big, which has been used as a bleaching ground since the city began. Here in summer time hundreds of booths are set up on piles, sometimes quite out over the water, and here of an evening the citizens come to sit on the mats and drink tea or mild potations of saké, and enjoy the cool air and the lights twinkling in the river. Sometimes all the family come, from Oji San (grandpapa) to the baby on somebody's back, and perhaps relatives or friends meet there, too. The ladies group together and discuss the children and the household, and the latest bit of gossip; the men talk business or politics, or maybe wax poetic and intone a Chinese couplet or Yamato *tanka* to O Tsuki Sama, my Lady Moon, rising over the mountains; while from other booths comes the tinkle of the samisen and bursts of laughter at the poor little geisha's latest sally. Hearn, in his "Kokoro," tells a sad little story of the Street of the Geisha, which lets one nearer than anything thus far written to the inner life of these hard-working butterflies. Not that many of them are like Kimiko; she is an ideal, though by no means an

impossible one. Sacrifice, in some form or other—
that is the watchword of a Japanese woman's life.

It was on the Go-jo (Fifth Street) bridge that
Yoshitsune first met the giant Benkei, sometime monk
of the convent on lake Biwa. Benkei had made a
vow to take a hundred trophies in single combat; he
needed but one, when he encountered the stripling
Minamoto and proposed to make short work of him.
But Yoshitsune, trained by the mountain Tengu,
leaped and danced around Benkei till with a shrewd
blow he brought the giant to his knees. Like
Little John, when vanquished by Robin Hood,
Benkei at once took service with Yoshitsune, and
from that moment never left him till they died
together.

There are three great festivals in Kyoto, besides
lesser monthly matsuri; they are the Inari in early
April, the Gion in June, and Bon, the Feast of the
Dead, in the middle of July. Nearly all April the
city is more or less *en fête*, for the Inari deities have
their celebration first, then make a visit to the divinities at Ise, and return in their gorgeous sacred cars
some time in May. As for Gion machi, it might be a
matsuri there all the year round, for the street is
always crowded, always lined with booths for the
same toys, sweets, cheap nicknacks and side shows
that follow from temple to temple on the Day of the
Horse, Day of the Bird, or the Monkey, or whoever's
turn it may be. Amusement is Gion machi's trade,

and was in the old days even more than now, when its pleasures for the most part are cheap and tawdry, its brocades faded and frayed. Yet even so, Gion festival is still popular—perhaps the most popular of all among the common people. Great pagoda-like shrines are carried through the streets by a complex framework of poles borne on the shoulders of some forty or fifty men at a time, and the crowd straggles in irregular procession before and after, carrying banners and emblems and lesser shrines. As the day goes on, everybody becomes more and more hilarious; the bearers are inspired, perhaps, by the saké flask, and they work themselves into a kind of frenzy, shouting, running, leaping in a rude dance, and even tossing the high pagoda into the air and catching it again on their shoulders. Such a feat must require a unity of action absolutely perfect; one can only guess how it is possible at all after watching a band of coolies lift some huge mass of stone or timber to the wail of a dolorous chant, making many hands do the work of hoist or crane. Just so, doubtless, those wonderful walls were raised at Nagoya or Hikone or Osaka, or at the Nijo palace here in Kyoto.

The Bon festival, or Feast of the Dead—sometimes called the Feast of Lanterns—is held on the 13th, 14th and 15th days of the seventh moon, reckoned by the old calendar, which brings it in the middle of August, counting by the new one. For these three days the spirits of the dead who have died within the year are believed to come back to their old homes, and lanterns are lighted and special offerings made at the graves, as well as before the name-tablets in the house—food and wine, and a peculiar dish of red beans and rice. Fresh flowers are arranged, too, and incense burned before the name-tablets and at the graves; and the house has been cleaned and purified and adorned as if for the new year, that the unseen guests may know they are made welcome. All households feast and exchange gifts, and the third day is the 'prentices' holiday—one of the two days in the whole year which every master must give. The children have a fine time, and think Bon almost as good as New Year's Day. On the third night the dead must go back across the sea to the dim land where they dwell, and all along the coast tiny boats, holding torches, are set floating on a falling tide, that the lonely souls may not go out into the utter dark.

This last night is called the Dai Monji in Kyoto, and they celebrate it by lighting huge beacon fires on the mountains, piling brushwood for days beforehand in long clearings cut to make various forms—the Chinese character for *dai* (great), and a torii, a ship, a "dai reversed," and other signs, traced against the wooded hills in half-mile lines of flame. The city, too, is a blaze of lights, lanterns hung at every house, strung across every bridge, dancing and bobbing among the eager crowds that fill the river bed; while out on the hills, below the glowing bonfires, constellations of torches mark the enclosures where the dead are laid.   The Dai Monji is at once gay and sad, the most characteristic and perhaps the most appealing of Kyoto's many festivals.

CHAPTER XI.

LAKE BIWA AND ARASHIYAMA.

"The land of Yamato
 Has mountains in numbers,
 But peerless among them
 Is high Kagayama;
 I stand on its summit
 My kingdom to view.
 The smoke from the land-plain
 Thick rises in air;
 The gulls from the sea-plain
 By fits soar aloft.
 O land of Yamato!
 Fair Akitsushima!
 Dear art thou to me."
 —From the "Manyoshiu."   Aston's translation.

"Isles of blest Japan!
 Should your Yamato Spirit
 Strangers seek to scan,
 Say— Scenting morn's sun-lit air,
 Blowsthe cherry, wild and fair!"
     —Motoori. Nitobé's translation.

FEW cities have more romantic surroundings than Kyoto. Mount Hiezan, three miles to the northwest, rises two thousand seven hundred feet, and prolongs itself southward into a long ridge and a series of foothills reaching almost to the Kamogawa; on the north

Bamboo Grove

the mountains close about the narrow valley of the river, heaping again around the west side into a high barrier, through which the Katsuragawa breaks in foaming rapids, and, emerging suddenly around the turn of a sharp hill, widens out and curves gently across the little plain to join the Kamogawa, near Fushimi. North and east, directly across Mount Hiezan and the ridge, lies lake Biwa, most beloved and most berhymed of all the waters of Japan. This it was that, tradition says, came there in a night, being the hollow whence Fuji as suddenly arose, so that, in the morning, where the fields had been, there was rippling water, and far over from the tops of the mountains lifted the white cone, where no mountain was before. Therefore the lake and the mountain are believed to be mysteriously one, and when you trail your hand in the water it is as if you touched the cool snows of sacred Fuji.

In poetry the name of the lake is Omi, but it is commonly called Biwa, Lake of the Lute, because the shape is thought to resemble a Chinese musical instrument of that name. It is a very considerable body of water, thirty-six miles long and about twelve miles wide throughout its upper part, though the southern end, which forms the neck of the lute, is much narrower. In many parts the shores are high and indented, and mountains, near or distant, make a picturesque setting all the way around.

The outlet of the lake is a small river flowing out

of the southern end, too small and swift to be used for navigation, except in its lower part. In old times a small canal continued from the point in the river to which boats could go as far as Fushimi; but this could only be used by small boats, and all cargo from the sea had to be transferred at Osaka, thirty miles away. This has been replaced by a large canal, fit for vessels of considerable size, which is cut through the hills between Kyoto and the lake, going part of the way by three tunnels. To manage the descent, an incline was built at a point just beyond the Awata suburb of Kyoto, by which the boats are hauled up on cradles by a wire rope; this is worked by an electric power-house at the foot of the incline, the power being furnished by the water from the canal above, which, after doing this service, collects into a canal again and finishes the distance to the Kamo-gawa canal, and by this reaches the river near Fushimi. In this way boats can come up from the sea at Osaka and carry freight or passengers through to the end of the lake, some sixty miles in all. The plan of hauling the boats up the incline is much the same as the old Morris canal in New Jersey. The enterprise was the suggestion of a young engineer, who made it the subject of a graduation thesis at the Imperial University. His proposal was accepted, and he was given charge of carrying out the scheme, which has proved exceedingly successful. Part of the water is turned aside at the top of the incline and used to irrigate the plain to the north of the city, and also to run another electric plant which supplies most of the city light, operates a trolley street-car line, and furnishes power for some fifty factories, smaller and larger.

It is a beautiful ride from Kyoto to lake Biwa, over the old Tokaido. Crossing the river, from the main part of the town by Sanjo bridge, and keeping through the continuous suburb of Awata—famous for beautiful china—it curves around Maruyama, keeps for some distance near the canal, though not often in sight of it, and climbs gradually to the top of the ridge, where stood the first barrier out of the city. Thus far friends conveyed their departing friends or kin ; here they came to meet them after absence ; and the hill was called The Hill of Meeting. A few minutes later the lake appears below, and the jinrikisha men race down the half-mile slope of smooth road, among a motley crowd of foot passengers and men with carts, toiling up or running lightly down, their bodies thrown back and shafts held high. Then there is a sharp rattle through the streets of Otsu, and you are at the shore of the lake and the landing for the steamers that ply up and down, calling at the various little ports.

To the east, the country around lake Biwa is level and rich, the hills standing back towards Sekigahara, but always in sight across the rice-fields. Mount Hiezan is close by on the south, and from the north the highlands of Echizen send down long spurs into the water. The upper portion of the lake is rather wide to be picturesque; the most beautiful part is the lower end—the neck of the lute—and it is just this that has been sung and celebrated by Japanese writers and painters for more than a thousand years. Characteristically fanciful are the "Eight Beauties of Omi"—eight, it may be noticed, being a favorite number for such categories. They are the Autumn Moon, from Ishiyama; the Evening Snow, on Hirayama; the Sunset Glow, at Seta; the Evening Bell, at Miidera; Boats sailing back from Yabase; Bright, Windy Day, at Awazu; Rain by Night, at Karasaki, and Wild Geese Settling, at Katata. Not having reached the age of steam, and become altogether practical and materialistic, a Japanese is not ashamed to gaze with delight upon a beautiful scene and recite an appropriate poem, such perhaps as this:

> " Unto each beholder's heart confiding
>   Whatsoever thought she stirreth there,
> Through the autumn night serenely gliding,
>   O'er yon peak the moon shines calm and fair."

Certainly Miidera deserves to be ranked among the most beautiful places. It stands high on a hill above Otsu, looking over the flat roofs of the town, which is rapidly growing into an important place, and therefore an unbeautiful one. The lake lies below, picturesquely winding, the steep green shores sloping away to the blue hills, and, for foreground, there is an old temple of Kwannon, one of the original " Thirty-six Holy Places." It was from Miidera that the merry giant Benkei stole the great bell—this was in his conventual days—and carried it off on his shoulder to his masters, the rival priests of Mount Hiezan. But the bell would not be content, and its murmurs frightened the priests, who thought they could hear it crying, " I want to go home ! I want to go home !" So they threw it over the hill, and it rolled and rolled till it reached its own temple again. There it is now, with the scratches on its sides that it got from rolling down hill ; and they show, too, the great iron kettle in which the naughty monks brewed the bean soup with which they bribed Benkei. So it must all be true.

Past and present meet together at Miidera, as everywhere in Japan ; the smoke of the steamer trails across the classic water, and smart young soldiers from the barracks, in the uniform copied from Europe, walk about the venerable temple, side by side with worshipers in the coolie's blue and white cotton, or the peasant's rain-coat ; or respectable town matrons, in sober, dark gowns and small, flat sashes—for, as at most shrines, it is chiefly the old who have time to come and worship.

Of the great monastery on Hiezan, little remains but a small group of buildings on the slope of the mountain, and these were not the original temples, but those erected after the others were destroyed.

No other establishment in Japan ever equaled this monastery on Hiezan; the shrines of Ise were far more sacred, and other Buddhist seats more popular with the multitude, but the learning and political influence of the monks of Enrya-kuji left all the rest behind. Indeed, their position was not a little like that of the Vatican, except that the Emperor's prestige as representative of the gods greatly outweighed theirs, at least in theory; in actual practice they were not much more submissive to him than the feudal nobility were.

Dengyo Daishi is supposed to have founded the monastery, at almost the same time that the Emperor Kwammu removed the Court to Kyoto and laid out the present city. The mountain stood on the northeast, the "demon quarter," and much of the influence of the monastery rose from the fact that it protected the palace from the danger of evil influences, just as the later temple at Uyeno, in Tokyo, protected the Shogun's palace. Many of the ideas about demons seem to have come from China, along with Buddhism itself; at New Year time, both in China and Japan, the evil spirits are supposed to be especially active, flying about like birds and trying to enter people's houses. One of the Japanese customs for the first part of the year is to go out on the seventh day and gather seven herbs, which are to be chopped up for soup; in some parts of the country the master of the house must cut them himself. Some say that this chopping of the herbs is a reminiscence of the Chinese habit of thumping on the walls to frighten away the ill-omen birds; in Japan, at the present time, when going through the dangerous rapids in certain rivers, the boatmen keep up a continuous thumping on the gunwale of the boat; and Hearn speaks of a woman who did the same thing when rowing him among some perilous rocks on the coast, on the way to a sacred cave. In some provinces they sing a song while cutting the herbs—

> "Birds of ill-hap pass us by,
> Never here from China fly;
> Flit and hop, flitting, hopping,
> Chip-a-chop, chopping, chopping."

The Enrya-kuji on Hiezan belonged to the Tendai sect, which was one of the earliest brought to Japan from China. Dengyo Daishi and his companion, Kobo Daishi, went to China to study, and brought back many books and images and much learning; and others less distinguished followed the same course during a number of centuries. It was Dengyo and Kobo Daishi who gave the name Shinto (Way of the Gods) to the old Kami worship, developing and pressing the explanation of the Kami as manifestations of the one supreme deity, and thereby doing away with antagonism between the two faiths.

A memorial to the throne in 901 shows that even by that time, only a hundred years after Hiezan was founded, the priests had already waxed fat on imperial favor, and held large estates around their monasteries;

whereby they were becoming haughty and puffed up.
Further, the disputes between the "eight sects" began
to be conducted with other than spiritual weapons; at
Hiezan, at Nara, at Miidera and elsewhere, the monks
had already begun to keep military bands and to train
their priests in war. The custom spread, and before
long nearly every temple had its soldier monks; but
nowhere were they so many or so haughty and turbu-
lent as on Hiezan. If the priests objected to the ap-
pointment of an abbot, or were not satisfied with his
rule, they donned their armor and marched down to
Kyoto to enter their protest at the very palace. Sometimes they took the sacred car of the gods from the
temple and bore it with them through the streets, com-
mitting all sorts of violence, and threatening the palace
itself; in such a case the officers were afraid to deal
forcibly with them, because of their sacerdotal character, and their lawlessness was a constant menace to the
capital.

From time to time an Emperor availed himself of
their temporal aid as well as their prayers; thus Go-
Daigo gained their interest through his son, the priest
Morinaga, and used them in his struggle against the
Hojo regents. The Ashikaga unsettlements gave them
new opportunity for power, and no one dared meddle
with them till Nobunaga made his attack. He pro-
fessed that their evil lives were a scandal and disgrace
to the nation, but his real grievance was that they had
sided against him in his recent difficulties with the

Prince of Echizen. He sent them a message, summoning them to repent and amend their ways, but they refused, and he proceeded to punish "all who indulged in meat or violated the law of celibacy." At that time Hiezan was like a fortified camp ; walls rose behind walls, and within them were the temples and vast monastery buildings—it is said that there were five hundred in all—and beautifully laid out gardens, besides images and pictures and a magnificent collection of books, which drew students from every part of the country.   Within the enclosure there were several thousand persons, priests, monks, and fighting men and attendants, besides many women.   Nobunaga's generals were aghast at the thought of attacking so sacred a place ; but he replied, " I desire to restore peace to the empire and authority to the Emperor, and for this I put myself in peril every day ; but so long as these monks defy me order is impossible.   I have given them their choice ; they would not accept safety."

Mazelière compares the taking of Hiezan to the sack of Rome by the Constable de Bourbon.   Nothing was spared ; the temples were burned, the library and priceless works of art destroyed, and all the inhabitants put to death.   It was a crushing blow for the Tendai sect, which never recovered its complete supremacy, although later, when Ieyasu again encouraged Buddhism, the monks were allowed to return to Hiezan and rebuild on a much smaller scale, not on the top, but on the slope of the mountain.

The view from the top sweeps over all the surrounding country ; on the one side is the city in its girdle of green fields, on the other the blue lake and the mountains. The Kyoto missionaries have made themselves a summer home here; at first they camped in tents, but gradually houses have been built, and quite a large community gathers here to enjoy the cool air. It is very much cooler and fresher than the city, for the top of Hiezan is higher than Nikko.

The loveliest part of the lake is along the lower end, between Otsu and the point where the Seta flows out at its southeastern corner. The road skirts the lake, under an avenue of pines, and to the right lie the rich fields, always full of picturesque life. (From an artistic point of view it is certainly a crime for farmers to wear anything but faded blue cotton and occasional dashes of red.) At Seta a long bridge crosses the river, or rather two bridges, resting partly on an island in the middle of the stream ; this double bridge has been painted and sung for generations, and so has the "temple of the stony mountain," Ishi-yama-dera, which stands a quarter of a mile or so farther on. It is one of the Thirty-three Holy Places, and a very popular shrine; most of all famous because it was here that the authoress Murasaki wrote her great work, the "Romance of Genji"—*Genji Mono-gatari*. It is a marvelous tale of the adventures of a knight who belonged to the Genji or Minamoto family, and whose love affairs fill page after page, all written in a style so poetical and perfect that it set a model for Japanese literature in the eight centuries that have followed. When Murasaki composed the *Genji*, the fit of genius came upon her so suddenly and with such violence that, hardly knowing what she did, she wrote her tale upon the back of a sutra, or Buddhist gospel. Afterwards, to atone, she wrote out a copy with her own hand, and it is shown at the monastery, along with the ink-stone which she used.

Near the middle of the east shore is the little town of Hikone, interesting chiefly for its white-walled castle, part of which remains—thanks to the Emperor, who stopped here on his way to Tokyo while it was being pulled down, and ordered the work to stop. It was the seat of Lord Ii Kamon, kinsman of Tokugawa and one of the chief Daimyo, the Regent appointed by the Bakufu to help them through the perplexities which Commodore Perry's coming stirred up, and who was assassinated in Yedo by the Mito Ronin. There is an excellent inn directly in the palace grounds, with a beautiful garden about it, and a most lovely view of the lake ; the place was formerly a villa used by the Daimyo when he retired in favor of his son.

On the west shore of the lake, about four miles from Otsu, and still on the neck of the fancied lute, there is a wonderful old pine tree—so old that nobody knows when it was young. It is nearly a hundred feet high and over two hundred and fifty feet across, and the immense spreading branches trail far out over the water, making music, the Japanese poets say, when the rain trickles softly through its leaves. Oddly enough, this great pine tree of Kawasaki is not numbered among the "eight beauties of Omi."

Quite away on the other side of the city is Arashi-yama, where the *yamazakura* grows—the lovely wild-cherry blossom, emblem of Japanese knighthood. From the mountain to Kyoto is a five-mile stretch of level road across the fields, that in April are like an impressionist poster done in washes of pale green and yellow—the vivid, unnameable yellow of the rape. Three months later, where the green barley was, young rice is pushing through the mud ; and by the time the maples turn in the gorge all the plain is covered with the harvest, a sweep of gold and amber from the city to the hills. Here, in spring, the slopes beyond the Katsuragawa flush into delicate bloom, and then it is that the poet bids one come at dawn, and, looking on the sakura flower, " learn what is *Yamato damashii*," the spirit of Japan. At least one may learn why the poets sang of the wild cherry, for it is indescribably lovely, far lovelier than the sumptuous double blossoms of Mukojima ; the slender, willowy branches seem lost in a pearly pink mist, ethereal as the faint fragrance, seeming to melt into the pale light of a Japanese sky. The wild sakura is the emblem of the *Bushi*, the Samurai, because the flower falls in its perfection, before the first breath has marred its purity ; even so, the code taught, a knight should fall in his prime, without the shadow of a stain upon his honor.

Japanese literature is full of allusions to the sakura. "Three things should be endured with patience—the clouds that hide thy moon, the wind that scatters thy cherry flowers, and the man who seeks to pick a quarrel with thee."

Or this, in which the whole law of Japanese knighthood is summed up—the law that bade every man seek for honor at whatever cost:

"If she puts not forth her blossom, who will tear the branches of the sakura? The tree is her own foe."

The custom of cherry-viewing is attributed to an eighth century Emperor, who, on an expedition in the mountains, sent back to the Empress a branch of blossoms, with a verse to the effect that if the single twig delighted the eye, the beauty of the whole tree would drive away sleep.

These trees on Arashiyama were planted by a fifteenth century Emperor, though no one could guess that they had not grown there of their own accord, so perfectly wild and natural is the effect of the forest.

Arashiyama is scarcely less charming in autumn, when bars of mist lie across the hillside in the morning and afternoon, and all Kyoto comes out to see the maples. This is the time of times to shoot the rapids of the Katsuragawa. They begin far up the river at a little village called Yamamoto, a three hours' ride from Kyoto; the road is hilly, and not too good

traveling in places. There you take a boat, putting
in kuruma and men, in order to be sure of getting
back from Arashiyama to the city; they are queer
long, narrow boats, and very flexible, as they have
need to be for such sharp turns and swift water; but
the boatmen are most skillful, and except after heavy
rains it is only exciting, not really dangerous. The
distance is thirteen miles, and the whole way down
the gorge is wild and picturesque. The river swirls
down it in a series of rapids, now broken with
islands, now rushing straight between precipitous
banks, now winding and dodging among a throng of
rocks. At Arashiyama there is an excellent tea-
house, and for those who have not come down, boats
can be hired for a little row up the river, to the end
of the last rapid. It is an admirable place to see the
good people of Kyoto enjoying themselves in their
best apparel, for a Japanese damsel would as soon go
cherry-viewing in her ordinary clothes as one of the
" Four Hundred" would appear at the opera in a traveling dress. The flash of sunlight on light crapes and
gorgeous sashes adds not a little to the picturesqueness
of Arashiyama.

CHAPTER XII.

THE THEATRE.

IT is written in the Nihongi that when Prince Fire Fade subdued his elder brother, Prince Fire Shine, by the help of the magic tide jewels, the elder brother humbled himself and promised to be subject to him forever. And in token of his humility, Prince Fire Shine thereupon danced a pantomimic dance, imitating the action of one who is drowning, as he himself was about to drown when Prince Fire Fade drove back the flowing tide. He stripped off his clothing, and bespattered his face with reddish mud, and " lifted his feet and stamped and walked. Then he turned over the soles of his feet, as if the tide began to wet them; and when it reached his knees he lifted up his legs. Then he ran around when it reached his thighs, and he placed his hands over his breast when it reached his sides; and when it reached his neck he waved his hands."

This sort of play was no doubt much like those descriptive dances performed by the American Indians and other savages, and which are little removed from the telling of a story in sign language, as the Indians of our plains do so graphically. As in all countries, they branched out two ways—into the sacred Kagura dances of the Shinto shrines, and the comic *Saru-gaku* or monkey dances, the ancestors of true comedy. These were probably danced at first to no other accompaniment than the *tsudzumi*, the small hand-drum shaped almost like a short hour-glass, which they smite with the hand and arm, much as Italian girls use a tamborine.

There is no lack of popular dancing to the present time. Whenever there is a local festival or matsuri, they set up little platforms in open spaces by the side of the street, and here, above the heads of the passers-by, girls or boys sway and turn and posture to the sound of a drum and some harsh nasal singing. It is not high art, or high anything else; but it is an evident survival of historic dances, and for anything that I know may have a religious significance both for spectators and performers.

As soon as intercourse began with China, Chinese music was introduced—with modifications, if we may judge by the present state of music in the two countries. It undoubtedly influenced Japanese music, except in the service of the Shinto temples, where, as in their architecture, the national type was preserved with the greatest purity. From early times dramatic dances, with music, were performed at Court, the Chinese and Korean varieties side by side with the Yamato, or strictly Japanese. The chief instruments used were the koto or harp, the drum, and the flute or flageolet.

In the twelfth century there seem to have been two kinds, known as the men's and the women's dances, the one using swords and spears, and the other discarding them for beautiful women's dresses; and from these, in the next two generations, was developed the historical and lyric Nô, which stands between the mere pantomime dance and lyric drama proper.

What the Nô added was an explanatory song, occasionally sung by the dancer or dancers themselves, but more often by a special chorus which took no part in the action, but expounded motives and expressed moral sentiments in the true spirit of the didactic chorus everywhere. Like the miracle plays of Europe, the first object of these Nô was instruction; their authors were Court nobles and priests, Buddhist or Shinto; but the greater number were written by Buddhist priests. Their subjects were drawn from mythology, history and romance, such as the events in the lives of the gods, or tales of the heroes and pious men and women; some also were taken from Chinese history, and from the Buddhist writings of India. The Japanese themselves claim that many of the most beautiful passages in their literature are imbedded in the stilted, archaic phraseology of the Nô verses, and Aston seems to bear them out.

A good Nô performance is an exceedingly impressive thing—very much more so than the Kagura dances of the temples, because those are marred for Western eyes by the tawdry-looking headgear of the virgins who officiate, and the thick plaster of whiting which overspreads their impassive faces, and gives them a strained, lifeless appearance; their garments, too, are bulky and almost grotesque, though the color is often very beautiful. The Nô performers, on the other hand, are clad in the armor of knights, which at once gives height and dignity to the figures. Masked and helmeted, and carrying great swords or spears, they stand on a raised platform and go through a series of gestures and poses, advancing and retreating, lifting and thrusting the huge weapons, all in time to the wailing music of the flutes and the high-pitched, straining voices of the chorus. The poses would be violent, if they were not so slowly, rhythmically made that you feel the reserve force— the restraint of power, and the perfect balance, as of a Phidian metope, which makes such postures possible.

Down to the present era Nô dances were considered an appropriate accomplishment for young Samurai; several might practice them together, part taking the movements, part the chorus. It was hardly thought of as an amusement, but as a useful exercise for mind and body. The language is so antique and obscure that at present only scholars who are up in classical Japanese undertake to understand a Nô chorus.

In the history of the feuds between clans there is

a story which illustrates this practice of the Nô among young gentlemen. It is a story of the struggle between loyalty and the individual sense of right, such as must have tormented many a noble soul in those days. The lord of a province, smarting under a defeat, told some of his young knights that he wished a special service of them ; it was to get into the castle of his enemy and assassinate him. One of the young men, named Koben, begged his master to reconsider such an unworthy proposal; another reproached Koben and called him a coward. The youth withdrew, and prepared to commit harakiri. But his mother, overhearing his preparations, came to his room and questioned him ; and when Koben related what had happened, she told him that it was his duty to obey his lord, no matter what he required. Koben therefore said farewell to her and departed on the hateful errand.

To get himself admitted to the castle he had already a plan ; he presented himself as a wandering knight, and when asked what he could do, modestly claimed some skill in Nô dancing. The attendants brought him before their lord, and Koben's beauty and grace so won the prince that he invited the young man to take service with him as a page. This Koben did, and remained with his new master many months, being always about his person.

At last one night Koben, who watched by the prince's side, roused him with a cry, " Rise up, my lord! Your enemy is before you!" The prince sprang to his feet and confronted the page, who briefly declared why he had come, but that he could not strike in the dark, and now bade him fight for his life. For a few minutes they clashed swords; then the guards rushed in and took Koben prisoner. The prince then told him he had known his intent long before, and that his old master was now dead, slain in a recent battle—ending by a frank forgiveness and an invitation once more to take service with the new lord, whom he had learned to love. But Koben sadly refused; the death of his master could not end his duty so far as to set him free to serve that master's sworn enemy. The prince then bade him go unmolested; and Koben went out, and found his old master's head where it was exposed on the castle moat, and killed himself there. For once there is a woman in the story—the beautiful daughter of the prince's chief retainer, who was promised to Koben in marriage. She cut her hair in token of widowhood, and went to the house of Koben's mother, remaining with her as a daughter as long as she lived.

As the Shinto temples had platforms for the Kagura dance, so many of the Buddhist temples have such a stage for the Nô performances, the chorus sitting on side platforms well out of the way. Naturally many of these temple Nô enforce a moral, or exalt the power of the Buddhist priesthood, and the value of exorcisms and the like. Such is the famous " Stone of Death," founded on a legend concerning the desolate moor of Nasu, some distance to the north of Nikko. On this moor was a stone which no one dared touch, for whatever did so, whether man or beast or plant, was straightway killed. One evening a priest came across the moor, and stopping to rest beside the stone, heard a voice, warning him to depart. The voice—represented by the chorus—goes on to explain the reason. Long ago a wicked spirit took the form of a woman and dwelt in the palace, being greatly beloved of the Emperor, whom she bewitched with her charms; but one evening there was a sudden blaze of light about her body, and at the same moment the Emperor was seized with a fatal disease. The exorcisers were called, and compelled her to take her true shape, so that she fled away as a fox, and the dogs chased her even to the Nasu moor. When the chorus has finished the recital, the evil spirit herself appears, and confesses that it is she who haunts the Death Stone and does all the mischief. The priest performs a Buddhist exorcism, and the troubled spirit is laid forever. The moral needs no pointing.

Between the parts of the severe Nô it was usual to offer mental relief in the form of a Saru-gaku, or monkey-play—usually the broadest kind of a farce, conducted in pantomime, with a little choric assistance. Just so at present, in the Tokyo theatre, a bit of broad farce is introduced to relieve the tension, say between the tragic deaths of the Forty-seven Faithfuls and Asagao's pathetic adventures in search of her lover.

Another early form of dance was the Odori, the modern representative of which is probably the maple-dance or the butterfly-dance, and the other graceful posturings of the Tokyo and Kyoto geisha. These Odori were danced by girls then, as at the present time.

Now, about the year 1602, a beautiful girl, called Okuni, appeared in Yedo, with her husband, and they opened a kind of a theatre, where they gave a new sort of exhibition. It was a combination of Nô, Saru-gaku and Odori, accompanied by flutes and drums and stringed instruments. This girl had been a *miko*, or virgin, at a Shinto shrine in Idzumo; but she fell in love with a Ronin and ran away with him to Yedo. While they were on the way they met another Ronin, who joined them and traveled with them for some time; and he, likewise, fell in love with the beautiful dancer, perceiving which, the first fought with him and killed him. Okuni's beauty and grace, and the novelty of the dramatic dances, made the new style all the fashion. She remained in Yedo and acted as long as her husband lived; but when he died, she cut her hair and became a nun, spending her life in prayers, not only for him, but for the Ronin whom he killed for love of her.

According to another version of Okuni's story, she began her career by going about from temple to temple, dancing the Kagura and collecting funds to rebuild the Idzumo shrine. At this time a literary knight used to write dramatic recitations for her to weave with her dances, and he afterwards married her, for which he was discharged by his feudal lord. They then went to Yedo and opened the theatre, as already related.

Meanwhile another element of the drama was developing. This was the historical recitation, with or without the accompaniment of a biwa, or Chinese lute, a custom that seems to have come down from the period before writing, when professional reciters held office at the Court. Later, when the development of writing made this office useless, it was dropped; but tales continued to be written and recited, under the name of *katari*, or *gatari*, like the "Genji Monogatari" of Murasaki. To the monotonous chant in which they were uttered, the rhapsodists sometimes added tones borrowed from the Buddhist invocations, or from dance music, with intent to make the recitation livelier or more impressive.

Words and action were now almost ready to unite into the drama; but, oddly enough, the medium which brought them together was a kind of Punch and Judy show, or Italian marionette theatre—a recitation given along with the performances of cleverly-made puppets. This, which was called *gidayu*, originated in Osaka, and went from there to Kyoto and Yedo; and it became exceedingly popular, largely because almost at the same moment a real dramatist, Chikamatsu by name, appeared and began to write plays for the purpose. The manager was likewise an excellent reciter, who rendered the speeches with great force and made his puppets take the parts very entertainingly. Even now there are story-teller's halls in Tokyo and elsewhere, in which the gidayu are recited to music, usually without the puppets.

A word concerning these story-teller's halls. There are fifty of them licensed in Tokyo, and no amusement can rival them in the popular mind; at least, if the reciter knows his business. A huge, square paper lantern hangs at the door, bearing the names of the story-tellers who are reciting there at the moment; there is generally one star narrator and three or four pupils or associates, who fill up part of the evening, since, unlike the regular theatre, these halls are open only at night—a sure token that it is the working and the student classes that they appeal to. At the door are the usual numbered shelves for the shoes, because you must check these in Japan, as you would an umbrella in America. The hall is matted with tatami, and the story-teller sits on a little platform, with a stand in front of him and a hibachi at his side; the audience place themselves on the floor, sometimes hiring thin cushions from the attendant, at a fraction of a cent a night. The admission itself is only a few sen.

There is no action whatever; hardly even a gesture of the hands or body. The reciter emphasizes a point at times by tapping a fan on the stand in front of him, as the Buddhist priests also do in their sermons. Contortions of the face there may be, especially in the funny pieces; but that is all. Nor is it even a recitation of something already written down; it is story-telling, pure and simple, spiced with puns and jokes, like an American minstrel-show.

They say the first professional story-teller was a Kyoto man, who came up to Yedo to present a petition, and waited three years in vain. After that he was ashamed to go back home; so, by way of a livelihood, he sat by one of the castle gates, reading and explaining a certain book of chronicles of the deeds of the Taira family. The readings became very popular, and others took up the idea; but, instead of reading history, they soon began to enlarge on a given account out of their own imaginations. Besides hero tales, these story-tellers relate fragments of the drama, love stories, exciting recent events and the latest piece of scandal, domestic or political—all embroidered with sensational details, and punctuated with dramatic pauses and sharp raps of the fan on the little stand.

The star performer always comes last—the invariable rule in Japan—and he sometimes recites a single piece, or more often a continuous story, lasting through the whole two weeks which make the usual run; and he takes good care to stop each time at the most thrilling point. The better grade of these

reciters are often employed to enliven dinner parties
and other entertainments, and they are said to get
very good fees.

The theatre proper is a much more serious affair.
There is no mere evening performance here; in the
good old days the play used to begin at daybreak and
last till midnight; and though now the show is
restricted by law to eight hours, from eleven in the
morning to six in the evening seems to the American
mind quite an undertaking. In old times the performance used to be announced by beating a big
drum, as they do still for the wrestling matches; it
was an imitation of the signal which summoned
retainers to the castle in times of danger. The old
theatres are disappearing, too, replaced by large new
ones, slightly different in plan, and protected by tiled
roofs and thick fire-walls.

The chief theatre in Kyoto is in Gion machi, by
the popular Gion temple. In Tokyo it is the Kobi-
kiza, where Danjuro plays; this is quite near Shin-
bashi station, and almost on the edge of Tsukiji, the
foreign Concession. Great colored posters beside the
door announce the play that is running, or rather
plays, for besides the chief piece, they generally give
parts of three or four others in lighter vein.

The floor of the house is entirely divided up by partitions a foot or so high, making little boxes of a "half
mat" each—that is to say, three feet square. These
boxes are occupied by four or even five persons, which

speaks for the modesty of ladies' draperies in Japan, as well as the slightness of their figures. In the Kobi-kiza theatre, there are also boxes raised in tiers at the sides, and a gallery at the back, where you may have the privilege of paying three prices, and sitting in a chair with your boots on.

Two passage-ways, one wide and one narrow, cross the floor of the house at a level with the top of the partitions between the boxes; and by these the actors usually arrive and depart, although there are also entrances at the sides of the stage. Over the left entrance is a little balcony, hidden by a screen, where the chorus sits, and joins with voice and instruments when required — not infrequently while the actor is still speaking.

The arrangement of the stage itself is peculiar. In the middle of the space, occupying most but not all of it, is a round platform which revolves on a pivot, like a turn-table, and is worked by men under the stage; partitions divide it into thirds, and each third represents a scene, so that by turning the platform about a new scene is presented without further delay or trouble. Scenery in the ordinary sense flanks the platform, and the curtain descends in front of all. On this platform, and the spaces before and beside it, the actors strut and pose in the stagiest of attitudes, attired in wonderful garments, modeled after the age they represent; armor, gorgeous court robes, or the Samurai's dress of ceremony, with the broad, stiffened folds over the shoulders. They discourse in a strained, high-pitched voice, most unpleasant to the ears, but made necessary by the constant interventions of the chorus. No woman may act upon the Japanese stage; men actors are usually trained to take women's parts, and it is one of Danjuro's glories that he acts equally well either as a man or a woman. The gestures, too, are set and extravagant, and it is impossible to forget for many moments the dance from which they grew.

Another and at first very amusing feature of the stage is the "blackamoor," who attends to clearing things up after a fight, disposes of "property" that is no longer needed, and makes matters smooth generally. They are dressed—there are usually two or more on at a time—in black clothes and hoods, and by a stage fiction they are supposed to be invisible; they crouch in some obscure corner, ready to run noiselessly out and gather up a discarded cloak, or take a fallen knight by the heels and remove him to some limbo behind the scenes.

Ichikawa Danjuro, the "Henry Irving of Japan," as his admirers call him, is the ninth actor who has borne the name. The first was a youth who played in Yedo in the latter part of the seventeenth century, or about sixty years after Okuni and her inventions; Ichikawa Danjuro was not his real, but his stage name, which he left to his son. The name Ichikawa he bestowed on all his pupils; for the actor's was a guild like all the rest of the employments, and the new ones had to be apprenticed as to any other trade. In the nine generations there have been four adoptions made, because the holder of the name had no son; the seventh member is counted the ablest of them all, and the present representative is a son of his. He is no longer young, but must be in the fullest of vigor, for he acts for hours in the tremendous poses of the Japanese stage —exercise, surely, that one of our gymnasts would hesitate to undertake. Mr. Osman Edwards gives a pleasant description of a call on the great man, who, he says, has none of the affectations of many Western actors when off duty; he declares that Danjuro "becomes less of an actor and more of an archbishop in proportion as he realizes every year the growing prestige and veneration attached by the bulk of his compatriots to the chief of the Japanese stage."

Favorite plays are the adventures of Yoshitsune and Benkei, such as the scene at the Hakone pass, when Benkei so cleverly got his master by—Danjuro told Edwards that this was the rôle he liked best—or the time that they and their followers were all in danger of being shipwrecked through the malice of evil spirits, and no one could do anything, till Benkei came to the rescue. Stationing himself on the prow of the ship, he lifts a rosary, and chants an exorcism that quiets wind and waves; ship and crew are saved, to the wondering joy of all.

Other plays deal with the misfortunes of the Emperor Go-Daigo, victim of the disloyal Hojo and Ashikaga.

They recount how he was exiled to a little island; how the good islanders contrived his escape on a little boat; and how, to their dismay, the government officials came down to search for the missing prisoner. There was just one hiding-place possible, under a great pile of dried fish; and into this unpleasant refuge the Emperor crept, and lay in safety till the officers satisfied themselves that all was right, and went away. And again, when he was once more a prisoner, a brave young knight, named Kojima, followed the escort who were taking his master again into exile. For many days he sought in vain for some means to communicate with the Emperor, that he might at least bid him take heart, knowing that his followers were still faithful. At last one night Kojima managed to get into the courtyard of the inn where the train had stopped, and planing with his sword the bark of a cherry — the Samurai's flower—wrote thereon a poem:

> "O Heaven! Destroy not Kosen,
> For he hath yet a Hanrei."

In the morning the soldiers found the writing, but were too ignorant to read it, and asked the Emperor to tell them what the characters meant; nor, when they heard the poem, did they see anything of importance in it. But the Emperor understood the allusion to a Chinese Emperor, who, after twenty years of fighting, at last overcame his enemies through the valor of the faithful knight Hanrei.

That all these things move the spectators deeply is very evident; but to those who are not very familiar with the story it is not always easy to follow. The fact is the audience are likely to be more entertaining to a stranger than the play itself. They are mostly of the middle class, and they come with all the family and settle down for the day, grandma and baby and all. Men and women smoke, the teapot man goes his rounds, and by and by the tea-house next door— through which everybody purchases theatre tickets— sends in its deputies bringing trays of lunch boxes, and every one falls to between acts. The women sit demurely, or chatter among themselves; the men yawn and stretch mightily, and the children run up and down along the narrow partitions, and even on the "flowery way" reserved for the actors. If the play becomes too pathetic, the ladies of the party disappear into their long sleeves, or even retire from the audience to weep unrestrained.

But, after all, hampered though it is by wearisome conventionalities, by exaggerations and restrictions, it is not to be denied that Japanese drama is both interesting and at times deeply impressive, even to one who looks on without comprehending a word, and with only a vague notion, at the best, of what the actors are trying to express. Also, in judging of its merits, we have to remember that till thirty years ago—the time when all, or nearly all, the plays were written, and when many of the actors now on the boards learned their art—it was against the law for a Samurai to enter a theatre. That is to say, he was not actually forbidden to enter, but it was one of the places where he might not go wearing a sword; and not to wear a sword was to be, for the time at least, no better than another man. So, if a knight entered such places at all, he had to do so in disguise; and as a consequence, the theatres had to draw their contingent from the ordinary people—the merchants and the artisans, who were not the lettered class at all. It is only since the beginning of Meiji, with its reforms and wholesale destruction of the rigid class lines, that all men have begun to frequent the theatre whenever they wish to do so; and even ladies attend at times. There can be no question but that this prohibition of the gentry had much to do in forming the style of the plays, and in keeping the drama from reaching a place in the national literature at all to be compared with Sophocles or Shakespeare.

CHAPTER XIII.

FETES AND FLOWERS.

"Hark! on the snow-laden branches
 Nightingales sing;
  Do they take the white drift on the plum tree
  For petals of spring?"
      —From the "Kokinshu."

"No man so callous but he heaves a sigh
 When o'er his head the withered cherry flowers
  Come flutt'ring down. Who knows? The spring's soft showers
May be but tears shed by the sorrowing sky."
      —Chamberlain.

New Japan recognizes eleven national holidays; the first, third and fifth days of the new year; January 30, the anniversary of the death of the late Emperor; February 11, the festival of the Constitution, which was signed in 1885, on the anniversary of the accession of Jimmu Tenno; the spring equinox, March 20; April 23, the death of Jimmu Tenno; after which they skip all the way to September 23, kept as the autumn equinox. The first harvest thanksgiving (the Divine Tasting) is on October 17; the Emperor's birthday on November 3, and the second harvest thanksgiving on November 23.

247

These are the official holidays, when banks and
schools and public offices are closed; but the people
keep many more, mostly religious ones; or, at least,
religious in their origin.   About the year 900 the
Emperor Uda (whom Michizane served) established
five festivals, all in the odd months, and each on the
day corresponding to the number of the month—the
first of the first month, third of the third, fifth of the
fifth, and so on, all the way around to the ninth of the
ninth month, the festival of chrysanthemums.   It
must be remembered that these months were reckoned
by the Chinese lunar calendar, and that New Year's
day fell some time in February; so that the seventh
month was our August, or perhaps part of September,
and the ninth of the ninth month would come late in
October, or early in November.   But each month in
the year has some special festival, celebrated more or
less universally throughout the country. The greatest
of all is the New Year, and after that in popular esti-
mation stands Bon, or, more properly, Urabon, the
Feast of the Dead, in midsummer.   At these two festivals gifts are universally exchanged, and in each
one day is set apart for the apprentices' holiday, the
only seasons in old times when they were absolutely
free to go where they would.   By an arrangement, which must have been convenient for the
masters, the 'prentices' day falls each time at the
end of the feast; but, as members of the master's
family, they had already shared all the home fes-

tivities, as well as the labor of the preparations for the feast.

For each of the festivals, and for all the months, there are certain designated flowers; in fact, one might spend half one's time the year through "flower viewing" at one or another famous garden, and find the people as interesting as the blossoms, for everybody goes, gentry as well as *bourgeoisie*, and all the women dress in their best—not in gaudy geisha costumes, but exquisitely delicate crepes; light colors even in winter, because the flowers suggest spring, and one must be appropriate. To tell the truth, it usually feels anything but spring-like when the plum blossoms begin; they come first and stay longest, flowering by the end of January in sheltered places. Little dwarf trees in close bud are forced carefully for New Year congratulation gifts, since the Western world has driven back the calendar to fit its own wintry feast. The Japanese love their *umé* blossoms just because they are first, as we love trailing arbutus, and as our English kin love the May; their charm is to brave the frost, and if a snow comes—the rare, brief snow of the south—half Tokyo rushes to Kameido to see the whiteness on the flowers, and to see them shake it off, only the fresher and more fragrant for the chilly load. Then, too, it is in order to write poems of just thirty-one syllables, on thick, narrow poem-papers, and hang them on the branches. Such as this :

"Were she belated, the umé could not vie with the sakura; because she is first, the prize of color and fragrance is hers."

Or this:

> "How shall I find my umé tree?
>   The moon and the snow are white as she.
>   By the fragrance blown on the evening air,
>   Shalt thou find her there."

But, unhappily for sentiment, the pasteboard takes a drenching much less safely than the flowers do, and after a storm the effect of a tree strung over with these draggled scraps is anything but decorative.

The trees at Kameido are the famous "Creeping Dragons," old, old trunks, twisted and almost lying on the ground—the older, more bent and gnarled the tree, the greater the delight in its delicate bloom, as a gentle woman, they say, shows fairest in adversity. The trees out at Omori are less wonderful in this way, but make up by a profusion of bloom and the beauty of the situation, so that they are scarcely less popular.

Conder quotes a pretty story of the daughter of a certain poet, whose favorite plum tree was sent for·by the Lord High Chamberlain, to replace one that had died in the imperial garden. Of course she could not refuse, but she managed to tie a little poem out of sight among the branches:

"Claimed for our Sovereign's use,
　　Blossoms I've loved so long—
Can I in duty fail?
But for the Nightingale,
　　Seeking her home of song,
How can I find excuse?"

The Emperor found the poem and read it, and the tree went back to the bird and the maiden.

The umé lingers with the lingering southern spring; the nightingale or warbler, *uguisu*, sings month after month in the branches, his note growing more plaintive, they say, as April draws near:

"Cry, Uguisu; spring comes not again for a year."

February is the month of Inari Sami, the fox god, and his temple reaps a rich harvest from the devout, who hope he will help them to get rich in the coming year. As the god of rice fields, he receives special attention from the country people; and at his festival, on all the roads leading to the Inari temples, posts are set up and hung with oblong paper lanterns, bearing rude pictures and homely texts, such as the most unlearned can understand. All the small boys have access to a great drum in the temple court, and on the days of the festival they thump it from morning till night. Two months belong especially to children; March to the girls (how ever did they happen to come first?) and May for the boys—the third day of the third month, and the fifth day of the fifth month, respectively.

The girls' day is called Hina matsuri, the Feast of Dolls. Each household where there are daughters has a set of little figures, often handed down for generations, representing the Emperor and Empress in splendid robes, five Court ladies in white overdresses and scarlet skirts, and five musicians to play to them; all seated on a set of portable shelves made for the purpose. Other dolls of less dignity are seated on the lower shelves, and before each is placed an array of real food on tiny dishes, along with miniature household utensils and toilet cases, writing materials, in fact, tiny models of everything that any one could use in real life, often made of the finest porcelain and lacquer. The holiday dish of rice and red beans is prepared for them, and a kind of mild, sweet wine, called shirosaké; and when the doll nobility have been served, be sure the little mistresses get their share. All the girls have holiday and are dressed in their best, and the family dolls go visiting friends and relations, and are entertained with their mistresses on dainty sweets; and when it is all over their majesties and all their train go back to their silk bags and boxes till the day comes round again, other ordinary dolls staying out to be played with through the year.

The boys' day is very properly a more active and out-of-doors affair; it is really a military feast, a reminiscence of the victory over the Mongol armada,

Boys' Festival

and flags and toy swords are much in order. The *tokonoma* in the best room is set with pictures or figures of three famous heroes, the Taiko Hideyoshi, his general Kato Kiyomasa, the conqueror of Korea, and a semi-fabulous brave named Watonai. But the chief characteristic of the occasion is the custom of flying huge paper carp, like flags, on high bamboo poles—a fish for every boy in the household. The meaning is that the carp, like the salmon, swims up streams and even waterfalls, and so is the emblem of courage and perseverance in overcoming difficulties— the model which all small boys should follow. The paper fish are sometimes twenty feet long, two or three sometimes fluttering on a single pole far above the roofs; they are hollow, and have a ring at the mouth and a hole at the tail, so that the wind sweeps through and makes them dip and struggle and undulate in the most life-like manner, precisely like a fish struggling against the current. As Mrs. Iwamoto puts it, " the fish are nothing more than the outward expression of the fond parents' wish for their boys, that they may be as aspiring and as courageous as the *koi*."

The war of kites, too, delights the youngsters on these windy spring days, and many a grown-up enjoys the sport, with his little brother or son for an excuse. The strings are armed with sharp pieces of glass, tied near the kite, and the object is to cut the other boy's string and release his kite, while saving your own from a like fate. In some provinces the kites are

immensely large, made of as many as two thousand
small sheets of paper, pasted together; in others they
are small, and around Nagoya the smaller they are,
the greater the honor of getting them to fly high.

On the birthday of Buddha, which falls in April, a
curious ceremony is performed at some of the temples.
The priests place an image of Buddha in a tub in the
temple court, and make a temporary roof over it,
adorned with green branches; then they fill the tub
with a decoction of hydrangea, called *ama-cha*, or
sweet tea, which is said to taste rather like weak
black tea. A long-handled ladle is provided, and
with this the devotees ladle up the ama-cha and pour
it over the image; and after making a small contribution to the temple, carry home some of the tea as a
remedy for sickness.

On the first " Day of the Horse," in April, the villages of Omi province, on the east shore of lake Biwa,
keep a peculiar festival. All the women walk in procession, each carrying on her head as many earthen-
ware pots as she has had husbands. Now it is no
disgrace for a woman to marry again after she has
been divorced or widowed, yet still it is higher honor
to have had but one spouse; and a considerable number rather implies that the dame is of a shrewish
tongue, or otherwise an undesirable companion, and
so has been frequently tried and found wanting. But
it will not do to cheat; they firmly believe the gods
will punish any one who does not produce her full

tale. They say that one woman who had had several husbands thought she would get out of it neatly by setting a number of little pots inside a large one, which stood for her present goodman; but she was rightly rewarded, for as she walked with the rest she tripped, and the pots came tumbling down, the big one broke, and the little ones rolled out for all the world to see.

With April a tide of pink sweeps over the world—the faint cloud-pink of cherry bloom; at classic Yoshino in Yamato, at Arashiyama, at Uyeno in Tokyo, at Mukojima and out at Oji; all along the castle moat, between the greening willows; flaunting over hedges and behind high yashiki walls—everywhere they are in flower, delicate, elusively sweet, crowding every twig with lavish blossoming, only to fling a storm of petals on the first rough wind.

"Cherry-blossom Sunday" at Uyeno park is one of the prettiest sights in all Japan. The wide avenue sloping up from the town is an arch of pink mist, leading to acres of pale rose-color against a background of pine and cryptomeria and live oak; the people throng, and the tea-houses have spread their best red blankets on the matted platforms, which serve for seat and table. Here will come a couple of *betto*, or running grooms, crying, "Hai! Hai!" before some grandee's carriage; there is a line of jinrikishas, a dignified old gentleman at the head and his family behind; yonder is a party spreading a blanket under the trees and sitting down to picnic delightfully on rice sandwiches; and again a group of young men, carrying each a cherry branch over his shoulder, and at his belt a saké gourd, which he means to have filled and refilled at the various wine-shops, till he is gloriously and entirely drunk—at which point they will all fall sound asleep, and the nearest policemen will pack them into kurumas, two and two, and send them safely off home; for nobody is allowed to be intoxicated in a public place in Japan.

Saké seems to be inseparably connected with cherry blossoms; the first allusion to them in literature is in the fifth century, when an Emperor went on a picnic and the petals fell into his wine-cup. And another Emperor wrote a poem, saying, "Without wine, who can properly enjoy the sight of the cherry blossoms?"

To tell the truth, a good deal of extra license is permitted in cherry time and in certain specified places. The wildest doings of Tokyo are at Mukojima, where for three miles a double avenue of cherry trees stretches along the far bank of the Sumida beside the road, which runs like a dike between the river and the rice-fields. In a meadow at the end of the avenue flags fly and booths are set up, drums beat — tum! — tum-tum! — you would recognize a Japanese drum-beat anywhere by the queer time— and a squeaky brass band plays "Marching Through Georgia" and other festive tunes; for they made a patriotic war song to old Georgia in '95, and it is entirely naturalized under the Sun Flag.

Tea booths stand all along the bank under the trees, and between them surges a dense crowd, absolutely given over to carnival. Of course, no Japanese gentlewoman is ever seen there, and for a foreigner it is decidedly better not to understand what is said; but the crowd is good-humored and entirely harmless, and does not go beyond carnival jests; the police would not permit that. More or less drunk it certainly is, and wildly hilarious; mummers rush about in all sorts of fantastic costumes, men dressed as women, or in harlequin garments, red and white, the color of spring and happiness. Presently, with great shoutings, comes the shrine of some god, dragged on a car or carried on men's shoulders, and ringed about with a dancing, singing crowd. The river, too, is gay with roofed pleasure boats, where the geisha's samisen twangs all day long. Probably the ancient Bacchanalia and Saturnalia were not very unlike cherry time at Mukojima.

The proper flowers for May are the great peonies, *botan,* and the azalea and Wistaria. The botan is too delicate to do well in the open ground without a great deal of sheltering from wind and sun and rain, and it is to be seen in perfection only in special gardens; but the azalea is wild all through the mountains, and will grow almost anywhere; so in May the flower fairs at night are full of them, and hillside gardens are a blaze of splendid color. The special place for them in Tokyo is the suburb of Okubo, where the trains make extra stops in the azalea season. And another beautifully planted garden of them covers a steep slope in Kojimachi, not far from the palace, in the midst of which an irregular slab of granite marks the spot where Count Okubo was assassinated. It was no mere brutal crime, but an affair of intense political conviction; the Count stood for progress and the increase of foreign influences, and the band of fanatics who killed him verily believed they were saving their country from destruction in the good old way. Standing on the hillside among the bushes, where the children play tag and string necklaces of the fallen flowers, it is hard to realize that all this *Sturm und Drang* of transition was only twenty years ago.

For a Japanese, a cardinal point in the enjoyment of flowers is that they shall be appropriate to the season, and arranged in a natural way; iris, for instance, is used for decoration in several months, and each time the habit of the plant at that part of the year must be duly considered; in spring the leaves are straight and stiff, and the flower-stem short; in summer the leaves are full and spreading, and the flowers have "much spirit"; in autumn the flower-stems are long and the leaves bent and curled—all of which must be properly emphasized in making the bouquet for the tokonoma. The vases, too, must have attention; for riverside plants a flat dish is appropriate, with or without pebbles strewn over it; a morning-glory should have a hanging vase of bamboo, and pine goes well in a handsome bronze decorated with figures of storks. Indeed, the variety of material and form is endless, and utterly bewildering to the outsider, who can only guess at the symbolic meaning of tall, short, wide and narrow, basketwork and porcelain. Yet it does mean something, and, after all, it is like so many puzzles—plain as day when you once know how to do it.

They do not make bouquets of flowers in our sense; as Conder says, "Whereas the Western amateur devotes his attention mainly to the blossoms, the Japanese lover of flowers bestows his admiration on the whole character of the plant or tree"—and what they are trying to do is to make it seem to be actually growing. So they include under *hana* a great deal besides flowers; such as pine, bamboo, willow branches, grasses and autumn leaves.

The art of flower arranging is said to have come from India, and to have been originally intended to preserve the flowers used in ritual from the effects of the tropical heat; and that it came to Japan with Buddhism. As might be supposed, it was one of the arts seized upon by the cha-no-yu devotees, who developed it into a fine art, and added unto it fancies and esoteric mysteries after their own hearts. It stands to reason, also, that an artful naturalness and a crafty simplicity were what they strove after, and attained, too, for themselves and their followers, by means of innate taste and a multitude of exact rules.

The theory of it is perfectly simple; it is only to arrange the flowers so as to form a triangle, the " principal branch " long, the others on each side of it shorter by one-half and two-thirds, respectively. All the branches must curve a little, and each in just the right way; the central one bends out and returns to make nearly a vertical line from top to bottom; the second and third follow its lead. If there are more branches, they come in as " supports " between the others; there may be five in all or seven—never an even number; and the number of blossoms should also be uneven. Buds are preferred to full-blown flowers, both because they keep better and because, like the Greeks, the Japanese love the promise of youth.

Here are some of the things that may be expressed by flowers:

Aspiration. Decayed wood and climbing creeper.

Affection. Pine branch with Wistaria twining around it; the vase should be bronze.

Serenity. A bronze vase in the shape of a boat, and small white chrysanthemums arranged to represent the masts and rigging of a ship in port.

Austerity. Suzuki grass and the field flower called patrina in a small bronze vase.

" Many of those who take a fancy to this art do not really love flowers," wrote a certain tea-master a century ago. " They are only trying to show their skill

in arranging them, and they treat them cruelly, bending, twisting and plucking leaves and flowers without
mercy. Those who cherish flowers in reality should
strive to change the natural form as little as possible,
and to preserve them as long as possible by dipping
them deep in pure water." Which seems to be very
sensible advice, such as even Americans may comprehend.

In June it is proper to ride up the river past Mukojima and out across the plain to the iris fields at Hori-
kiri. They are not the common early irises which
flower in April; these are the large "Japanese"
variety, which need irrigation to do their best, and are
planted in patches divided by little dikes, like so
many tiny rice fields in an acre or two of level meadow.
Gentle grassy slopes rise all around, tastefully set
with shrubbery and a few trees, and small tea-houses
stand about at the prettiest points, overlooking the
field spread out below like a white and purple carpet.
The paths wind in and out among the shrubbery and
along the dikes, and people wander about admiring
beautiful individual flowers; and in the tea-house they
sell cut blossoms and colored prints of the newest and
choicest varieties. The imperial purples and clear
lavenders accord well with the early heat of June, and
the showery, muggy days that begin the rainy season,
which is due the 11th of June, but, needless to say, is
not always punctual. Delayed rains mean plenty of
trouble for the farmers, for the young rice must have

water, and as you ride back across the fields you sometimes see a peasant carrying two buckets on a pole or treading a small water wheel, laboriously irrigating his little plot. In such seasons the roads get very dusty, and the sun beats down pitilessly, while the shrill *zeeing* of the cicadas seems to aggravate the tense heat.

With full summer comes the lotus, flower of Buddha, and introduced with his teachings; it is not the Egyptian Nelumbo, but the great rose lotus of India, growing high above the water among large blue-green leaves, and looking like a bit of the tropics, although the pond it grows in may have had a skim of ice an inch thick in January, and they flourish even in the ice-bound Hokkaido.

Because of the place where it grows, the lotus is a symbol of purity under trial and temptation, much as we speak of a lily from a dust heap:

"If thou art born in a poor man's hovel, yet hast wisdom, thou art even as the lotus flower growing out of the mud."

The correct time to visit the lotus ponds is at sunrise, when the buds are supposed to open so suddenly that you can hear them crack; and many devotees do go at that hour in spite of the early habits of a July sun. If one fails to hear anything very startling, at least one may see a lovely pearly dawn, and bars of mist floating up across the Uyeno pines.

The morning-glory, or asagao, too, must be viewed

before the day is well begun, and this may be one reason why the cult is rather an esoteric one—that, and the great difficulty of getting the fancy varieties in perfection. It is not surprising, therefore, to find the flower a favorite with the cha-no-yu masters, in whose reunions, indeed, the cult originated; Rikyu, the master cha-jin, having been an assiduous asagao cultivator. The delicacy and perishable nature of the flower made it especially fit for the severe simplicity of the cha-no-yu room, and for the freshness of those early morning meetings.

They say that a famous general heard of Rikyu's wonderful morning-glories, so one day he called to see them. But though there were morning-glories in the garden, the general saw none that struck him as particularly remarkable till he entered the tea-room and beheld Rikyu's favorite arrangement—one flower and one leaf. Seen thus apart, the color seemed purer, fresher and lovelier than any other. He gazed delighted, exclaiming, "Now I understand."

Double asagao are the most highly prized varieties, chiefly, no doubt, because they are excessively difficult to propagate; the initiated distinguish four main types, going off into varieties past the knowledge of any but the learned. The asagao is a great favorite with poets and artists, the most famous verse of all being one composed by a young girl who went to her well, and, finding a morning-glory had twined about the rope, rather than disturb the flower, begged water

from her neighbor in a dainty poem of the regulation
thirty-one syllables :

> " Asagao ni
> Tsurube torarete
> Moraiye midzu."

Which is to say, alas, far less gracefully :

> " By asagao
> Is my bucket filched away—
> Water give, I pray."

Aston quotes another equally characteristic poem of
the didactic sort :

> " Oh for the heart
> Of the morning-glory,
> Which, though its bloom is for a single night,
> Is the same as that of the fir tree
> Which lives a thousand years."

Aston adds a commentary on the poem from Kiuso,
the eighteenth century philosopher :

" Living for a day, let us fulfill the Way for that
day and die ; living for a month, let us fulfill the Way
for that month and die ; living for a year, let us fulfill
the Way for that year and die. If we do so, there
will not be an atom of regret, even if we die in the
evening after having learned the Way in the morning."

The seventh of the seventh month is kept as the *tanabata* festival. In that month, according to Japanese
mythology, the goddesses wash their garments in the

Milky Way, which is the River of Heaven, Ama-no-gawa. At that time all the younger members of the family write something on a slip of fancy paper, and tie them to a branch of bamboo; the branch so laden is called tanabata, and it is fastened to the house-top or in the garden for the first seven days of July. On the evening of the seventh the tanabata is thrown into the nearest river, and the popular belief is that it will float away till it reaches the River of Heaven, when the heavenly goddesses may pick it up and read it. If they are pleased, they will reward the writer by causing his or her penmanship to improve—something the boys and maidens are very ambitious to attain.

But the great feast of July is the Festival of the Dead. Back in the country they still keep to the old calendar for these religious feasts, but everywhere that the railroads have gone the spirits must return for their welcome in the new month.

The origin of the festival is said to be this: Among the disciples of Shaka was a certain very holy man, who became possessed of supernatural powers, so that he could gaze into the lower regions and see what was happening there. To his horror, he beheld his own mother, condemned for her sins to suffer perpetual hunger. The son instantly offered her a bowlful of rice, and the hungry spirit turned eagerly to it, but as she tried to eat, the food became burning coals. In deep distress, the son cast himself before the merciful Buddha, and implored his help. And the merciful

Buddha told him, " Get together the priests from all the ten directions, and cause them to read prayers for thee and for thy ancestors to the seventh generation. Then, when thou hast set a bountiful repast before the priests, the condemned among thy ancestors shall be able to partake of thy offerings."

With the Buddhist priests, therefore, the 14th, 15th and 16th of July are observed as a time of special prayer and meditation, followed by a magnificent service on behalf of the hungry spirits.

With most people, however, it is rather the sense of the return of the spirits, the welcome that must be set for them on their brief visit, that makes the essential quality of the feast. The ihai are given a special stand, hung with bamboo and bright berries till it is like a bower, and lanterns are placed by the road and incense sticks burned, that the returning souls may not miss the way. In country places still, a tub of water is set by the house, and toy horses and oxen, made of egg-plants and cucumbers, are placed there for the spirits to use on the journey. But the straw boats set on fire are not often seen now, for the government has forbidden the practice on account of the danger to shipping, though it is winked at sometimes, they say, in out-of-the-way places on the coast.

In the country, too, they still dance the Bon-odori, the special dance of Bon. Men and women, young and old, all dress up in fanciful garments and dance in line, winding, doubling, like a game of " Follow my leader," with fantastic waving of arms and clapping of hands. They say it is symbolic of the joy of the rescued spirits.

On the night of the 16th, when the spirits go back over the sea, it is not good to be abroad upon the water; for the sea is troubled with strange currents, and quivering through it are countless pale lights—the glimmering lamps of the departing ghosts.

The fifteenth night of the August moon is devoted by the literary to a moon-gazing feast, wherein to watch O Tsuki Sama rising over some mountain or reflected in a still lake; offering to her rice dumplings and bouquets of suzuki grass, and repeating or composing verses. There is a delightful tale of a celebrated poet who was in the habit of wandering about the country cultivating his art by poetic contests, and who came one evening on a party of rustics engaged in one of these moonlight feasts; they dragged him into their midst in spite of protests of ignorance, and bade him compose instanter a *haikai* on the full moon. The poet, who happened to have invented that particular form of verse, with many grimaces, slowly begins, " 'Twas the new moon."

Howls of glee from the audience. "The new moon! But it is to be the full. No, listen : "

> " 'Twas the new moon;
> Since then I waited,
> And lo—To-night!"

The thing is perfect; the scoffers bow to the earth, and learn that the simple guest is no other than Basho, most renowned of verse-makers.[1]

This moon festival really belonged to September, the time of the harvest moon, as we call it; but the new calendar has pushed it back, leaving September rather bare of festivities. Artists paint for it the "Seven flowers of autumn," or a part of them, epecially the suzuki grass and the pretty purple lespedesa. At this season the women are busy bleaching and fulling their homespun cloth, pounding it with wooden mallets, or dipping and wringing and spreading it on the bank beside the river. The graceful postures, the sleeves tied back by the bright *tatsuki,* and blue and white kerchief over the hair, make one feel as if some of Hokusai's sketches in the "Occupations of Women" had come to life again.

October also is a dull month, when there is little doing at the temples, because all the gods are supposed to be off visiting the gods of Idzumo. Conservative people would not think of undertaking a wedding or betrothal or any important affair during this month. On the other hand, Idzumo is over-well provided with divinities, and they say many farmers in the province still lock their doors at sunset, and on no account venture out before dawn, lest the gods should feel themselves spied upon and insulted.

The Idzumo people keep a strange holiday con-

[1] Aston: "Japanese Literature."

nected with this visit of the gods, which is called the Laughing Festival. They say the origin of it is that the first time the gods came together for the yearly reunion, one of the divinities made a mistake in the date, and did not arrive till just as everything was over; whereat the rest laughed at him unmercifully. Therefore, in memory of the gods' merriment, all the villagers assemble once a year, and all the old men and all the children march in procession, the men first, carrying two boxes of oranges and persimmons run on bamboo sticks, and then the children, carrying in their hands oranges and persimmons spitted in the same way; one bears a large paper gohei. With decorous solemnity they march to the temple, and when they reach it, the oldest man turns round, and facing the children grouped about the gohei, he orders them to laugh—and is promptly obeyed. The spectators join in the merriment, and everybody spends the rest of the day in feasting and laughter.

But whatever October may lack, November makes up for by harvest thanksgivings and chrysanthemums and maples. It has kept the old festival of the ninth of the ninth month, when, from the days of the Emperor Uda until now, it has been the custom to hold garden parties at the Court and elsewhere, to view the chrysanthemums and drink wine and make verses. By great good luck the Emperor's birthday falls on the 5th of November, when the chrysanthemums are at their height, for, as every one knows, *kiku* is the imperial flower, as *kiri*, the purple Paulonia, belongs to the Empress. We are so used to identifying chrysanthemums with Japan, that it is rather a shock to find they are not native, after all, but one of the many borrowings from China, though, as usual, the loan has been improved upon by the borrowers. The Emperor's crest is a sixteen-petaled chrysanthemum, curiously like an Egyptian lotus-rosette—so like, indeed, that one wonders if it can be pure coincidence, and whether they had not both, perhaps, a far older prototype somewhere back in the unknown heart of Asia.

Such beautiful chrysanthemums are raised now in America that people are sometimes disappointed not to find anything much more wonderful than they have seen before. The truth is, you very seldom see finer specimens in Japan than in American hot-houses; the charm and the wonder is in the abundance of them, in the beauty and perfection of hundreds of plants together at an ordinary *en-nichi* on the streets at night, and the bundles of great stalks piled up in the flower shops; all of which give a pleasing sense of beauty, lavished without stint—somewhat, perhaps, like the delight of California roses in mid-winter. Exceedingly beautiful plants are grown in the Emperor's garden, and now and then an imperial garden party gives favored ones a chance to enjoy them. Count Okuma, too, is a great chrysanthemum lover, and raises many new varieties at his beautiful half-English park, Waseda. It is pleasant to hear that the garden and green-houses escaped the fire which lately destroyed the Count's residence. Most of the plants are grown out of doors, sheltered from wind and too much sun or rain by a light bamboo shed, just as peonies and morning-glory are protected.

The most famous chrysanthemum show, and certainly the oddest that could be imagined, is at Dango-zaka, over toward Asakusa temple. The place is a rather steep street, full of the usual stands for cakes and toys—delectable little owls, made of suzuki grass, are a specialty—among which, on either side of the street, stand a succession of big sheds, rather suggestive of circus tents, which you enter for a fee of a few sen to behold the show. It has nothing whatever to do with fine plants, though there are a few very beautiful ones, as it were incidentally ; the real exhibition is a collection of life-sized figures, the heads and hands made of *papier maché*, and the rest, gorgeous robes and armor and all, entirely composed of little red and white and yellow chrysanthemums—not cut flowers, but growing, on fine wire frames, into which the stems have been carefully twisted, the flowers all on top and the leaves underneath. The figures represent historical events, or scenes from some drama ; warriors and ladies in the ancient costumes and "stained-glass attitudes " of the theatre. Each platform is set like a stage and revolves, as in the Japanese theatre, to bring on new situations ; while, from time to time, ghosts and supernatural beings rise slowly through the floor, and disappear and rise again, with mournful groanings of machinery. Even recent events are depicted; scenes from the war, or some great earthquake or other catastrophe, such as the awful tidal wave of 1896, which was displayed at Dangosaka in the act of curling over a village in a foaming mass of green leaves and white petals. The crashing cottages and tossing limbs were quite too realistic to be pleasant. The ferocious, stagey Ronin are much better, or a poet rhapsodizing beside a flowery waterfall. It is all more curious than beautiful, but the skill and pains that can make things grow and bloom at such angles seem truly marvelous.

In Tokyo there is a very popular *matsuri*, held at a certain temple on the " Days of the Bird," in November. (The days of the Japanese month are called after twelve beasts and birds, namely, the rat, ox, tiger, rabbit, dragon, snake, horse, sheep, monkey, cock, dog and bear; if the first day of the month happens to fall on " snake," the fourth will be on " monkey," and so on.) The Temple of the Bird (he is an eagle) is in the part of Tokyo called Shitaya, not far from Asakusa and its entertainments; it is not a very elegant quarter, but thousands of people flock there in November, mostly peasants and mechanics and small tradespeople, to pray at the shrine and buy the charms, which they think will bring good luck for the year. There are three things: potatoes ready to

sprout, token of humble ambition, buried yet growing; millet dumplings, the name of which means to
hold, and hence means that you will keep what you
get; and, most important of all, a small toy rake
with curved teeth, such as is used to gather up stalks
of grain lying in the field; a head of rice is tied
across the teeth, and a little square rice measure and a
tiny piece of gold leaf is pasted on. All along the
street leading to the temple there are rows of booths
for the sale of these things, and, many as they are,
they must do a fine business, for custom forbids bar-
gaining for the charms, lest the luck should be spoiled.

There are few amusements for December, and no
flowers; if there were, nobody would have time to
see them, every one is so busy getting ready for the
New Year. In every house there is the sound of
pounding *mochi*—the sticky rice cakes—a dainty as
indispensable and almost as deadly as Christmas can-
dies; the men are settling all their affairs, that no debt
may be left unpaid, and merchants often stay up till
daybreak on the last night of the year; while the
women are in the midst of a frantic bout of house-
cleaning, for every tatami—mat—must be taken up,
aired, beaten, or renewed; the floors and every par-
ticle of the woodwork scrubbed, clothes brushed,
broken screens recovered, bedding aired or made over
—in a word, every cranny set in the most immaculate
order, that no evil thing may have excuse to linger.
On New Year's Day, on the other hand, there is no

sweeping or dusting, for fear of sweeping out the
" new atmosphere." As a last purification of all, on
New Year's Eve, the old-fashioned country dame was
wont to fling out a handful of dried peas, in token of
turning out last year's evil spirits—just as she is doing
in one of Hokusai's inimitable sketches. A few days
earlier, Tokyo is hazy with the smoke of bonfires
burning up old worn-out things, such as shoes and
brooms and household gear, replaced perhaps at one
of the fairs held through the month in different parts
of the city.

All the last days, every corner fairly bubbles with
excitement; up and down the streets people are selling the needful decorations—straw ropes, either inch-
thick strands and tassels and the knot which must go
over every door, or mere cords with dangling straws
attached; all these are to put across the doorways, in
memory of the rope with which the young god Susa-
no-o closed the cave, that his Sun Goddess sister
might not again hide herself from the earth; and,
incidentally, these ropes are believed to keep out evil
spirits, which roam about at this time looking out for
a residence. With the straw decorations are hung
strips of paper, cut in a peculiar way, and a few fern
leaves, an orange, and a boiled lobster. This last is
said to be a symbol of living till the back is bent
with age, like the fish's. Platforms for semi-sacred
dances are set up beside the street in many places, and
exorcists go about from house to house—usually a

man, conducting two or three little boys in huge grotesque masks, who posture and tumble and turn hand-
springs, to the monotonous thumping of a drum ; the
whole being a purifying rite, and probably a very
ancient one.

All the first days of the year, too, girls and women
go about in pairs, under big pointed straw hats, twang-
ing the samisen and singing charms ; they are called
tori-oi (bird chasers), and they are supposed to drive
away those evil spirits which are flying about in the
form of birds.

Under the eaves of the Gion temple in Kyoto a
small lamp burns night and day. On the last evening
of the old year people come to the temple and light
tapers at this year-old flame, with which to kindle the
little light burning before the god-shelf in each house.
Two hours after midnight, at the " hour of the tiger,"
the priests rekindle the lamp from a fresh fire ; this is
called the rite of pine shavings. A priest reads the
ritual, and meantime other priests rub together two
pieces of wood, kindling a spark upon the pine shavings in a large iron lamp. From this they light the
small lamp under the eaves, and the charred fragments
of the pine are sold to the worshipers as charms
against disease.

About the 28th of December carts of green begin
to arrive from the country, and the prettiest act of all
begins—the setting up of a bit of pine and fresh
bamboo at every house, emblems of long life and

happiness through the year. Some can only afford a
sprig, others plant a thick, short pine on either side,
and with it three green stems of large bamboo, cut
off at different lengths; by others again—and this is
prettiest, as well as commonest—the long stalk is left
uncut, and the slender green feather of foliage waves
far above the low roofs. By New Year's morning
the leaves dry from green to an exquisite silvery
shade, and among them are flags innumerable—the
white national flag that bears a red ball for the rising
sun. Down each street, under the silvery-green arch,
little girls are playing ball, and young and old batting
shuttlecocks, the hard little seed keeping up a con-
tinual tap-tapping against the gaily-decorated wooden
battledores; the burr of kites fills the air, and the
jinrikisha men dodge frantically among the humming
strings. All the men are paying calls; high func-
tionaries dash past in their carriages, passing petty
officials, stiff and unhappy in tight frock coats and
silk hats, that see the light but once a year, and seem
to date—some of them at least—from the earliest
years of Meiji. Then there are stately old gentlemen
in beautiful silks, and family parties—first the master
of the house, then the daughter-in-law with her
mother-in-law, a son proud of military blue and cadet
cap, and the little girls, riding two and two, awe-struck
in their best crepes, and afraid to smile for fear of
cracking the powder on their faces. The children
carry willow wands, on which hang many-colored

objects made of dried *mochi* paste, such as a fish, a clam, round cakes marked with lucky characters, and a mask of O Kami San, round-cheeked and smiling— she who danced to lure the Sun Goddess from her cave.

Indoors, just within the vestibule, lies a pile of three big, round *mochi* cakes on a little square stand covered with white paper; these represent the mirror with which Susa-no-o coaxed his sister from the cave. The cakes are decorated with the same symbols of luck and plenty as are over the door, the fern leaves and seaweed, a twig of pine, an orange and some dried persimmons, and a lobster. People who cannot afford a real *ebi* can buy a red plaster copy, which does to bring the luck.

Mrs. Iwamoto—whose charming essays should be better known—thus describes New Year's morning in a modern Tokyo household:

"The children come in smiling, in holiday attire, and they notice that father, in *haori* and *hakama* (a costume answering to your evening dress), is sitting at the place of honor, with his back to the tokonoma (alcove) in the guest room, where the feast is spread on this particular morning. The mother sits next to him, and the rest of the family all know their places by the names on the paper chop-stick cases, all so new and white. . . . When all are seated the mother greets the father, saying '*Omedeto gosarimasu*'—i. e., 'I present you my congratulations.' The greeting is returned, and the children, beginning at the eldest, all do the same to father and mother, and to each other. After this the servants come in and present their congratulations to the family.

"Then it is the custom for the family and servants all to take a sip of a certain spiced sweet wine called *toso* from three dainty lacquered cups arranged on top of each other; but in Christian homes, and where temperance is emphasized, this is omitted; so we hail the *zoni*, or soup with mochi in it, and prepare to enjoy our chief New Year dish. While the children plunge their rather clumsy new chop-sticks into the soft pieces of mochi, mother takes the side dish and takes out a little of the 'three things' prepared for the family in three lacquer boxes fitting on top of each other; these are not so much of a delicacy as 'good omened' food; first *mame*, boiled black beans, the name having the same sound as the adjective *mame*, healthful; then *kazunoko*, a kind of roe steeped in sauce, emblematic of multiplicity and prosperity; and *gomane*, small dried sardines, for good luck. Other delicacies are served up, but all must have the above dish. . . . But the boys' sharp ears catch the growl of the kites, and they begin to get fidgetty, and the girls, too, are eager for a game with their new battledores and shuttlecocks, so they are all excused to enjoy themselves to their heart's content on this day of all days, while the father hastens to his New Year calls and the mother prepares to entertain the visitors at home."

Indeed, the mother's day will be a very busy one, for every caller must have food offered, and wine or tea. In non-Christian houses special offerings of dainties are made before the ihai, name-tablets of the ancestors on the god-shelf, and in the poorest cottage the vase in the tokonoma holds a sprig of pine and a budding plum branch, before the traditional New Year kakemono, which is always a red-headed stork flying or sitting on a pine tree, always across a red rising sun.

For, of course, it is really a sun-feast, a rejoicing over the return of spring, like all the rest from Osiris down; and it has a myth of the sun's hiding as naively grotesque as any German tale of kobolds. Thus it runs: One day as Amaterasu, the Sun Goddess, sat spinning among her maidens, her riotous brother Susa-no-o, the god of clouds and wind, playfully flung through the roof the bloody skin of a newly-killed horse. His sister found it a sorry jest; in fright and wrath she hid herself in a cave, and all the world grew dark and cold; but she would not return, though all the gods besought her. At last a giddy young goddess bade the rest bring a tub and turn it upside down, and she dressed herself splendidly and sang and danced on the tub with such comic gestures that all the gods laughed and applauded, and Amaterasu could not help peeping out to see what the fun could be. Then her brother cried, " Here is one far lovelier than Amaterasu!" and he thrust a mirror before the crack, so that she saw her own beaming face; whereat she was so astonished that she opened the door a little wider, and her brother drew her out and clapped the door to behind her, and made it fast forever, hanging straw ropes across, and Amaterasu hid her face no more.

Therefore henceforth men hang the knots of twisted straw, and dance the sacred dances, and feast and keep a three days' holiday at O Sho Gatsu, the August New Year.

CHAPTER XIV.

NARA.

NARA stands to Kyoto somewhat as Canterbury does to London, in that it was the capital in an early romantic period, and kept its religious prestige long after the Court had departed. The "Nara period" is a sort of Age of Charlemagne—a heroic, brilliant period, when art was young and literature flourished, and the Court led the way in all; when the Emperor was the actual and not the nominal ruler, and when women had a position and freedom that later Chinese influences stole quite away.

In the beginning, when an Emperor died, it was the custom to move the capital to a new city, much as some primitive peoples desert a hut in which there has been a death. By really historic times—say 500 A.D.—changes were made less frequently, but always, so far, within the boundaries of Yamato, the sacred province first ruled over by the Divine Ancestors— which, when divested of mythology, doubtless means the first region settled by in-coming waves of migration. But Nara was the first capital that can fairly be called permanent, its period of occupation being nearly a hundred years, coinciding almost exactly with the eighth century; and the fact that it was so long occupied of itself marks an advance in the stability of the government.

It was an Empress, Gemmyo, who first chose Nara as a residence. She was one of the three or four Empresses who ruled during the seventh and eighth centuries, and she seems to have been an able and energetic lady, who "enjoyed the confidence and affection of all," as one chronicle declares. By her time Buddhism had become firmly established—indeed it may be considered to have been so for two or three generations previously, along with Chinese and Korean arts and civilization generally; a Code based on the laws of the Tang dynasty had been promulgated shortly before, and the Court remodeled on Chinese lines, while art had passed the stage of mere imitation and was beginning to create in its own way. Scholars studied the Chinese classics, sometimes journeying to China for the purpose; Korean teachers, artists and workmen were encouraged to settle in the country, and many did do so at this time, as well as before and after.

It is generally acknowledged that a large share of the credit for the rapid advance in development during this period belongs to the Buddhist priests; and it is no exaggeration to say that the spread both of art and science—as the age understood science— was the direct consequence of their labors. Many of

Pagoda, Nara

the priests, after their journeys to China, traveled up
and down Japan, building temples, making or extend-
ing roads, putting up bridges, digging wells and
storage ponds and irrigation canals; in a word, opening up barren country and contributing to the material
prosperity of the people almost as much as to their
moral welfare. The increasing size of the temples
called for improvement in carpenter's work; and the
demand for images and sacred books and pictures,
and temple hangings, vases and other sacerdotal furniture, provided just the impetus that was needed for
the development of a national art.

Here, too, at Nara, early in the eighth century, the
first authentic book was compiled, the *Kojiki*, which
was a history of the creation and the Age of the Gods,
and of all that followed, down to the reign of the
Empress Suiko, who lived about a century before the
founding of Nara, and who issued rescripts on several
occasions encouraging the spread of Buddhism. The
Nihongi, a second authorized history, was published a
little later than the *Kojiki*, and a collection of all
known poetry, called the *Manyoshiu*, was compiled a
few years later still. There are traditions about other
books, said to have been written before the *Kojiki*,
and to have been part of the source from which its
records were drawn; but all of these were lost, and it
is probably because printing was introduced from
China about the close of the Nara period that these
three works have been preserved.

One of the earliest Nara Emperors established a university at the capital for the study of the " Four Paths of Learning,". which were history, Chinese classics, law and mathematics. Its object was the training of officials. At about the same time the *kana* syllabary was invented to express words phonetically, instead of entirely by ideographs, as in Chinese. They did this by taking Chinese characters, shortening them down to a few strokes, and using this abbreviated form to express the sound that the original character represented. Thus the character for the word *ho*, which originally had ten strokes, lost all but the cross and two dashes which made its lower right-hand corner; and henceforth it stood for the syllable *ho*, without regard to meaning. Instead of a true alphabet, therefore, Japan has forty-six syllables, each consisting of a consonant and a vowel—ka, ki, ku, ke, ko ; ra, ri, ru, re, ro, and so on. But some syllables are wanting, because the Japanese cannot pronounce them ; and others have the consonant modified by the vowel that follows it—ti, for instance, becoming chi, and tu, tsu. Later, Kobo Daishi composed a verse bringing in all the sounds in use, and children recite this as we do the alphabet ; it is called, after its first three syllables, *Iroha*. But Chinese characters are used almost universally in place of the kana, the character being used which expresses the right meaning. The same character may often be pronounced either as a Chinese or a Japanese word ; the character for way, for instance, may be read either as *tô* or *michi*.

To this period, too, belongs Prince Shotoku, priest and statesman; and Gyogi, traditional inventor of the potter's wheel; and Shodo Shonin, who exorcised the Nikko demons. Altogether it was a stirring, heroic age, when much legend was in the making, if not a great deal of authentic history.

There is a curious bit of mythological story told in the annals as to the way some elements of Korean civilization got to Japan, in a time supposed to be shortly after the Age of the Gods. A Korean farmer, says the legend, was once going to the fields, driving an ox, and carrying provisions for the men who were working there. On his way he met a great lord, who spoke to him angrily, and accused him of taking the ox in order to kill and eat it. The poor man vainly protested his innocence, and at last, to appease the nobleman, gave him a shining red jewel that he had hidden in his girdle. The nobleman took it and carried it home, and laid it by his couch.

Now the jewel was not really a stone at all, but the daughter of the sun and of a beautiful girl whom he fell in love with as she lay sleeping on the shore of a lake. When, therefore, the noble carried her home to his house, she became a woman, and the noble loved her, and made her his wife. But after a time he grew tired of her, and treated her rudely; and she said to him, " Now I shall go away to my home in Japan."

But he thought nothing of it. But while he slept, she rose up and took a boat and fled away over the sea. Then when her husband saw that she was indeed gone, he also took a boat and pursued her; but a storm arose, and broke his ship, and cast him ashore on the coast of Japan. Yet he saved the treasures he had brought with him; these were two strings of jewels, a wave-shaking scarf, a wave-cutting scarf, a wind-shaking scarf, the mirror of the sea and the mirror of the shore. Then he married the daughter of a Japanese lord, and stayed in that place, and taught the people many things.

When the Court departed, Nara at least gained the safety of obscurity, and escaped the periodic burnings which overtook Kyoto in the feudal wars; and this is exceedingly fortunate, for many of the oldest and finest specimens of art are here and at the monastery of Horiuji, a few miles away. Many of these early works are not Japanese at all, but Korean, and all are very Chinese in manner. The paintings are formal, almost, as a Byzantine mosaic, but show far more knowledge and vigor; the bronzes and wooden statues are especially broad and noble. The best of these that are visible at all are in a museum near one gate of the Daibutsu temple, where there is an exceedingly interesting collection of fine lacquer, embroidered vestments, pictures and images. Some of the statues are portraits of priests, with beautiful, kindly old faces, recalling Fra Angelico's childlike saints at San Marco.

The Daibutsu is marred by an ugly sixteenth century head, and still further by the gilded wooden nimbus set up behind it, and the bare, ill-proportioned hall in which it stands. It is rather larger than the Kamakura Daibutsu, and only the lower portion dates from the eighth century, when it was first built; the other parts are restorations made after fires had twice destroyed the temple and melted the head, besides doing other injury to the figure. The pose is graceful and impressive; less utterly still than the Kamakura figure, it is yet calm and benignant, and is worthy of much, if not all, of the praise Gonse bestows on it.

A good deal of the legendary mingles with its history. In the first place the Emperor Shomu, who built it, seems to have had certain misgivings as to whether the Shinto Kami would approve; they were his ancestors and protectors, and he wished to be sure of their permission before making images of strange gods. The energetic Gyogi, the potter priest, was sent on pilgrimage to Ise, and returned with a reassuring dream; and the Emperor began the work, and carried it through in spite of many discouragements. It is said that gold was discovered in Japan just in time to be used in making the alloy; and many other wonderful things happened.

The artistic tradition which first came to Japan was the Hindu Buddhist type of the south of India, modified on the way by Chinese and Korean influences;

the Chinese share being all in the direction of coldness
and restraint, like their own early bronzes, and a sharp,
thin treatment of drapery growing out of their love
of line—the hard, incisive line of Chinese ideographs.
On the other hand, the Koreans thoroughly understood
pottery and excelled in modeling, and Fenollosa claims
that they passed on "Chinese dignity softened by a
more mellow line." Of this type are the Horiuji
figures, and a carved wooden Buddha attributed to
the artist-priest Prince Shotoku, also some fine paintings at Horiuji almost certainly done by Korean
artists; all of these being about a century earlier than
the Nara epoch.

Then came another wave of influence, what is known
as Græco-Buddhistic art finding its way from the north
of India through China, and so to Korea and Japan.
Its ancestor was the Hellenistic style of Persia under
the Selucidæ and the Sassanid reigns, a style which
admitted a great deal of action, not to say violence,
along with much grace. Even filtered through three
Oriental races, it kept something of movement and
force, with many Greek architectural details used
purely ornamentally; indeed, Gonse cites a bronze
vase in the Horiuji collection which he considers to be
actually of Greek workmanship, and which must have
served as an example. It was this Græco-Buddhist
manner that reached Japan just before the Nara
period, when Japanese artists were engaged by imperial command on bronze altar-pieces and images for

Girl Painting

the new temples. "A beauty almost Greek in its sensitiveness slowly emerges," says Fenollosa; a combination of "Korean hints and Japanese genius;" and it established a canon for all future images of Buddha.

It would be hard to dream of a more peaceful spot than Nara; the town itself is sleepy enough, but the temples are removed even from this, standing as usual in a beautiful park among tall trees. As you enter the long avenue, the sound of wheels brings a score of spotted brown deer bounding about the kuruma, nosing for salt biscuits, laying cool muzzles in your hand without a shadow of fear, for nothing has ever hurt them or can hurt them in this sacred wood. Mossy, time-worn lanterns almost wall the road and crowd about the temples—so many, they say, no one has ever been able to count them. The great Shinto temple and its companion buildings are strong red, and the galleries are hung with hundreds more lanterns of polished brass, making a wonderful depth of glow and richness in the cathedral twilight of the wood. The divinities are ancestors of the Fujiwara family, and their Wistaria crest—*fuji*—appears on the filmy robes of the girls who dance the sacred Kagura dances; they wear, besides, a white under-dress and wide, full trousers, of an odd shade of red. They have their hair down their backs, tied just at the end, after the old Court fashion, and wave branches and little bells as they sway and pose to the wailing Shinto flutes.

Farther over there is a large Buddhist temple, perched on great piles and crossing timbers, built out from the side of the hill; it is reached by a high flight of wooden steps, and it, too, is hung with countless lanterns of brass and bronze. One feels that lanterns must surely be the *meibutsu*, the keepsake of Nara, but instead they sell little painted images called *ningyo*, dolls, representing the Nô and Kagura dancers, and sticks of India ink of a particularly excellent quality—which does indeed seem appropriate for so artistic a place—also fans, and trifles made of deer horn. A third great temple, founded in the Nara period, was burnt a couple of hundred years ago, and has little left but two pagodas and a hall full of admirable wooden statues.

Foreign travelers often stay some time at Nara; two of the hotels give more or less European accommodation, and it is near enough to Osaka to get supplies from there, if needful. For rest or sketching, nothing could well be lovelier; but it is not particularly cool in summer, and winter behind paper shoji is something strangers should not lightly attempt. The loveliest time is spring, when the plum is in blossom at Tsukigase, seven *ri* up the valley—unless by now modern progress has done away with the trees. Or, better still, come in autumn, when the rains are over and the plain lies in dreamy haze and all the maples are aflame. On such a day, instead of offering the customary gifts, Sugiwara Michizane, the faithful premier, wrote at one of these temples:

> " Nought bring I to-day;
>   May the gods take lavish fee—
> Crimson, gold inlay,
>   Brocade of the maple tree,
> From the sides of Tamuké."

CHAPTER XV.

ACCORDING to the *Kojiki* and *Nihongi*, the eldest and the youngest of Prince Fire Fade's four sons met one day in the palace in Kiushiu and consulted as to the best place for their future seat of government. They decided to go east, and passed up through Kiushiu, and, from the northeastern part of that island, sailed over to the part of the main island that comes down to the straits of Shimonoseki. There, in what was afterwards the province of Aki, they remained eight years, subduing the previous settlers, who are known to the *Kojiki* as "Earth Spiders" and "Reed Men." Murray compares their progress to the migrations of the hordes of Goths in Europe, who moved, with all their belongings and all the tribe, young and old, women and children; and they stopped long enough to cultivate the ground, as well as hunt and fish and fight.

After the eight years, they sailed across from the shores of the Inland Sea to a harbor at the mouth of a river, which they called Naniwa, or Nami-hana—Wave-blossom—because of the dashing spray through which they had to land. From here they proceeded to Yamato, and the elder brother was shot by an arrow while fighting the barbarians, and soon afterward died; but the younger, Jimmu Tenno, went on and overcame all the demons and ogres and other opponents, and established the line of the Sun Goddess in the sacred province.

Naniwa seems to have been a small seaport from a very early period, and for a time it was also the imperial capital. Thus it happened that the first Buddhist temple in Japan was built there, in 522, and a Korean mission established. But, fifty years later, a severe epidemic broke out, and one of the Emperor's advisers protested against the foreign religion, declaring that, both in his father's reign and his, the pestilence had ravaged the country, "so that the nation is about to be destroyed. The cause of these ills is the impiety of those who have established this religion of Buddha." The Emperor was convinced, and gave orders to prohibit Buddhism; the temple was burned down, the statue of Buddha thrown into the river and the monks imprisoned; but the pestilence did not cease, and two Emperors died within a year. Before the end of the century, the Empress Suiko and Prince Shotoku restored the priests' privileges and gave Buddhism a position from which it could not again be shaken. Shotoku is worshiped as one of the patron saints of Osaka, at the temple which he is said to have founded. People come there and make petitions to the saint for their departed friends, asking him to show them the way to paradise. There is a bell for the worshipers to ring, set in a shrine by itself, and in another building a stream of sacred water pours from the mouth of a stone tortoise and flows across the floor, and here the people drop in slips of paper, on which they have written the names of their dead. The sacred stream carries them away to Shotoku Daishi, and thus the departed will be sure of a kindly reception from the saint.

The name of the place was apparently changed to Osaka in the fifteenth century. At that time it was an important stronghold of the monks, and after Nobunaga had destroyed Hiezan, the priests of the Hongwanji stirred up a holy war against him and fortified themselves at Osaka. Nobunaga besieged them, and would probably have made another wholesale massacre if the Emperor had not interfered and caused their lives to be spared; but their fortress was given up and became an imperial castle.

From this time the prosperity of Osaka rapidly increased. Hideyoshi protected the merchants and encouraged commerce, and in 1583 chose Osaka for his capital, and built there the great castle which stood till 1868.

Osaka is not actually on the sea, but near the mouth of the Yodogawa, which drains lake Biwa, and ocean-going steamers cannot come to it. Kobe, fifty miles away, is the port for the long distance trade. But for internal commerce it is well fitted ; the products of the whole region around lake Biwa and Kyoto can come directly there by water, and the small vessels of the coasting trade find their way around from all the ports, as well as from the Inland Sea. The river winds in a double curve like an S, cutting the city into two unequal parts ; then it divides, reaching the sea by two streams. An island at the fork was granted as a foreign concession by the early treaties, but the port was not actually opened till 1867. The Concession is a pretty place, well built up with substantial houses, and shaded by trees along the water ; but as a commercial centre for foreign trade Osaka has never been a success, and much the larger part of the foreigners residing there belong to the various missions. In 1897 the exports to foreign ports were only a twentieth of Kobe's and half Nagasaki's, and there were only about a hundred foreigners, not counting Chinese. Such firms as there were have mostly moved to Kobe or sold out to Japanese.

Yet Osaka is the second city of the empire, a place of half a million inhabitants, " compact and well laid out, clean and animated," thinks the author of " European Settlements in the Far East." Clean it certainly is, but, unfortunately, subject to severe epidemics, largely due to an execrable water supply. The situation is in itself not bad ; the tide affects the canals which run all through it, but it lies too low and flat for a perfect city. Modern it certainly is, and well compared to Manchester, on account of its immense manufactures of cotton and silk and rugs, as well as many other industries. The imperial mint is here, founded in 1868 by the initiative of Count Okuma, with English managers and English machinery, but now for many years entirely run by Japanese; and the arsenal, where likewise there is foreign machinery and native service; besides iron works and shipyards and the big spinning mills, and entirely too many of the worst features of American factory life.

This practical, go-ahead spirit is not new to the place; the people of Osaka seem to have always been different from the rest of Japan, more hard-headed and worldly. From the time of Hideyoshi, Osaka merchants enjoyed privileges no other city possessed, not even Yedo, the Shogun's capital. In Yedo even the richest merchant was inferior to the lowest Samurai; in Osaka the great guilds dictated terms to princes, and their position was strikingly like that of the Free Cities of Europe in relation to the knights. Under the Tokugawa, Osaka paid no tax to the central government except an annual "gift" of ten thousand *rio;* it had its own local administration, its own assembly of elders; besides these, there was a mayor and two magistrates appointed by the Shogun, and over all the governor of the castle, which belonged to the Tokugawa.

But, above all, Osaka was the port of departure for the rice of the south. Sendai sent direct to Yedo,

Osaka Castle

Osaka Castle

but the other two centres—Kumamoto and Niigata—
were required to deliver theirs to the merchants of
Osaka, who shipped it to the Shogun's capital. When
the Daimyo got into difficulties, the Ōsaka guild
endorsed their paper, and refunded themselves when
the next rice crop was sold at the Exchange; and before the end of the Tokugawa régime many a prince
was practically at their mercy. Under the Constitution the city is still favored; one of the seven higher
courts sits here, and it has a flourishing Board of
Trade, the first in the country, with many lesser privileges that keep up the old prestige.

The enclosure of the castle is now used for the garrison, and a special pass is needed to see it. Besides
the wonder of the great walls, it commands a vast
map-like view of the city and the wide plain in which
it lies; the endless dark roofs netted in a mesh of
shining canals, and the river winding through, half
hidden sometimes under the throng of brown junks
and the forest of masts. Far down is a glimpse of the
green island where the townspeople come out on summer evenings to play, and among the low roofs, straight
and high and hideous, rises chimney after chimney
rolling out clouds of sooty smoke.

One of the marvels of Hideyoshi's castle was that
he built it in three years, laying many Daimyo under
tribute to supply the materials. The hewn blocks are
even more enormous than at Tokyo or Nagoya; like
those, they are squared or polygonal, cut to the finest

joining, and fitted together without mortar. It stands on a hill not greatly raised above the plain, and a part of the river has been turned a little aside to fill the moats, which, with the wall, are all that remain of Hideyoshi's fortress.

It was here that Hideyoshi's son, Hideyori, made his last stand against Ieyasu. The battle of Seki-gahara had established the Tokugawa power, and made Ieyasu the acknowledged master of the country; but he left Hideyori his two provinces and the castle, waiting for some excuse to take these also. It was fourteen years before this excuse finally came, when Hideyori dedicated the great bell at the Daibutsu temple, in Kyoto, and Ieyasu pretended that two Chinese characters in the inscription were so worded as to imply an insult to himself. The two characters, read in one of the possible ways, made his own name, and he affirmed that Hideyori was calling down a curse upon him, and insisted upon an inquiry as to the loyalty of Hideyori's followers. Thereupon these followers flocked to Osaka and fortified themselves there. Ieyasu summoned the other clans and be-sieged the castle for a year; then peace was made, but broken the next year, when a still greater number of retainers entrenched themselves at Osaka. But the year before Ieyasu had had the moats partly filled in, as one of the conditions of peace, and the clans took the castle without great difficulty. When it was evident that they could not hold out, Hideyori set fire to the castle, and he and his mother threw themselves into the flames; his chief followers killed themselves. But the fire was put out and the place repaired, and it became a Tokugawa fortress of the first rank.

In 1868 the ex-Shogun, Prince Tokugawa, retired to Osaka, after an interview with the Emperor at Kyoto; and it was from here that he marched to the fatal battle of Fushimi. When that day was lost, he fled back to Osaka, and went on board a ship, first warning the foreigners—who had only entered the Concession a few months previously—that he could no longer guarantee their safety. His retainers pillaged the castle and set it on fire, and then followed, escaping with him to Yedo; and when the Imperialists arrived they found only burning ruins. A few months later the Emperor himself came to Osaka, by the advice of some of his ministers, who thought—and very wisely—that it would be far easier to make the necessary reforms from a new capital. But he soon after returned to Kyoto, and chose Tokyo instead, this being partly because his advisers believed his presence there was the best possible means of gaining over those who were hesitating between loyalty to the ex-Shogun and to the Kyoto Court. The event has proved them entirely right. If the people's awe of their hidden lord is somewhat less, now that he is visible, their love and loyalty are surely more.

32425

CHAPTER XVI.

KOBE.

THE treaties of 1858 granted three open ports for residence and trade — namely, Nagasaki, Kanagawa (afterwards Yokohama) and Hakodate; and they promised two—Niigata, on the west coast, and Hyogo, which is generally known by the name of its foreign half, Kobe. These were to be opened within a year or two after the others, and likewise residence "Concessions" in Osaka and Yedo. Black, in his "Young Japan," gives a vivid picture of the negotiations, the vexatious delays and disappointments to which the government was driven to resort by fear of outrages from lawless clansmen and Ronin, if the aliens were admitted too soon. The fact was that the fatal "Richardson affair" of 1862, and other attacks, provoked though they nearly always were, had made the foreign representatives willing to put off dangerous experiments; and the two new ports and Concessions were not actually opened till the beginning of 1868. The Concession at Osaka had been insisted upon, because it was known to be the second city in the empire, and of the greatest importance commercially, which made the foreigners suppose there would be large opportunities for trade. They either did not know or did not realize that in the absence of a harbor for sea-going vessels they would gain little. The government, on its side, tried to make matters run smoothly by creating a trading corporation of twenty Osaka merchants, and giving them importance by titles of rank and grants of income.

Thus when the time at last came everything began smoothly. But the foreigners were scarcely settled when the battle of Fushimi precipitated the so-called Tokugawa rebellion, and the Shogun warned the representatives that he could no longer guarantee their safety at Osaka. They went accordingly to Kobe, where their ships were at hand as a refuge, in case of necessity. It must be remembered that it was with the Shogun's government that the representatives had been treating, and up to this time the Kyoto Court had had nothing but hostility for them. The representatives of the Powers were nearly all on the side of Tokugawa, until Sir Harry Parkes arrived, and by his keen insight discovered where the real sovereignty of the empire ought to rest. The foreigners in Kobe not unnaturally felt themselves in an uncertain position, and had a number of frights, the worst of all when some retainers of Bizen fired on a couple of French soldiers who accidentally crossed their line. Luckily no one was killed; but the guards were called out, two or three people wounded, and the entire

Settlement thrown into the wildest alarm. Mitford, who was there with the British legation, tells of all sorts of martial effervescence. "If it had not been for the serious nature of the offence given, which was an attack upon the flags of all the treaty Powers, and for the terrible retribution which was of necessity exacted, the whole affair would have been recollected chiefly for the ludicrous events which it gave rise to." The retribution of which he speaks was the death of the officer who had given the order to fire on the Frenchmen, and who was condemned by the government to commit *harakiri*.

All that is long past, and rough coolies and drunken sailors of the "flags of all the Powers" are now the only breakers of the peace. Kobe-Hyogo "grew up like a mushroom," as a Japanese wrote ten years ago, and it is growing still. In 1898 there were about a thousand Europeans and Americans, and as many Chinese, besides over two hundred thousand Japanese. It is a prettily situated place ; the business part lies on a level space a mile or more across, between the harbor and the hill, where the residences are—pleasant cottages and green gardens bowered in trees. A fine stone bund, or retaining wall, runs all along the water front, and there is an iron pier and two railroad piers, likewise two docks and the imperial shipyard, capable of dry-docking vessels of two thousand tons ; and a custom house, warehouses, clubs, cricket ground, gas and water and newspapers, and all needful requirements for a bit of Western life set down on the edge of the East. All the liners call at Kobe, foreign and Japanese alike, and all the coasting service—a little fleet in itself—besides the small steamers plying about the Inland Sea. Except for some severe heat in midsummer, the climate is considered unusually pleasant, and altogether Kobe is the favorite port with the foreign residents.

Hyogo proper is altogether Japanese ; it lies across the Minato river, which meanders, after the habit of Japanese rivers, among the stones of an immensely wide bed. lying a great deal higher up than the surrounding country ; and every year or so, after the rains, it disports itself in a flood that threatens the embankments, and even the stone bridge connecting the two towns. Kiyomori of Taira banked up its present bed in the twelfth century, and likewise made other improvements, part of which still remain.

There is not much of interest just around the city itself ; outside there are a few pretty walks and rides, such as the trip to Nunibiki gorge and its pair of waterfalls, or to Ikuta temple, in a splendid grove of camphor trees ; or to the baths of Suwa-yama, or to Cape Wada, beyond Hyogo, where there is a pretty tea-garden and a glorious view of the sea and the nearer islands ; while among the hills there are plenty of longer climbs for the energetic. Hyogo possesses a Daibutsu, nearly fifty feet high and only less ugly than the Kyoto one, and a beautiful little bronze

Amida on a stone pedestal, before a pond of lotus.
Relics of Kiyomori are at many temples, and of Nitta
Yoshisada and Masashige, faithful generals of Go-
Daigo the unlucky, who fought a great battle here in
the river-bed and were utterly defeated.

This battle of Minatogawa was the culminating
act of a life-long tragedy, and the cruelest pity of it
is that the Emperor was anything but worthy of the
romantic devotion paid to him.   It was not that he
failed in courage; the story of his escape from exile,
hidden under a pile of fish, proves him no palace dar-
ling.   But he was open to flattery; instead of reward-
ing the faithful knights who had fought for him, in a
way to strengthen their hands, he set them aside for
men who could make soft speeches, and, worse than
all, he believed the traitor Ashikaga Takauji, against
his own son.

Three generations before Go-Daigo there had been
two lines of succession in the imperial family, de-
scended from two brothers, who had both reigned.
For nearly a century the Emperor had been chosen
from one or the other, according to the will of the
military rulers at Kamakura.   Go-Daigo, who came
to the throne in 1319, enlisted the aid of his son, the
Buddhist priest Morinaga, and with him and the
priests of Hiezan laid a plot against the Kamakura
government.   The Regent, Hojo, sent an army against
Kyoto, with orders to arrest the Emperor; but Morinaga gave warning, and Go-Daigo fled with the impe-

rial insignia to Mount Kasugi, near Kyoto, where he assembled an army of his partisans. The Regent thereupon proclaimed the heir apparent Emperor, in place of Go-Daigo, marched against Kasugi and took it, and sent Go-Daigo to honorable retirement on an island in the Inland Sea; his two sons were banished to Sado, on the desolate west coast. This ends act the first.

The two heroes of the struggle now come on the scene; first, Kusonoki Masashige, then Nitta Yoshisada, who was a member of the Minamoto family, and at first on the side of his Kamakura kin, but was won over by Prince Morinaga. Ashikaga Takauji was also sent against Kyoto, but he, too, went over to the ex-Emperor, not from any loyalty, as afterwards appeared, but from hatred of the Hojo Regents. Go-Daigo now escaped from his island, Morinaga gathered an army, and they all marched up against Kamakura. It was then that Nitta threw his sword into the sea, and, with the help of the sea-god, entered the city and destroyed it.

Go-Daigo, as ex-Emperor, now returned to Kyoto in triumph, and at once began his series of blunders; finally allowing Ashikaga to arrest Prince Morinaga on a charge of conspiracy and imprison him at Kamakura, where, after a year of confinement, he was secretly put to death. Ashikaga then proclaimed himself Shogun, and Go-Daigo sent Nitta and the rest against him and defeated him. He raised another army, in the name of the reigning Emperor, and defeated them. So it went, back and forth, year after year.

At last, in 1336, the loyalists found themselves hemmed in at Hyogo, an army coming against them by sea and another by land. Believing themselves overmatched, they prepared for a last desperate stand; and it was then that Masashige sent for his young son and bade him farewell, commanding him to escape and train himself to fight for his lord. The boy pleaded to be allowed to die with his father; the father sternly refused, declaring that duty required of him life and service. The scene is very dear to the Japanese dramatists—the boy's youth and distress, the father's sternness, breaking for a moment into tender messages and counsel, and the final calm parting, make together the Samurai's ideal of conduct. The son went away, in charge of faithful retainers, and did grow up to fight for his master, and to die for him a very few years later. Masashige went into the battle of the river-bed and fell there, with nearly all his following; and shortly after Nitta, too, was surprised and set upon by an overwhelming force, and, when mortally wounded, cut off his own head with his sword. Two years later Go-Daigo himself died, still clinging to the imperial insignia, which he had kept through all the struggle, and imploring his followers not to rest till the succession came back to his line—a command which they vainly tried to obey, at the cost of another twenty years of war.

There are several delightful excursions by rail from Kobe. The Japanese go most to Naka-yama-dera, one of the Thirty-three Holy Places, where there is a beautiful view and some hot springs; and to the pines of Takasago, beloved of poets, a place that is as the Rhine or the Trossachs in Japanese literature. More than one Nô drama is laid here, and many scenes of the Taira-Minamoto War of the Chrysanthemums. Here was the tragic death of Atsumori, the fair young knight whom Kumagai was forced to kill, lest he fall by a baser hand, and for whose sake he renounced the world. And prettiest legend of all, the Spirits of the Pine Trees, typifying a wedded couple in happy old age, who appear as two nice old people raking up pine needles in the sun. Their song in the Nô drama is sung at Japanese weddings, and is too pretty for me to resist quoting a fragment from Aston:

> "On the four seas
>   Still are the waves;
>   The world is at peace.
>   Soft blow the time-winds,
>   Rustling not the branches.

> "The dawn is near,
>   And the hoar-frost falls
>   On the fir tree's twigs,
>   But its leaves' dark green
>   Suffers no change.

> "Morning and evening
>   Beneath its shade
>   The leaves are swept away,
>   Yet they suffer no change."

(Verse.) "Though many a mile of mountain and river separate them, the ways of a husband and wife whose hearts respond together with mutual love are not far apart."

Only a few miles beyond Takasago is a fine castle in excellent repair—Himeji—which also goes back to poor Go-Daigo and his rebellious Ashikaga Shoguns; the five-storied keep, though, and the turrets and most of the building, are the work of Ota Nobunaga, Xavier's friend, a great general and brave and loyal gentleman, who brought order out of the lawlessness of the sixteenth century, and made the way ready for Tokugawa Ieyasu. More of the buildings remain than at Nagoya, and the situation is very lovely.

Last, farthest from Kobe and most frequented of foreigners, is Arima, fourteen hundred feet up in the bed of a dead volcano; reached by rail and chair (or afoot) over the Rokko-san pass, three thousand feet high. There are some hot springs, and the place is cool and pretty. Not a few come over from China to summer at Arima because of its convenience to the port, and it is a favorite haunt of Kobe and Kyoto people.

CHAPTER XVII.

MIYAJIMA AND THE INLAND SEA.

PROBABLY if the captain of a Pacific liner were asked about the charms of the Inland Sea, he would denounce it as the worst piece of water in his course, so winding it is, so beset with islands and rocks and shoals. But at least it is for the most part smooth and still, and few waters can well be lovelier to look upon, not even the long harbor of Bermuda, which it resembles considerably; though, instead of twenty miles, as at Hamilton harbor, it is here two hundred and thirty from Kobe to the straits of Shimonoseki — the end of the Inland Sea—and one hundred and fifty more around the west coast of Kiushiu to Nagasaki. The sea lies nearly east and west, shut in on the north by a long arm of the main island, and on the south by Shikoku, and closed at its lower end by Kiushiu, which makes, with the end of the main island, the narrow Shimonoseki straits. It is divided, moreover, into five great basins, separated by narrow, rocky channels, two of them so strewn with islets that the free passage is only a few hundred feet wide. The larger islands are very mountainous, their peaks running up to fifteen hundred feet; the greater part of them is not wooded, as the coast is farther north, but green, nevertheless, the year through, and all repeating emerald and opal and violet in the shining water. Tropical the sea is not, only a little warmer, a little softer than the rest of Japan, and by just so much the lovelier than even Odawara or Matsushima or Volcano bay.

Part of the charm is the picturesque life along the shore, the brown villages and the rice-fields, and the flock of fishing boats, beached in rows along the sheltered coves, or stealing in and out among the narrow channels. The ways of the people are exceedingly primitive; those who are afraid Japan is "getting spoiled" need only take one of the local boats among the islands to find themselves quite away from modern life.

Just beyond the turn of cape Maiko, as you leave Kobe to enter the sea, the island of Awaji lies almost across from shore to shore, leaving only a narrow channel at either end. According to tradition, Awaji was the very beginning of Japan, the first-born of the creator pair Isanagi and Isanami; and in the southern part of it they show the first islet piled up from the drops of mud on Isanagi's spear—a mound in the midst of low fields. The upper end of the island is a long, mountainous point, thrust out like a finger toward Kobe; the lower end is exceedingly rich and fertile, and very populous, the people living partly by fishing and partly by farming, as they do everywhere along the coast.

Shimonoseki

On Awaji, they say, there is the tomb of an Emperor who died there in exile. The Empress Koken had reigned before him, and having no heir, she had adopted him and abdicated in his favor; but apparently he was not sufficiently submissive to her will, and, moreover, she had a favorite, a priest named Dokyo—this was in the latter part of the Nara period, when the Buddhist priests had great influence at Court. At any rate, she dethroned and exiled the Emperor, and took the throne herself again. After some months, he tried to escape from Awaji, but was caught and brought back, and died there within the year, some said by assassination. The priest was made prime minister, and affected the state of a prince; and his followers began to say openly that if he were Emperor, the country would be prosperous. Upon this, one of the nobles consulted an oracle at one of the shrines, and the answer was, " No subject can become an Emperor; the difference is fundamental. Let the evil-doer be banished." This oracle greatly incensed Dokyo, and he had the venturesome noble exiled; but the Empress took the warning to heart, and chose a new heir from the imperial house.

After passing Awaji there is a wide open space, the next to the largest of the five *nada*, or basins, into which the sea is divided. Where it narrows again, the important town of Okayama lies on the right; it used to be on the sea, but is now five miles inland, and a small port has grown up for convenience on the har-

bor. The castle garden at Okayama is famous as the
most beautiful in all Japan; it is large enough to contain real lakes and hills, and rocks and streams and
bridges, and besides the usual pines and maples and
flowering trees, there are some beautiful palmettoes,
growing in perfection in the warm, equable temperature.

The castle of Takamatsu, on the Shikoku side, was
attacked by Hideyoshi, who laid siege to it in a remarkable way. The castle is surrounded on three sides by
water, a lake and two small rivers, so that it was
nearly impossible for an army to get close enough to
storm it; and Hideyoshi decided that the only thing
to do was to drown it out. He therefore set his men
to dam the rivers, and the water gradually rose and
rose, till the besieged prince had enough, and offered
to make peace. Just at this moment Nobunaga, for
whom Hideyoshi was acting, was set upon and killed
by one of his generals. Hideyoshi sent word to the
lord of Takamatsu, saying that Nobunaga's death did
away with the treaty, and that he might either renew
the peace, or fight; it was quite immaterial to Hideyoshi
which he decided. The lord naturally preferred peace
to any more water, and his castle was allowed to stand.

To a Japanese the whole reach echoes with memories of great fightings, clan against clan, Kiyomori of
Taira slaying the Minamoto, Yoshitsune of Minamoto
annihilating the Taira at Dan-no-ura; memories, too,
of Xavier's mission at Yamaguchi, and again of the
"Shimonoseki Affair" of 1863, when the Daimyo of

Choshiu tried to close the straits to foreign vessels, and the Powers responded by bombarding his forts for three days with eighteen ships. As Black rather quaintly remarks, "Choshiu was converted"—namely, to the necessity of learning the game before trying to play it.

All the world knows how well they had learned that game by 1895, when Marquis Ito and Li Hung Chang met at Shimonoseki to arrange the terms of peace with China; and it knows, too, how the three bullies—Russia, France and Germany—forced Japan to give up Port Arthur, in order that Russia might take it as soon as she was ready. Japan submitted to the insult, because her statesmen knew that she was in no position to undertake another war at that moment, even against less overwhelming odds; but she will not soon forget, and England and America may some day have to regret that they did not so much as enter a protest against that injustice.

Pleasanter memories belong to Hiroshima, a lively town standing a little back from an excellent harbor, from which the troops embarked for Korea and China. The Emperor spent the winter of 1894–'95 at Hiroshima, enduring some quite real discomfort in order to cheer and encourage his soldiers. The town is prettily situated in a little plain sheltered by hills that lie around and behind, and looking out on a bay dotted with islands. The largest of these islands draws pilgrims from all over the empire, for it is one of the

San-kei, or "Three most beautiful places" in Japan, the sacred mountain island Miyajima.

There is something half unreal about Miyajima; in part it is the feeling that comes to one most often in misty dawns and twilights, a sense of something not quite of earth, lent for a moment from some dream-world just beyond our ken. Partly, like the dawn-mystery, it is an effect of vagueness and mere physical loveliness, partly, too, of a certain consciousness of being set apart, dedicated. *Numen in est,* said the Roman of such haunted spots. Ages since men believed in this divine presence, and their faith has been handed on and multiplied in millions of devout souls, till the influence of it lingers, as burnt-out incense lingers in the very air. What vision began it? Was it the spell of the fair island set in a pale sea, or the flash of phosphorescent ripples breaking at midnight over its wide sands? One would like to fancy so, would like to forget that primitive man is not apt to be over-sensitive to beauty of landscape, that there is far more of fear than joy in his religious awe. And the traditions of Miyajima point back to a worship very primitive and very ancient, perhaps pre-Japanese. Like ancient Delos, and like Kinkwazan in the north of Japan, no one may be born, no one may die on the sacred soil. The sick must be rowed across to the nearest shore—or at least this was so in the old days; now many rules are relaxed even in sacred places.

In truth, since the beginning of their history the

Japanese have been proverbially sensitive to natural beauty, and thereby, no doubt, the fame of Miyajima's sanctity was much enhanced; still its great renown dates only from the time—in the twelfth century—when Kiyomori of Taira won a great battle hereabouts, and having hewn the Minamoto hip and thigh, built here a splendid temple in remembrance. Since then many princes have added to its adornment, till it is one of the richest shrines in Japan.

It should surely have been the temple of a sea god. The great camphor-wood torii which marks the entrance stands far out in the bay, and the temple buildings wade, as it were, into the water; at low tide you may pass on stepping-stones from shrine to shrine, but at flood the sea sweeps in across the sands, lapping against the slender piles supporting galleries and bridges, until the whole group seems afloat, like a fleet of small ships moored against the shore.

At festival times, instead of a sacred car, gaily-decorated boats wind at night in long procession among the shrines, bearing the emblems of the gods; and hundreds of lanterns star the galleries and trail long ribbons of light in the water below, while every wavelet breaking against the piers ripples back in cool phosphorescent light. No dogs are allowed on the island, and tame deer wander about the shore, and stray out on the balconies to nibble the paper from the very lanterns.

Behind the shore the mountain rises steeply to eighteen hundred feet, thickly covered with a forest of magnificent trees, and broken by romantic gorges and valleys. There are many temples on the slopes, and at the very top a shrine where a lamp has been burning for centuries.

The last reach of the Inland Sea is an open sheet, some sixty or seventy miles long, almost without an island. The wide Bungo channel leads from it into the Pacific, between Shikoku and Kiûshiu, and on the other side the strait of Shimonoseki makes the narrowest of gateways to the Japan Sea. Bold headlands guard it on either side, and an island lies directly across the outer end, forcing vessels to make a sharp turn directly under the cliffs and the masked batteries that tunnel their green sides; and through this narrow channel the tide races with great speed, making it difficult for vessels to anchor on the northern shore. On the other the little town of Mogi has a good harbor, and has grown into quite an important place since the Kiushiu railroad was built to it, though it is less picturesque and attractive than Shimonoseki, on the main island, and has not the same soft, sheltered atmosphere.

Here in these swift tides, say the fisher people, pale faces rise sometimes from the waves, and flashes of armor, and black, disheveled hair floating on the water; and the forms stretch their hands, crying in ghostly voices for the loan of a dipper. Then the

fishermen hasten to give it; but first they are careful
to knock out the bottom, else the spirits would quickly
bale the sea into their boat and swamp it.   Most of
all at the Feast of the Dead they come, for these are
the ghosts of the Taira, who were drowned or slain in
that last terrible battle; and here at Dan-no-ura,
where the bay narrows into the strait, is the place
where they fought.

These provinces along the upper shore of the Inland
Sea were Kiyomori's territory, and his followers held
many castles here and there on the coast.   But Yoshitsune had driven them from Hyogo and destroyed
the palace that Kiyomori built; and he had pursued
them from place to place, as they fled with their wives
and children, and with the young Emperor Antoku,
Kiyomori's grandson.   Reaching the shore at Dan-
no-ura, they took to their ships, hoping to escape to
Kiushiu; but Yoritomo's ships overtook them, and
crowded as they were with women and children, they
made a last desperate fight.   At first the Taira onset
was so fierce that the Minamoto were thrown into
confusion; but Yoshitsune urged his followers with
mingled taunts and encouragement, and they drove
their boats up close, and leaping among the Taira,
slew men and women and children without mercy.   It
was when she saw that all was lost that Kiyomori's
widow took her grandson, the child Emperor, in her
arms, bearing with him the mirror, the sword and the
jewel, and sprang into the sea.   A small remnant

fled to Kiushiu; they were relentlessly pursued, but a few hid themselves in the mountains, where their descendants are said to be living still, poor, proud and suspicious, resenting any interference from strangers. But others say a portion of them escaped far over the sea and settled in Mexico, and that they were the ancestors of the Mexican Indians.

I am not sure whether it was in this fight or another that one of the combatants raised as a standard a fan, on which was painted the red sun, believing that no one would dare shoot at it for fear of striking the sacred symbol. But one archer was seen to bend his bow, and as the arrow passed, the fan fluttered from the pole into the sea. Then every one was astonished, and rowing to the fan, they picked it up, and found the archer had not touched the fan itself, but had shot away the pin that held it to the pole.

Another arrow, shot by the Minamoto, was plucked out and returned by a Taira bowman, piercing one of the Minamoto men. Yoshitsune cried to them to shoot it back. The archer took it, and said, "It is too weak;" and taking out another, shot two men on the Taira ship. Greatly elated, the Minamoto sent a shower of arrows against the Taira, killing many. For months afterward, they say, the fishermen drew up in their nets or found on the shore the armor and bodies of the slain.

Another bit of the history of this region belongs much farther back. On the northern shore of the strait is a tomb, which is said to be that of the Emperor Chuai, whom the energetic Empress Jingo tried to rouse to that expedition against Korea that she afterwards accomplished herself. According to the chronicles, one day when the Emperor was playing on his lute, the spirit of divination came upon the Empress, and she prophesied of a wonderful land to the west, which the gods bade him go forth to conquer. And the Emperor was moved by her words; but one of the high lords of the palace said, "Westward, so far as the eye can reach, is no land, but only water and sky. This is a dread message, my Sovereign; cease not to play on thine august lute." Then Chuai's hand wandered again over the strings; but, of a sudden, the sound died and he sank down, smitten of an unknown disease, and all were awe-struck, believing the gods had slain him because he did not obey the heavenly vision. But the Empress called together the men of war and bade them make ready an expedition, for that she herself would lead them; and they went forth to the western land and conquered it. And the memory of this conquest of the Empress Jingo was revived in 1895, for the encouragement of the soldiers who sailed out from Shimonoseki to defend Korea against Chinese encroachment.

CHAPTER XVIII.

NAGASAKI.

"The Mitsu Bishi Dockyard and Engine Works, Nagasaki. No. 1 dock takes vessels up to a length of 500 feet, and of a draught of 26 feet. New granite dock, patent slip, shipbuilding yard. The engine works are extensive, and contain machinery of the latest type. Boilers, land and marine, built to order. Telegraphic address, 'Dock, Nagasaki.'"

SEEING an advertisement like this, one naturally expects to find the whole town of the same bustling, mechanical order; or, at least, as modern and enterprising as Osaka. But nothing could be farther from the facts. The docks and iron works lie apart, and over most of the place there broods an atmosphere of sleepy calm. The foreign part of the town is not large; it lies mostly along the bay, where there are several warehouses and a few hotels, among them one really good new one, built lately. The residences are on the hill overlooking the bay, and the Japanese town runs out in the other direction. Although it was the one entrance to Japan for a couple of centuries, and has been an open port for more than forty years, Nagasaki has been left behind by Yokohama and Kobe, and exports little to foreign markets; indeed,

320

Nagasaki Harbor

if it were not for the convenience of coaling, it is doubtful whether the liners would call here at all. Nagasaki coal is cheap, because the mines are not far away; but it is soft and dirty, and decidedly inferior to the Hokkaido article. The vessels coal from barges in the harbor, and women do much of the work of carrying baskets, a few men shoveling and directing. For once, the babies are left at home.

Nagasaki harbor is one of the most beautiful in the world. It lies near the head of a deep inlet, almost steep and narrow enough for a Norway fiord, surrounded by hills several hundred feet high, that are covered with forests of maple and evergreen oak and great camphor trees. There is not much space between the water and the steep slopes of the hills; the houses of the town have soon to begin climbing, roof above roof, like a city tilted on edge. The docks are on the far side of the harbor. They were the first in Japan, having been built by Dutch engineers, commissioned by the Daimyo of Hizen; the Shogun's government bought them from him; and, after the Restoration, they were turned over to the imperial government and finally sold by it to the great banking and commercial firm, the Mitsu Bishi Consolidated Company, somewhere in the eighties. A year or so ago the Company built an ocean liner of six thousand tons, with all the latest improvements in water-tight compartments and plans and machinery, and her mate is being constructed now.

If Nagasaki was chosen as the one port for foreign trade with an eye to keeping the strangers well away from the rest of the country, the selection could hardly have been better. The place lies on a ragged, mountainous peninsula, in the province of Hizen, which again is a sort of projection from the northwest corner of the island of Kiushiu. To have landed an army there and attempted to march into the country would have been worse than useless; any one trying it would have been held in a trap of mountains, as Ieyasu probably realized when he gave his sanction to the traders.

The Portuguese account of their first visit to Japan has to be taken with a grain of salt. They say that, in 1542, three shipwrecked Portuguese were taken up by a Chinese vessel, which, in turn, came to grief, and was driven on an island off the southern coast of Kiushiu; an educated Chinese interpreted for the party, by writing, as he could do quite easily, since the Japanese use the Chinese characters to write their own language, as well as the numerous words and expressions borrowed from the Chinese. They employ the ideographs to render Japanese words of the same meaning—as if we should be able to put down a sign meaning "dog," which a German could read *Hund* and a Frenchman *chien*. Through this interpreter they obtained what they needed, and made a return gift of guns, which were afterwards forwarded to the Shogun.

A few years later Mendez Pinto made a visit, with

several other Portuguese, in a Chinese ship—or one that claimed to be Chinese. They landed on a large island, directly south of Kiushiu, and the Daimyo received them with kindness and much curiosity, and apparently asked many questions, which they answered, without troubling greatly about facts, in whatever way they thought most likely to enhance the glory of their country in his eyes. Presents of firearms were the most acceptable gifts; but, unluckily, the Prince's son nearly brought them all to destruction, by trying experiments when Pinto was not by. The arquebus exploded and the youth was seriously injured. Fortunately Pinto was allowed to attend him—having already showed his medical skill by curing the Daimyo of gout—and the young Prince recovered so rapidly that Pinto was honored more than ever. He taught the armorers how to make gunpowder, and they imitated his firearms so well that, in the five months that he stayed, he declares they made six hundred guns.

Again Pinto came on a trading expedition, and this time he took away two Japanese, who ran down to the shore pursued by horsemen, and, wading out into the surf, begged to be taken on board. Pinto took them to the Portuguese settlements, where they were educated and converted, and afterwards returned with Xavier to Japan. One of the two was the famous Paul Anjiro.

Xavier's party went to Kagoshima in Kiushiu, which was Anjiro's birthplace. The Prince of Sat-

suma allowed them to remain, and gradually they began
to preach, Anjiro's family being the first converts.
Xavier's delight in the kindly reception is well known,
and his praises of the people, their gentleness and
courtesy. The beauty and earnestness of his own character must have carried conviction, and there can be no
doubt that there were very many who truly accepted
Christianity as far as they understood it, although the
interest and apparent encouragement of the princes
probably belonged to their material and not to their
spiritual gifts. Xavier got permission to go to
Kyoto, and did make the journey there afoot, under
great physical difficulties; but the Ashikaga troubles
were absorbing everybody, and he could make no
headway, so that, after two years spent in Japan, he
left some priests and lay brethren at Yamaguchi, on
the Inland Sea, and returned to establish a mission in
China, where he died shortly after.

Nobunaga now appears on the scene, with his deadly
hatred of the Buddhists and his desire to humiliate
them in any possible way. The Christian fathers
basked in his favor and thought him in a fair way to
conversion, but it is evident that, like Xavier and many
others since, they took toleration and politeness for
interest in religion. Nobunaga allowed them to build
a church at Kyoto, and another at his own castle
town of Akechi, on lake Biwa, evidently for the sake
of thwarting the monks.

Hideyoshi also at first encouraged the Christians,

but afterwards suddenly turned on them and issued an order for all priests and teachers to depart within twenty days; and though the traders were still allowed to come, they were forbidden to bring any foreigner who belonged to a religious order. The Japanese Christians, however, were not yet interfered with.

The most plausible reason for this order is the usually accepted one, that Hideyoshi heard of the boastings of a Portuguese sea captain, who said his king easily conquered such countries as Japan; that the way he did was first to send out missionaries, who converted the people to his religion, and then to send an army, which joined with the converts and got possession of the land without trouble. The boast seemed so close to the facts that Hideyoshi lost no time in putting a stop to it.

Meanwhile some of the Daimyo along the Inland Sea provinces had been converted, and were more intolerant than the priests of the native faiths; destroying temples and taking from the Buddhists their revenues and estates. One lord offered his people the choice between Christianity and banishment. This, of course, stirred up the wrath of the Buddhist priesthood against them.

When Ieyasu succeeded to the Shogunate, he also at first allowed the Jesuit fathers to come to the country, and even gave an audience at Kyoto to the bishop; but shortly after he sent out a proclamation, banishing them and forbidding any one to embrace Christianity.

Before this time the Dutch and English had arrived, and were busily trying to get their share of trade. The first comers were the English pilot, Adams, and his Dutch captain and half a dozen Dutch seamen, who were driven on the southern coast in a destitute condition. They were cared for, and the captain and others sent home on Chinese vessels, but Adams was retained to build ships and lighthouses for Ieyasu. A Dutch ship followed soon after and took home a promise of trade and residence and protection, on the strength of which they sent out another ship and established a factory at Hirado. The English followed; but, as Murray says, though these two nations could combine against the Spanish and Portuguese, "it was not easy for either of them to look on with complacency while the other secured for itself advantages in the matter of trade supremacy." After an expensive struggle the English gave it up and retired. Meanwhile the Dutch cleverly worked upon the Japanese fears of Spanish encroachment, and gave a handle to the Tokugawa, who did not wish Satsuma to gain the advantage that foreign trade must have given them. The Spanish and Portuguese were finally ousted entirely, and the Dutch alone permitted to trade at the one port of Nagasaki, well out of everybody's way.

Even so, the conditions were exact and humiliating

for the Dutch, and could only have been borne for the sake of the immense profits to be gained. Their factory was on a small artificial island in the harbor, called Deshima; only a certain number of Hollanders might come, and but one expedition in the year. They were not permitted to preach or teach, or to give or sell books, or to have communication with any Japanese except the interpreters and other officials appointed to take care of them and transact their business with the rest. Marvelously beautiful pieces of porcelain reached Europe through Dutch hands in those days, and such wonderful pieces of lacquer as are preserved at the Queen's palace, the "House in the Wood" at the Hague; besides untold quantities of gold, silver and copper, then cheap and plenty as compared with later times, when this drain of metals began to tell on the country. It is very certain also that very many books and much knowledge reached the insatiable Japanese students, in spite of the rigid prohibitions.

In Ieyasu's last years he began a determined effort to destroy Christianity, and this policy was continued by Iemitsu, who added a course of terrible persecutions. A price was set upon every Christian; children denounced parents and parents children, while others suffered torture and died for their faith. Of the forty thousand Christians said to have been in Nagasaki, at the end of three years the governor flattered himself there was not one left; all had either recanted or fled, or had been put to death. Finding some still lingered, to finish things the authorities invented the ordeal of trampling on the cross; the officers made a house-to-house inspection, requiring every inmate to appear and tread on a rude crucifix brought for the purpose. Whoever refused was sent to the torture.

In desperation over these persecutions, the remaining Christians of Nagasaki and the neighborhood joined with the retainers of the Daimyo of Arima, whose exactions and cruelty had driven them to revolt. They took possession of a strong castle in Shimabara, and fortified and provisioned it for a long siege, knowing that if they were taken they would receive no mercy either for themselves or for the wives and children shut up with them. A large army was sent against the castle, but could make no impression; then the Shogun sent to the Dutch, and asked first for gunpowder, then for cannon, and finally for ships; informing them that if they complied, it would be much to the advantage of their trade in the future. All were sent to him, and two Dutch ships came and bombarded the castle for days, though with little effect. It was at last taken by assault, and every man, woman and child put to death by the Shogun's express order.

From this time Christianity was supposed to be entirely exterminated; yet it is now known that it lingered secretly in remote places, chiefly around Nagasaki; and the Roman Church has found least difficulty in making its way there, as if the people had an inherited toleration for the faith.

When Commodore Perry arrived, all his transactions with the government had to pass through Dutch, that being the only language the Japanese interpreters understood. Soon after, the prohibitions against Western books were relaxed, and the study of languages even encouraged; then a naval school was opened at Nagasaki, which was naturally one of the first ports thrown open to foreign trade and residence. This school was opened in 1855, under the care of the Dutch, and forty students were permitted to attend, selected from eight of the chief clans; later twenty more were added. One of the most prominent pupils was the late Count Katsu, whose family were Hatamoto, retainers of the Shogun—he who took the first Japanese ship to San Francisco. In his "History of the (Japanese) Navy" Count Katsu tells of the great difficulty the students had in comprehending what the professors tried to teach them.

"The daily recitation hours began at eight o'clock in the morning, and finished at four in the afternoon. Besides these indoor lessons, there was naval practice on the ships. It was not permitted to take notes of anything, but the students had to learn all by heart. Having not yet acquired a full knowledge of foreign languages, we were obliged to learn through interpreters, which was very difficult both for professors and students. Even those students who had an excellent knowledge of Chinese classics, and were highly esteemed by the other pupils, could hardly get on; much less the ordinary pupils. After hard struggles and patient application for months, we were able by degrees to understand the lessons, and felt hopeful." Some years later a naval school was established at Tokyo, and the Count was placed at its head; and shortly after the Nagasaki school was discontinued.

The people of Nagasaki being less unused to foreigners, there was no great opposition to them there, as at Yokohama, and students soon flocked to the place, eager to acquire all the learning of the West, but particularly languages and science. Many of the men who have made new Japan studied at Nagasaki in those days, and not a few with a bright young Hollander who had come out in 1859 as a missionary under an American board. Of the many foreigners who have helped Japan according to their ability, the greatest, wisest, and therewith the gentlest and most unassuming of all, was Dr. Guido F. Verbeck.

Books were scarce in those days, and the eager students no less impecunious than they are to-day. A certain young man named Fukuzawa possessed a prize —a Webster's dictionary—which he is said to have bought by selling his mosquito net; and if you want to know what that means, spend a warm night on the New Jersey coast when the wind blows off the swamps. Fukuzawa studied his dictionary all day and till ten o'clock in the evening, and then a friend of his borrowed it and finished the night. This young man actually made, not one, but two copies of the work,

Native Boats in Nagasaki Harbor

one of which he sold; his family cherish the other.
Count Katsu likewise made two copies of Webster,
one of which he sold for thirty yen, an exceedingly
useful sum for a poor student. And yet people say
the Japanese have no perseverance. This Fukuzawa
was he who afterwards opened a school in a private
house in Tokyo, which grew into the great college in
the suburb of Mita, and has influenced thousands of
the present leaders of Japan. Count Okuma, one of
the greatest, if not the greatest of the Meiji statesmen
who are still living, was long a pupil of Dr. Verbeck
at Nagasaki.

There are many beautiful excursions along the
shores of the bay, kuruma rides and walks, and also
a number of short steamer trips; there is good bathing, too, through all the long summer. The town
contains nothing of great interest, except the lovely
views; there are several temples of local celebrity,
but none of much beauty. They stand for the most
part far up the hill, and above them is a grove of
magnificent camphor trees, with great gnarled boles
that might be any age. The hills and the sea air
make Nagasaki pleasantly cool even in summer, and
those who live there claim that it is not only the most
beautiful, but has the best climate of all the five Open
Ports.

CHAPTER XIX.

KAGOSHIMA.

" Poverty makes great men ;
  Deeds are born in distress.
  Through snow are the plum-blossoms white,
  Through frosts are the maples red.
  If a man know Heaven's will,
  Can he live in slothful ease?

" A man succeeds by overcoming himself, and fails by loving him-self.

" In the Book of Saden it is written, Virtue is the source of which wealth is the outcome.   Wealth comes by replenishing the land and giving peace to the people.   The small man aims at profiting him-self; the great man at profiting the people.   The one is selfishness, and it decays; the other is public-spiritedness, and it prospers.

" Civilization is not fine houses and beautiful garments, but an effectual working of righteousness."

—Saigo's " Essays."   Uchimura's translation.

KIUSHIU, the southernmost of the four large islands of Japan, seems to have gathered into itself the essen-tial characteristics of all.   Lying almost in the fork of the Black Current, its lower end has far more heat and rain than Tokyo or Kyoto, though the difference in latitude is hardly more than between New York and Washington ; while, on the other hand, the upper

332

end is exposed to the northwest winds and their bracing chill. The centre of the island is a mass of mountains, and the only real lowland is along the many little rivers that flow down to the coast. The side toward the Pacific is uncommonly little broken, for Japan, but the other three sides are cut up into deep bays and islands and peninsulas, all mountainous and all green and picturesque. The principalities from which Kiushiu gets its name of "Nine Provinces" were all ranged around the coast, mountains forming nearly all of the dividing lines.

It is only a hundred miles as the crow flies from the northwest coast of Kiushiu to Korea, and between lie three good-sized islands and a number of small ones, all belonging to Japan. Tsushima, the largest, which lies just half-way over, is named in the *Kojiki* as one of the elder children of Isanagi and Isanami. And to the south of southern Kiushiu the Lu Chu islands stretch like a line of stepping-stones toward Formosa and the Malay peninsula. They were considered a dependency of the Prince of Satsuma. By these two routes the migrating tribes entered who made the Japanese race; and Kiushiu is full of traditions of the Divine Ancestors and the early Emperors. Not unnaturally, too, they are represented as leaving that country and coming to Yamato; for it was there that civilization developed, and that records began to be preserved. In the beginning of the Kyoto period, when Michizane was exiled to

Dazaifu, all Kiushiu was a half-barbarous country, little influenced by the Chinese civilization that had already transformed the region at the head of the Inland Sea.

It was on the coast, only a few miles from Dazaifu, that Kublai Khan's armada was utterly defeated and destroyed. This was the second invasion; the first was several years earlier, and that, too, was driven back, chiefly by a storm, after doing much damage in the midway islands, Tsushima and Iki. The defences, hastily raised along the coast of Kiushiu, were mere parapets of earth or loose stones, breast high, and only intended as a shelter for the bowmen. The Japanese expected to fight hand to hand, in single combat, as they had always done; but the Mongols landed in compact bodies and bore down the knights by mere weight of numbers, while from the ships they discharged poisoned arrows and stones from catapults, as the Venetians had taught them, and "balls of fire, that exploded as they fell." Still the Japanese slew many, and at last a bowman shot down their leader, a tall man in red armor; and a storm that night destroying many of their ships, they sailed away.

More embassies followed, but were either returned with scornful messages or beheaded at Kamakura or Dazaifu; and meanwhile the Regent, Hojo Tokimune, built ships and prepared better defences. The second expedition was enormous; the Japanese say there were over one hundred thousand ships sailing from Korea.

Again they landed at Tsushima and Iki, and swept everything before them; but when they reached Kiushiu they were met by a considerable fleet of small, swift boats, which hung on their flanks and made sudden dashes, doing much damage. Various exploits are recorded. Two brothers went out with a handful of followers, set fire to five junks, and came safely back with twenty-one Chinese heads. Another ship went out, and, by cutting her masts and letting them fall across the Chinese vessel, the knights boarded her. This was the kind of fighting they understood, and on the crowded decks the Mongols were no match for the swift Japanese swordsmen. But again it was the storm that finished the work—one of the sudden terrible typhoons of the Japan Sea, rising from a clear sky; or, so they believe, in response to the Emperor's prayers at the holy shrine of Ise. The clumsy, crowded junks were driven against each other, "like bulls," and ground to pieces, or dashed against the coast; those that the sea cast up the Japanese slew. A few escaped to the islands; but the Japanese pursued and killed them, except three, who were spared to carry home the news to their Emperor. The prestige of the throne was considerably increased, for all the people believed that the Emperor's prayers had saved them.

Splendid camphor trees have always been the glory of Kiushiu, and in old times they were carefully guarded; but since property has gone into the hands of many individual owners, the trees are being grievously wasted. In some parts of the country they use wild tea, letting the bushes grow in waste places, and burning off the shrub when it gets too high. Naturally, the tea is very poor stuff, and only used for making the coarse "block tea," put up for export to the Russian peasants. Sulphur is another product of Kiushiu, for the island has a full supply of volcanoes and boiling springs. The great volcano, Aso San, has an immense crater, ten to fourteen miles across, inside of which there are a great number of villages, besides a modern crater sending out frequent small showers of ashes. The mountain is over five thousand feet high, and two small rivers flow out of the crater through a break in the wall, which the mountain god obligingly kicked open to make an outlet for the water and leave the fields dry for the use of men. Aso San is nearly in the centre of the northern half of Kiushiu, about twenty miles from Kumamoto, the capital of Higo, which Hearn has made so familiar. The college in which he served still prospers, and the students have the reputation of being fine fellows, albeit somewhat rough and quick-tempered, as is the Kumamoto way.

The truth is that Kiushiu has always kept a rather independent attitude toward the rest of the country. Not that the princes were disloyal to the Emperor; they were at least as faithful as those who controlled the throne; but they did not readily come under the sway of the Kwanto. One of the tasks Hideyoshi

set himself was the conquest of Kiushiu; this done,
he was ready to attack Korea and China. And of all
the Daimyo, Satsuma was the most restive—the least
inclined to be submissive to the Tokugawa Shoguns.

Certainly they were well out of the Shogun's way.
The province occupies the lower western corner of the
island; its southern part, Satsuma proper, lying
between the Japan Sea and a great arm of the Pacific,
forty miles long and ten wide, which divides the lower
half of Satsuma from the neighboring province of
Osumi, which also belonged to Satsuma after the fifteenth century. Kagoshima, the Daimyo's castle
town, is on this arm of the sea, directly opposite the
volcanic island of Sakurajima. Tradition has it that
on the top of this mountain island, Ninigi, grandson
of the Sun Goddess, landed, when he came down
from heaven to subdue and govern Japan; and on the
place where he touched the earth he set up a heavenly spear, which is still there, just where he thrust it
into the ground. It is made of bronze, and certainly
is very old. Perhaps the sword which Amaterasu
bestowed on him was a better one, and more worthy
of being left to his descendants. This region is warm
and wet, and on the lower parts of the hills they raise
a great deal of sugar-cane, oranges and grape-fruit,
which last are known as pommeloes by the foreigners
in the Far East. These southern ones are very good;
those grown farther north are apt to be pithy and
tasteless. For some reason, no one raises lemons in

Japan; all that one can get there are imported from the Bonin islands, or even from Honolulu.

The only way to reach Kagoshima is by sea, in a long day from Nagasaki, or in forty hours from Kobe. This last is said to be an exceedingly beautiful trip, but as there is only Japanese food to be had, only those who are well used to the country are wise to venture. The other way takes you out of the deep pocket of Nagasaki harbor, down the west coast in view of mountainous islands and the lower, yet greener shore of Satsuma, around Cape Nomo, along the southern coast, and so into the long gulf leading up to the port. Just at the entrance of the gulf, on the Satsuma side, is the beautiful active volcano Kaimondake, known as the Satsuma Fuji. The form is really almost exactly like the real Fuji, only on a smaller scale. It is a little over three thousand feet high, and three sides of it rise directly out of the sea. On both sides of the gulf the mountains are very near, and even in the harbor the water is so deep that vessels cannot anchor except close in shore.

Kagoshima is a picturesque, attractive town, with wide, clean streets and an active, industrious population. It was here, or at least in a certain suburb of the town, that the famous Satsuma ware was made, under the express patronage of the Daimyo, for whom all the best pieces were produced, either for his own use or to serve as gifts, of which the princes had always to prepare a goodly store for all sorts of occasions. A little of the pottery is made there still, but no longer as in feudal times.

Most of the city is comparatively new, rebuilt since 1863, when the British fleet of seven vessels bombarded it, as the only way to obtain satisfaction for the death of the Englishman Richardson—he who insisted on riding in among the Prince of Satsuma's train on the Tokaido, and was cut down by Satsuma's retainers. It was in the middle of August, and a furious typhoon was blowing, but the ships destroyed all the Satsuma batteries and burned most of the town. After this the Prince of Satsuma saw the necessity of yielding for the present, and of studying the ways of foreign warfare. This attitude of Satsuma had much to do with the policy of the imperial government towards the foreign Powers after the Restoration.

The Satsuma men are the Spartans of Japan; they have always prided themselves on being made of sterner stuff than other Samurai, and to this day they are simpler in their habits and more blunt in manner. Satsuma students in Tokyo love to go about in wintry weather clad in the shortest possible garment, the heavy blue and white linen or cotton of their native province, and with bare feet thrust into a pair of geta. Indeed, in the old days the practice of music was especially enjoined on Satsuma Samurai as a means of softening their fiery natures.

There is a tradition that during the period of Yoritomo's exile, while he was half guest, half prisoner in the territory of the Daimyo of Izu, he secretly married that prince's daughter. When it was discovered, the Daimyo was greatly enraged. Yoritomo escaped to another province, and his wife and child were condemned to death; but a faithful retainer saved the boy, who grew up and became the ancestor of the Shimadzu family, the lords of Satsuma. Whether this is true or not, the family dates from Yoritomo's century, and by Hideyoshi's time had taken possession of a good deal of their neighbors' property, as well as their own. Part of this Hideyoshi took from them, but left them Osumi and most of Hyuga, besides Satsuma itself. Their power at this time and later rose largely from their contact with the outside world. It was on the island of Tanegashima that Pinto first landed with his gifts of firearms, and trade with China and Korea also flourished during all that period, till the Tokugawa put a stop to it by closing the country absolutely. Repressed for three centuries, since the Restoration Satsuma has led the way in almost every change, and the three allied clans who brought about the Restoration—Satsuma, Choshu and Tosa—still furnish the strongest and ablest representatives in the government.

Riding out from Kagoshima to the cemeteries, one cannot but be impressed with the appalling sacrifice of life those stones represent. It seems as if half a generation of Satsuma men must have fallen, and almost as many from the rest of the provinces; and with them lies the best and bravest of all, the great General Saigo.

Saigo was a typical Satsuma Samurai, blunt, unpolished, a man of iron, yet tender as a woman; above all, a man who followed absolutely the dictates of his conscience. It is said that he was a slow, silent boy, so stupid-looking that his companions nicknamed him the idiot. He was still only a child when he was called upon to witness the *harakiri* of a distant relative, who, before lifting the dagger, spoke to the boy of a life of devotion to his master and his country. Young Saigo wept, and the impression never left him.

Even as a boy, he loved to roam by himself in the mountains, and wrestling and all muscular sports delighted him. He studied the stoical Zen philosophy, "to kill my too keen sensibilities," he told a friend; but the greatest influence of his life was the doctrine of the Chinese Wan Yang Ming, of whom Uchimura says, "Of all Chinese philosophers, he came nearest to the Christian faith, in his great doctrines of conscience and benign but inexorable heavenly laws," and Dr. Nitobé, "Western readers will easily recognize in his writings many parallels to the New Testament."

While still a young man, Saigo went up to Yedo, and there came under the influence of one of the Mito clan, from whom he probably absorbed the dominating ideas of his life—a united Japan, and the extension of its dominion over Korea, and perhaps even China, "sc as to enable the land to stand on equal terms with Europe."

From these two ideals he never wavered. When he led the imperial army against the Tokugawa, it was to put an end to the dual system and unite the empire under its rightful head; and he was willing even to tolerate foreign ways for a time, in order that Japan might learn all that was necessary to make her as strong as the European powers.

His first quarrel with the government came soon. Korea had not received the notice of the changes in Japan with proper respect; Saigo wished to chastise her, and bring her into subjection to Japan. He wished to convey an embassy to Korea, and if she did not show the proper spirit, he was ready to lead an army to instruct her. At first the leaders of the Cabinet (of which he was a member) were persuaded by him; but just then Baron Iwakura started on his embassy to the Vienna exposition, and came back deeply imbued with the need of internal development along European lines; the Korea expedition was put aside, and Saigo resigned in disgust and went back home, there to brood over the demoralizing effect of Western influences—which were only too apparent—and to train a band of young men who came to him and put themselves under his teaching, both as general and moralist. It was these young men, and not Saigo himself, who precipitated the Satsuma rebellion. He joined it, in the faint hope of being able to prevent what he firmly

Japanese Junk

believed to be the ruin of his country, and his prestige
and ability made it an eight months' struggle before
the government army finally routed them at Nobeoka,
where eight thousand gave themselves up with the
town. Saigo and a few others fought their way back
to Kagoshima, "to be buried in their fathers' graves,"
and entrenched themselves on the castle hill over
against the town for a last resistance. There, while
waiting for the attack, Saigo plunged into a game of
go, the Japanese chess, which is said to be even more
scientific and intricate than the Western game. The
next day the imperial forces stormed the hill, and the
little band was soon cut to pieces. Saigo was wounded,
and retiring to a cave, took his life in true Samurai
fashion; and the remnant of his band followed his
example.

Uchimura gives many anecdotes of Saigo's kindli-
ness and the simplicity of his tastes. When Com-
mander-in-Chief of the army, and member of the
Cabinet, he lived in a shabby little house in Tokyo,
and could not be induced to dress otherwise than as an
ordinary soldier, "his usual costume being Satsuma
spun cotton stuff, girdled with a broad cotton *obi*, and
large wooden clogs on his feet." One day, as he went
out of the palace after an imperial dinner (this was
before the days of European dress at Court), he missed
his clogs, which he had left at the palace gate; so, not
wishing to trouble any one, he walked quietly out into
the rain without them. The guard at the gate, not being

used to barefoot men in cotton clothes at that entrance, asked his name; and when he gave it, declined to believe him. At that moment Baron Iwakura came out in his carriage, and picked the General up to take him home, before the eyes of the astonished sentinel. It is said that Saigo gave the site for the first national bank, refusing to accept payment. Gifts he would never receive, unless they pertained to dogs; there he was vulnerable.

One more story of Saigo's youth. After he returned from his first visit to Yedo, he identified himself with the anti-Tokugawa party, and thus it happened that one of the Imperialists came to him for shelter—a learned priest whom the Tokugawa had condemned to death for his political utterances. Finding that the priest was discovered and would certainly be taken, Saigo decided that honor required him to die with his guest; so the two slipped out into the night, and after pausing a few moments to enjoy the moonlight on the sea, they took hands and plunged in. Their friends heard the splash, and went to search for them; the bodies were found; Saigo was revived, and accepted life as the will of heaven.

CHAPTER XX.

FORMOSA.[1]

LAST year Formosa celebrated her sixth Japanese birthday, the anniversary of the treaty of Shimonoseki, by which the island was ceded to Japan as part of China's indemnity for the war.

Geographically, Japan claims that Formosa ought of right to belong to her, because it is the last in the line of islands that begins with the Kuriles, away up on the edge of the arctic circle, and continues on down past Kiushiu, by the Lu Chu islands, to within two hundred miles of the top of Formosa. For that matter, both Japan and China long laid claim to the Lu Chu islands, and they compromised by paying nominal tribute to both, until the last century, when Japan got decidedly the upper hand. At last she made a clever move, which settled her claim positively. In 1871 a party of Luchuans were wrecked on the east

[1] It was the wish of the publishers that this chapter should be written by Dr. Inazo Nitobé, head of the Bureau of Products and Industries in Formosa. As this proved impossible, Mrs. Nitobé has kindly given me access to numerous personal letters from Dr. Nitobé, on which I have drawn freely in preparing the following pages.

coast of Formosa and killed by savages or brigands, and Japan sent to demand indemnity from China. China shuffled and evaded, in her usual manner, saying that she did not undertake jurisdiction on the east coast. Japan then sent an expedition, under the present Marquis Saigo, brother of the great general. So wisely did he deal with the islanders, that to this day his name is remembered and honored by the tribes, and in one district, when the children wish to express delight, they clap their hands and cry, "Saigo! Saigo!" General Grant offered to mediate between Japan and China, and so did the British minister at Pekin, and the result was that Japan retired from Formosa, with her claim on Lu Chu fully acknowledged; and China, as usual, remained more puffed up than ever for the encounter.

Formosa, or Taiwan, as the Japanese call it, is two hundred and twenty-five miles long and about eighty wide. It lies from a little north of latitude 25° to a few miles south of latitude 22°, the tropic of Cancer crossing it rather below the middle. All the centre and east side—in fact, all the island except the west coast—is a mass of mountains; two peaks, Mount Silvia and Mount Morrison, reaching twelve thousand eight hundred and fourteen thousand three hundred feet respectively. A little snow lies on the higher peaks for a few months, but that is all. The Formosans say that the gods used to play chess on the summits of the mountains, and that a large flat stone was their chess-board. All these mountains are covered with dense primeval forest, great quantities of enormous camphor laurels and other valuable trees, and among them a tropical tangle of undergrowth and vines; especially the rattan, so much used in making furniture in China, and for this and a great many other purposes in Formosa. The tree grows to a height of twenty or thirty feet, and then begins to send out the long, vine-like branches, which grow hundreds of feet over the branches of neighboring trees. The Chinese go into the forests after it, and, while they are pulling down the long streamers, they became an easy prey to the watchful head-hunters.

On the west side of the island there is a great deal of exceedingly fertile plain, very little raised above the sea, in which small hills stand up like mounds here and there. These were probably islands, which have been gradually surrounded by the waste brought down from the mountains and piled up by the waves in the furious summer storms. In this way the coast is all the time changing; places that were on the sea a few years ago are now a mile or two inland. Across this plain many small rivers come down from the mountains, all of them having immensely wide beds— there is one in the southwest that is three miles across —and, after a storm, they become raging, destructive torrents.

It is not only that Formosa lies partly in the tropics; it is also almost in the path of the typhoons, which, indeed, do not spend their full force on the island itself, but on the Formosa channel to the west, where the Pescadores lie between Formosa and the Chinese coast. They, too, were ceded to Japan in 1895. On the east side the worst storms sheer off somewhat, and the northern part of the island is comparatively sheltered by the mountains; but navigation in this region is proverbially dangerous, especially in summer—as the old New England sea captains used to say:

> "July, stand by;
> August, you must;
> September, remember;
> October, all over."

The Black Current is largely responsible for the heat and dampness—that same *Kuro-shiwo* that makes the softness and beauty of Japan. It flows along the very edge of Formosa, only a few hundred feet outside in some places on the east coast, and the deep blue color is plainly marked against the lighter tint of the ordinary sea. Its moisture-laden winds strike against the mountains and discharge sudden torrents of rain, flooding streams and doing immense damage. The west coast is less deluged than the east; but that, too, gets a very rainy season for three months, from about the middle of January.

The result is a luxuriant tropical vegetation; all southern trees and fruits flourish — palms, bananas, pineapples, sugar-cane, and all the rest, besides peaches and many fruits and vegetables which properly belong farther north, and pine and chestnut and other such trees on the higher slopes of the mountains. Two crops of rice are grown in a year—sometimes five in three years; but, though the soil is exceedingly rich, these two crops do not yield as much as the one crop in Japan, probably for want of proper cultivation. With all this fertility comes the inevitable malaria and kindred diseases of heat and moisture, and frequent visitations of cholera and sometimes plague—this last the hardest possible thing to stamp out where there is a large population of Chinese, with their ineradicable love of dirt and darkness. Yet even in these six years the effect of Japanese sanitation is very marked, and if the mosquito can be proved guilty of malaria and by any means defeated, the worst material difficulty will be overcome. The Japanese doctors say that the fevers are seldom fatal, and that, if taken in hand quickly, an attack seldom lasts over two or three weeks. The south is much worse than the north, perhaps because the upper part of the island is more hilly and has better natural drainage. When the interior can be opened up, it will be possible to have health refuges on the mountains, which are now given over to the savage aborigines.

Though Japanese pirates probably visited Formosa at many periods of their history, they do not seem to have had much to do with the island, except during the latter part of the sixteenth and the early seventeenth century—that wonderful period of expansion, when Japan not only welcomed the Portuguese traders, but herself sent embassies to Europe and trading expeditions to China, Siam, and even to Mexico, and when Japanese pirates were the terror of the coast.

At this time there were already a considerable number of Chinese in Formosa. They probably went there always to some extent; but the first recorded visit was in the twelfth century, when a Chinese official was wrecked on the coast. He found a barbarous but kindly population, who helped him and his companions to repair their vessel and get safely away. The next to come was a Chinese pirate, who took refuge there from a fleet of war junks. He found the island much to his liking, and, with other pirates, made it his headquarters. To make themselves respected, they killed many of the savages and smeared the ships with their blood, thereby beginning the abiding hatred of the islanders for the Chinese.

In the seventeenth century Japanese pirates and adventurers also settled in Formosa and made colonies of a sort. Thus, when the Europeans arrived, there was already a considerable population of Chinese and Japanese on the island.

The Portuguese were first to reach there, and they bestowed the name Formosa—beautiful—which will probably remain to it in all European tongues, instead of Taiwan, the Chinese name, which is also used by

Japan. The Portuguese did not settle, but the Dutch did, in 1624, and they proceeded to annex the island and also to attempt to convert it. But their record in Formosa is not a bright one; they were harsh and exacting towards the people, and the Japanese soon withdrew. The Chinese and Formosans seem to have submitted to taxations and other requirements, but it is probable that they joined the Chinese pirate, who drove out the Dutch only about fifty years later.

This was one Koxinaga or Koxinga, the son of a Formosan pirate and a Japanese woman. The father fought against the Manchus, who overthrew the Ming dynasty and established the present one at Pekin, and was taken by them and put to death. The son fought under him, and afterwards overran the coasts, but finding himself unable to oppose the Manchus on land, he retired to Formosa, and proclaimed himself an independent sovereign there. His successors, however, were conquered by the Manchus about twelve years later, and from that time the island was considered a part of the Chinese empire—a dependency of the neighboring province of Fohkien. It was administered by a Taotai—"intendant of circuit," Pickering calls him—who resided at Taiwanfu, and was under the final control of the viceroy of Fohkien. The viceroy was supposed to make periodic visits of inspection, but if it was made worth his while he would stay away. Pickering tells of the alarm when on one occasion the viceroy sent word that he was really coming. There was a great scurrying round to smooth things up for his examination, and, among the rest, orders were given to take down the war junks and have them ready. Now these junks were beached when not in use, and were supposed to be floated and otherwise examined and repaired at due intervals; but the officials had been systematically appropriating the funds provided for the purpose, and the vessels had not been disturbed for many years, and meanwhile the sea had receded, leaving them a mile inland. Preparations were being made to put them on rollers and haul them down to the water, when a message came that the viceroy had given up his visit, and they were left to rot peaceably, as before.

This is only a specimen of the way things have been done in Formosa for centuries. Being well out of the way, the officials had an even freer hand for extortion than on the mainland; and in not a few cases they were characters unscrupulous even beyond the ordinary Chinese official—men who had been sent there to be conveniently disposed of. It was notorious that criminals were sometimes released on the condition that they would go to Formosa, and the island was used as a political dumping ground for generations. Justice was an affair of the highest bidder, and the substitution of one man for another who could pay well was a perfectly undisguised method of escaping punishment. Brigandage was unchecked; villages often paid blackmail to the bands to be let alone. They would hide in the long grass or the sugar-cane, and fire on the passers-by, so that in some parts of the country the people were forbidden to plant tall crops within two hundred yards of the road. Even at the present day the Japanese government is having hard work to put down these brigands.

In 1860 the treaty of Tientsin opened the principal ports for foreign trade, and a number of merchants settled there, chiefly for the purpose of exporting tea and camphor. Their tribulations with the Chinese merchants and officials are forcibly told in Pickering's entertaining book, "Pioneering in Formosa." In 1884 the French blockaded the ports during their war with China, and bombarded Kelung, doing a great deal of unnecessary damage, and gaining little or nothing for themselves.

There are four distinct classes of people in the island, exclusive of the Japanese, who are nearly all newcomers. They are, first, the aborigines, who are divided into wild tribes and half-civilized; then the Hoklos, Chinese settlers from Fohkien and Amoy; and the Hakkas, lawless Chinese, who came to the province of Canton some generations ago, and from there to Formosa, where they have been and are one of the most troublesome elements to deal with.

The aborigines are almost certainly of Malay descent, and must have reached Formosa from the islands farther south, probably in small and often repeated bands; many, no doubt, drifted there by accident in the strong currents that set along the shore from farther south. They speak a great many dialects, mutually incomprehensible, and the hill tribes enjoy much fighting among themselves and with their more quietly disposed neighbors. They inhabit all the mountain region in the east and centre of the island, except where a few little breaks in the barrier of cliffs along the coast has made landing possible, and small towns have been established, as at Kwa-renko, at the foot of a fertile valley, where the tribes are uncivilized, but friendly, and come down to the steamer to help land freight.

In the plains of the south there are a large number of aborigines who have come under some civilizing influence, and have become peaceable, and taken to agriculture in a simple way. These are called Jiko-ban by the Japanese, and Popohoan by MacKay and other English writers. They are no match for the Chinese, who get their land away from them almost as fast as they take it up and reclaim it. The Popo-hoans are very fond of drink, and when well filled they will part with anything, even the field and the crop on it. Davidson relates a story which he says is a popular Chinese anecdote: "Two Popohoans had together become the proud possessors of three dollars, but could not devise a means of dividing them equally. They sat down on the road, and each took a dollar, but there still remained another; how to dispose of it fairly was a poser. At length a Chinese came along, and they asked him to solve the problem for them, which he did by giving each one dollar and pocketing the third, leaving them lost in amazement and delight at this ready disposal of their difficulty."[1]

The Japanese call the wild tribes *Seiban* (" Raw Barbarians "); they are the famous head-hunters, among whom a man's position in society is determined by the number of skulls he has hanging on his wall under the eaves. At first they only desired the pig-tailed variety, regarding the cropped Japanese as a man and a brother; but unfortunately they have ceased to make distinctions. Yet they are capable of restraint, if exercised kindly and firmly, as has been shown by at least two Japanese officials who have been living among them on the southeast coast. One of these men is a connection of Marquis Saigo, and this predisposed them to think well of him; and he has checked head-hunting by cutting them off from the Chinese till they promised to behave properly. As their only way of getting salt and powder and such things was from the Chinese, to separate them entirely was a very heavy punishment. The officer has also made the chiefs promise to spend a certain part of the year in residence in a certain village, with their families; and there they come in contact with the Japanese, and a beginning of a school is provided for the children. The other guardian is also from Sat-

[1] J. W. Davidson: "Formosa and Its Inhabitants." *Far East*, June, 1896.

suma, and is one of the few survivors of General Saigo's band, having remained alive by the chief's express order, that he might care for the many who were left fatherless and widowed, or without sons. Here in Formosa he devotes himself to his little flock of "Raw Barbarians," and has won their confidence by justice and straightforward kindness.

At first the Japanese government divided the island into three prefectures, but this arrangement has been lately done away, and the administration centred entirely at the capital, Taihoku, or, as the Chinese pronounce it, Taipeh. This is at the northern end of the island, not on the sea, but on the Tamsui river, which empties about ten miles below. The port of Tamsui is at its mouth, but is not deep enough for anything but small boats. Kelung, about as far from Taihoku to the northeast, is the only real port of Formosa that deserves the name; and even this is anything but good, the anchorage soft and shifting, and the harbor disturbed by waves from the Black Current, which flows by only a few hundred feet outside. The vessels anchor in the harbor, and you go ashore in very poor Chinese sampans. It is a pretty place, a deep bay running up toward the hills, and with the mountains in view behind. A picturesque island lies in the midst, and the shores are brilliantly green with palms and bamboo. Around this northern end of the island the country is hilly, and a great deal of tea is grown—that which gets into the market under the name of Formosa Oolong.

The landscape is un-Japanese from the moment you reach the shore; the fields are larger, fenceless as in Japan, but less exquisitely trim; the houses are of brick or adobe, higher than in Japan, and in the Chinese part of the city crowded and dark; the very people working in the fields or pulling the jinrikishas show, even at a distance, the loose, angular build of the Chinese lower classes, and the baggy trousers and flapping coats, so unlike the tight nether garments and belted tunics of Japanese peasants. Some of the policemen are Chinese, and even they are not dignified, in their loose clothes, and with their cues wound round their heads and stuffed under straw hats; but they have proved useful in finding out what goes on among their countrymen, and especially in discovering contagious disease, which was often concealed from the Japanese inspector. A Chinese hospital has been established for them, and they are much less afraid to go to their own countrymen for treatment.

The Japanese quarter of the city is scrupulously clean, and the drainage excellent; deep ditches, with cemented sides, run along the streets, and are carefully cleaned each day, though water runs in them continually. Years ago the Chinese brought water from the mountains to another suburb of the city, called Banka; leading a stream through many feet of rock, and by a wooden aqueduct fifty feet high across a ravine. A third suburb is inhabited by the American and European population; this is outside the walls, and goes by the somewhat barbarous name Twatutia; the railroad station is here.

So far as can now be seen, it must be railroads and not ships that open the country, though a Japanese expert in harbors has lately been studying the possibilities of improvement. Anping, the old Dutch settlement, has only a roadstead, where vessels have to anchor two miles off shore, and passengers and freight are landed in boats which Prof. Chamberlain compares to "a tub on a raft." Takao is a little better off; it is at the mouth of a long lagoon, entered by a narrow channel between two hills. Tainan, formerly called Taiwanfu, the original Chinese capital, is not on the sea at all now, but two or three miles inland; it is a walled city, quite large and fairly clean and attractive; the better class of houses are screened by high hedges or bamboo fences, and abundance of trees. Tainan has the most European accommodation to be found on the island, and there are shops for some European goods, though the foreign population is small, and the Japanese count only two or three thousand, besides the officers and soldiers stationed there. This western coast is the home of a large Chinese population, agricultural and industrious, and on the whole well behaved; the women bind their feet, which the troublesome Hakkas do not, and thus the latter are the

stronger race, and get the better of the Hoklos whenever they come into competition.

That Japan has many most difficult problems to
solve in Formosa is not to be denied; and her reforms
are seriously handicapped by lack of money to push
them. Yet the natural resources of the island are immense, and the government has undertaken its task
with much earnestness for the real good of the Formosans, as well as of the nation at large, and the end
must be prosperity. It is satisfactory to read Pickering's opinion in 1898, three years after the treaty of
Shimonoseki gave the island to Japan; he thinks that
there will be no trouble with the savages—with whom
Pickering himself had considerable dealings—but that
"only the severest measures will subdue the Chinese,"
who he thinks may intrigue with the mainland, as well
as resist order and civilizing influences. But he con-
cludes hopefully, "There can be little doubt that the
change of government will ultimately benefit both the
Japanese and the inhabitants of Formosa, and that
the civilized world will be the gainers, though hitheito
the conquerors have not achieved any great results."

Let me close these rambling chapters with De la
Mazelière's parting judgment on Japan and her
people.

"With Oriental fatalism, the Japanese have accepted progress as inevitable; with an enthusiasm
which to us seems to belong not to the East, but to
Europe, they have joyfully repudiated what they

counted good, that in all things they might attain to yet better. . . . If the future requires of them reforms still more complete, be sure they will be ready to accomplish them. The work of Japan's transformation is not yet ended, it is scarcely begun; should she carry it to a successful conclusion, Europeans will surely find therein useful examples for the task which they have themselves to fulfill."

INDEX.